*Crucial Words of Leading
in the Lord's Recovery*

BOOK 1

The Vision
and
Definite Steps
for the
Practice
of the
New Way

WITNESS LEE

Living Stream Ministry
Anaheim, CA • www.lsm.org

First Edition, December 2004.

ISBN 0-7363-2774-6

Published by

Living Stream Ministry
2431 W. La Palma Ave., Anaheim, CA 92801 U.S.A.
P. O. Box 2121, Anaheim, CA 92814 U.S.A.

Printed in the United States of America

04   05   06   07   08   09   10   /   9   8   7   6   5   4   3   2   1

CONTENTS

PREFACE

This book is a translation from messages given by Brother Witness Lee in Taipei to the elders and co-workers from Taiwan from March through May 1986. Chapters 1, 2, and 3 have been published as *The Vision of the Age*. These messages were not reviewed by the speaker.

CHAPTER ONE

VISION IN GOD'S ECONOMY

Prayer: Lord, we trust in Your precious blood. May Your blood cleanse us. We long to live in fellowship with You. We do not want any sin, any evil, or anything that is contrary to You to veil our inner being; we do not want to lose Your light, miss our fellowship with You, or forego our enjoyment of Your presence. Lord, be our sin offering and trespass offering. We do not want to have some religious activities or busy outward works while missing Your inner presence and not touching You. Lord, in such a training, keep us so that we would remain in fellowship with You and that we would touch Your heart's desire and Yourself. We want to know not only the objective words in the Bible but Your subjective work within us, the work which You are doing in the church today. Lord, be gracious to us and speak to the depth of our being. We want to be taught and encouraged, but more than that, we want to know Your way and be preserved by You, gained by You, and sustained by You. May You grow within us, daily softening us, so that we would be truly mingled with You and be in one fellowship with You. May there be genuine growth within us, and may there be a broad pathway within us that will open all the doors in us.

Lord, in our sojourn on this earth it is unavoidable that we come short and are defiled all the time. Do forgive us of all our shortcomings. Cleanse us of all our defilements. Save us, and remove all filthiness so that our mind, heart, and spirit, including our conscience, would be clear. Lord, may our fellowship here be a pure flow, clear as crystal, without any shadow or covering. Grant us an open sky; remove all the veils. May both the speaker and the listeners be in one spirit. Whatever we would cover, may all of us touch the same thing, and may all of us get into it and pursue after it in spirit. Lead us into You to receive Your cherishing, care, and supply so that we may experience the genuine growth. Lord, guide us to speak the same thing. We have no preconceived decisions; we only want to move according to Your Spirit. Speak to us again and again the words that are in Your heart. Amen.

THE NEED FOR VISION AMONG THE SERVING ONES

In this chapter we will first consider the kind of vision that a servant of the Lord should possess.

What Is a Vision?

Among the serving ones, the two most important groups of people are the elders and the co-workers. According to the Bible, a servant of the Lord must be governed by a vision. We have been speaking about this point for many years. From the first day the work began here in Taiwan, we have been speaking about vision. Over twenty years ago, this matter affected some young people. They felt that they had seen the vision, and they called themselves the "vision group." They condemned the elderly saints for not having any vision.

Whether or not a person understands a certain biblical term is an important matter. Even when a person understands a term, it is very important to know if he understands it correctly and accurately. Proverbs 29:18 says, "Where there is no vision, the people cast off restraint." This means that without a vision, the people will become loose, like wild horses in their untamed state. The clearest instance in the New Testament where the word *vision* is mentioned is in the case of Paul. In Acts 26:19, while he was defending himself before King Agrippa, he uttered this word: "I was not disobedient to the heavenly vision." In order to understand the meaning of the word *vision,* we must understand the context of Paul's speaking in verses 4 through 23.

Prior to verse 19, Paul said that he was once a zealous Judaizer, being zealous for the religion and traditions of his forefathers. He was so zealous that he could not tolerate any different teachings or beliefs among his fellow Jews. Yet at that time there was a group of Christians whose words, teachings, actions, and works were different from the ordinances and the very root of Paul's Jewish religion. Paul's native town of Tarsus was at the crossroads between Asia Minor and Syria; it was a hub of communication and a historically famous academic town, a city of culture. In Tarsus there was a Greek school where Paul received the highest education. At the same time, he joined one of the strictest sects of Judaism and became a Pharisee, sitting under the most famous teacher, Gamaliel. We can see that he was a learned, ambitious, active, and aspiring person.

While he was yet a young man, he received authority from the chief priests in the Jewish religion to put many believers into prison. He even cast a vote to condemn them and to put them to death. Many times he persecuted the believers in the synagogues and compelled them to blaspheme. He was exceedingly enraged at them and persecuted them as far as the Gentile cities. He even requested a letter from the chief priests and took the lead to put into bondage all those who called on the name of the Lord. But while he was on the way to Damascus, the Lord met him and said to him, "Saul, Saul, why are you persecuting Me? It is hard for you to kick against the goads" (v. 14). Paul asked, "Who are You, Lord?" The Lord said, "I am Jesus, whom you persecute" (v. 15). Then the Lord told him that He had chosen him to be a minister and a witness both of the things in which he had seen Him and of the things in which He would appear to him. He would send Paul to the people and the Gentiles to open their eyes, to turn them from darkness to light and from the authority of Satan to God that they might receive forgiveness of sins and an inheritance among those who have been sanctified by faith. After testifying of these things, Paul concluded by saying, "Therefore...I was not disobedient to the heavenly vision" (v. 19). When Paul was serving God in the Jewish religion, he was serving by tradition, not by vision, but from the day the Lord met him, called him, and chose him on the way to Damascus, he became a man with a vision. From that time onward, his service was governed by that vision.

Concerning the word *vision,* our emphasis is not on its Old Testament meaning but on what Paul said in Acts 26:19. Of course, we can never ascertain a truth in the Bible by one verse alone. Every truth in the Bible requires the entire Bible for its explanation. This is like the various organs of the body; none can survive alone. They need the entire body to act as their support. In the same way, every truth must have the entire "body" as its support. The entire Bible is the whole "body," the supporting structure. In order to understand what the word *vision* means, we must consider the entire Bible.

Many Christians have read the biography of Hudson Taylor. The writer told us clearly that while Mr. Taylor was young, he felt that he needed to go to China for the gospel. He first joined a mission and went to northern Fukien for the gospel. Later, while he was back in England on furlough, he went to the seashore one day to spend some time alone with the Lord. As he gazed at the ocean, he felt that his eyes were brought across the seas to catch a glimpse of the interior parts of China, and he saw four hundred million dying souls. He felt that the Lord was calling him to consecrate himself entirely to those people and to send the gospel to the interior of China. Right there he accepted this charge and commission. Such a charge and commission became Mr. Taylor's "vision." Immediately he shared what he saw with the Christians whom he was acquainted with. Many responded to his word, and the China Inland Mission was formed. In the following forty to fifty years, hundreds and thousands of people were sent to the interior parts of China to preach the gospel.

It is debatable whether what Mr. Taylor saw can be considered a vision of the age. Of course, the vast China needed the preaching of the gospel. From this viewpoint, Mr. Taylor certainly received a commission, and it was certainly a vision. Yet it is questionable whether or not that is the vision that God has for this age. Concerning the matter of vision, we must come back to the Bible.

GOD'S VISIONS
THROUGH AN OUTLINE OF THE OLD TESTAMENT
From Adam to Samuel

The Bible has sixty-six books. The Old Testament begins

with God's creation, or the creation of Adam, and spans four thousand years until the birth of the Lord Jesus. The first two volumes of Level One of *Truth Lessons* give us a description and an outline of the Old Testament. The purpose of such a description is to show us the various visions God gave to men throughout the ages. We have to see that in every age, God gives only one vision to man. In Adam is seen God's redemption. In Abel is seen God's way of redemption. In Enosh is seen man's need for God and man's calling upon Him to enjoy His riches. In Enoch is seen a redeemed one walking with God on the pathway of redemption. In Noah is seen one who walked with God and worked with God to build the ark to meet the need of that generation.

Then in Abraham is seen God's calling, God's promise, justification by faith, the living by faith, and the living in fellowship with God. In Isaac is seen the inheriting of grace and the rest and enjoyment. In Jacob is seen God's selection, the transformation in life, and the maturity in life. In Joseph is seen the reigning aspect of the maturity in life. Following this, we see different things in Moses, Aaron, Joshua, and the judges. In Samuel we see the voluntarily consecrated Nazarite replacing the ordained priests, ending the age of the judges, and bringing in the kingdom age. In Acts 13 Paul mentioned this period of history and spoke of God's leading of the Israelites out of Egypt. Through Joshua He led them into the land of Canaan and divided the good land among them for their inheritance. After this, He appointed judges from among them until the time of Samuel, at which time He ushered in David. This period lasted about four hundred fifty years.

The Way of Reckoning in the Age of the Judges

We need to learn to interpret the Bible with the Bible. The Life-study trainings emphasize life; they do not pay that much attention to history, genealogies, and dates. This is the reason that they give detailed explanations of the things of life but spend little time to explain history and dates. In Acts 13:20 Paul says, "After these things, for about four hundred and fifty years, He gave them judges until Samuel the prophet." There are at least two or three authoritative interpretations of this verse. It is difficult to ascertain the exact number of years in this case. However, since this period of time has much to do with the vision given at that time, we must study the matter in depth. How do these four hundred fifty years come about?

First Kings 6:1 says, "Then in the four hundred eightieth year after the children of Israel had come forth out of the land of Egypt, in the fourth year of his [Solomon's] reign over Israel..." The Israelites were in the wilderness for forty years. After this, Joshua led for twenty-five years. Then there was the time of the judges, which lasted until the time of Samuel. The four hundred fifty years that Paul speaks of in Acts 13:20 surely include all these events. David's reign lasted forty years, and afterward there was the reign of Solomon. If we add up these numbers, we can see one thing: Paul's word in Acts 13 does not take Saul's years into account because at the time he was king, there was a rival, which was David. We can say that during that period of time there was no properly appointed king from God to unite the whole nation of Israel. Strictly speaking, before the Israelites were united as one nation, they were still in the age of the judges.

Although Saul was appointed by God to be king, in God's eyes his words did not count; only Samuel's words counted. Samuel held the positions of both a prophet and a judge. At that time, outwardly Saul was king, but in reality, in God's eyes, Samuel was still functioning as a judge. As for David, he was anointed early on, but at the beginning it was neither his words nor Saul's words that counted, but Samuel's words. Even after David became king, his first seven and a half years are not reckoned in Paul's word concerning four hundred fifty years because at that time the house of Saul was not yet removed; Saul's son Ish-bosheth was still king in Mahanaim (2 Sam. 2:8-11). In the eyes of God, that was still the age of the judges.

Based on the above, we can make a clear conclusion: The age of the judges was terminated only after David became king over all of Israel. David unified the entire nation of Israel and was officially recognized as king in Jerusalem. After this, there was no more confusion or disturbance in the land. This lasted for thirty-three years. According to 1 Kings 6:1, from the time of the exodus to the fourth year of Solomon were four hundred eighty years. Subtracting from that the last thirty-three years of David's reign and the first three years of Solomon's reign, we have four hundred forty-four years left. This somewhat matches Paul's word in Acts 13:20: "For about four hundred and fifty years." The difference between the two is only six years. This is the reason that Paul uses the word *about*.

Within the period of the time of the judges, which lasted approximately four hundred fifty years, was the reign of Saul, which lasted forty years. But God did not recognize him as king. The reason for this is that he did not serve as king according to a vision. Samuel, on the other hand, was recognized as a judge because he served with a vision. This can be proven by the fact that the age of the judges did not end until the termination of the ministry of Samuel. Of course, the final termination of the age of the judges began with the reign of David in Jerusalem. The period of proper kingship does not include the first seven and a half years of David's reign. In God's eyes, the throne was empty at that time because there were still contenders for the throne, and the nation was under the turmoil of war. During those seven and a half years, the Israelites did not serve according to a vision. Although both Saul and David (during his first seven and a half years of reign) were kings, the only one who served according to a vision was Samuel, who served as a judge.

SERVING GOD ACCORDING TO THE VISION OF THE AGE

We must be clear that in every age there is the vision of that age. We have to serve God according to the vision of the age. Consider the age of Noah. When we read the record of the Bible, it appears as if Noah's family, including himself, his wife, his three children, and their wives were the only ones who were serving God. Can we believe that at that time there were actually only eight people serving God, and the rest were worshipping idols and not serving God? Perhaps we have never thought about this matter. Whether or not others were serving God, one thing is certain: They were not part of those who built the ark. For this very reason their service was not recognized by God.

Some people might ask whether at the time Noah was busily building the ark there was not a single person on earth who feared God. We can deduce from historical data that at the time of Noah it is quite possible that his one family with eight people were not the only ones serving and worshipping God. The ancient Chinese were serving and worshipping also at that time. Their way of worship was in many ways similar to that of men in the Old Testament. Confucius was five hundred years prior to Christ. He once said, "To sin against heaven is unforgivable." In the parable of the prodigal son in Luke 15, the prodigal said to his father when he returned home, "I have sinned against heaven" (v. 21). In ancient times, both the East and the West considered "heaven" a symbol for God. The reason for this is that whenever men lifted their heads heavenward, they thought about God. We can assume that in the ancient times many people sought after God and had some knowledge of God. They served God according to the knowledge they had of God. Yet we must realize that though so many people were serving, only Noah and his family of eight served with a vision, and only their service was acceptable to God.

MOVING UNDER A VISION
AND FOLLOWING THOSE WHO HAVE THE VISION

When Jesus of Nazareth came, He also served God, and a group of Galilean fishermen followed Him as His disciples. In the eyes of man, these Galileans were just like little naughty children. Outwardly, Jesus was a Galilean; He did not move away from Nazareth the first thirty years of His life, and He received no formal education in serving God. Yet at the age of thirty He started a ministry, and a group of "ignorant" people followed Him. Even some women ministered to His needs. They followed the Lord Jesus for three and a half years. What do you think the Pharisees, chief priests, scribes, and elders thought of them at that time? Among these men were fishermen, tax-collectors, and relatives of the Lord Jesus. There was even a woman who was once possessed with seven demons.

Did they not seem to be children at play when they claimed that they were serving God?

At that time among the Jews, there was still a magnificent temple. It was built over a period of forty years. The Levites were divided into twenty-four orders and were offering sacrifices and ministering according to their orders. They were either taking care of the utensils, slaying the animals, or offering the sacrifices such as the daily burnt offerings and sin offerings and the weekly Sabbath offerings on the bronze altar. In the eyes of man, such services were certainly proper and dignified, but were they carried out under a vision? We are all very clear that the services of the priests in the temple were not carried out under a vision; they were carried out by tradition. It was the Lord Jesus and those who were following Him who were serving under a vision and whose service was pleasing to God.

The followers of the Lord Jesus were a blessed people. Among them was Peter, who was also a leader and one who took the lead to say foolish things. There was Mary the Magdalene who was once possessed with seven demons. There was also the other Mary, who loved the Lord fervently and who broke the flask of alabaster worth thirty pieces of silver to anoint the Lord Jesus. Outwardly they were all blindly following the Lord because the Lord Jesus was the only One who had the vision. Peter, James, John, Mary, and all the others did not receive that vision. Yet they were clear that the Lord's way was right and were determined to follow Him. When the Lord turned to the east, they followed to the east. When the Lord turned to the west, they followed to the west. When the Lord went to the sea, they followed Him to the sea. When the Lord went to the mountain, they followed Him to the mountain. When the Lord was in Galilee, they followed Him in Galilee. When the Lord went to Jerusalem, they followed Him to Jerusalem. They were resolved in their heart that as long as they followed the Lord, nothing would go wrong.

In John 11 Lazarus was dying. When the Lord learned about this, He did not do anything. After two days the Lord told the disciples that He would go to see Lazarus. The disciples said to Him, "The Jews were just now seeking to stone

You, and You are going there again?" (v. 8). The Lord answered, "Our friend Lazarus has fallen asleep; but I am going that I may wake him out of sleep" (v. 11). Verses 1 through 16 show that the disciples were truly following in a blind way. They were not at all clear what they were doing, yet they followed and went anyway. Perhaps in the eyes of men this is blind following, yet this kind of following pleases God, and this kind of following is done with a vision. They did not receive any vision individually, but the One whom they were following had the vision, and that was enough. As long as they were acting according to the One who had the vision, they were right in the eyes of God.

GOD'S VISIONS
THROUGH AN OUTLINE OF THE NEW TESTAMENT

Today many Christians criticize us, saying, "You are too proud. How can you negate all the denominations and all the Christians and say that only you have the vision?" Some brothers and sisters on occasion have been asked by others, "You say that the pastors are wrong, the pope is wrong, and everyone is wrong. Are you the only people who are not wrong? Are you the only ones who are right in following what you are following?" I believe sometimes such winds would even cause you to question yourselves. However, if we are clear concerning the vision in the Bible, we will have the confidence to say that we are in fact those who serve by following a vision.

The Service of Peter and His Companions

In the book of Acts, after the Lord's ascension, Peter and later Paul continued to serve in the ministry. In Acts 5, while Peter was ministering, the Jewish synagogue rose up to oppose the apostles and put them into prison (vv. 17-32). But the Lord's angel at night opened the doors of the prison and, leading them out, told them to stand in the temple and speak to the people all the words of this life. At daybreak the chief priests called together the Sanhedrin and asked for the apostles to be brought to them. When the officers arrived, they found the prison locked with all security and the guards standing at the doors, but when they opened the doors, they

found no one inside. While they were utterly perplexed, someone came and reported to them, "Behold, the men whom you
put in the prison are standing in the temple and teaching the
people" (v. 25). Then the captain with the officers went away
and brought the apostles to the Sanhedrin to be tried.

After the Sanhedrin listened to the apostles, they wanted
to do away with them. One Pharisee, Gamaliel, a teacher of
the law honored by all the people, stood up and said, "With-
draw from these men and leave them alone; for should this
counsel or this work be of men, it will be overthrown; but if it
is of God, you will not be able to overthrow them, lest you be
found to be even fighters against God" (vv. 38-39). Gamaliel's
word was correct, but this does not mean that he had the
vision. The only ones who had the vision were the apostles who
were imprisoned and the simple ones who were following them.

In Acts 12 Herod began to persecute the church. He killed
James and put Peter into prison. A large group of women
gathered in the house of Mary, the mother of John, to pray for
Peter. In the night the Lord's angel opened the door of the
prison and took Peter out. Peter went to the house of Mary
and knocked at the door. A maiden came to answer (vv. 1-13).
In the eyes of the Sanhedrin, the chief priests, and the Pharisees, these women were foolish. They would not go to the
proper temple and would not abide by the tradition of their
forefathers; they chose to follow a group of Galilean fishermen and mingle with them. Could it be that all of their
forefathers were wrong? Could it be that David, Isaiah, and
all the others were wrong and that these Galileans alone
were right? Moreover, they had even been imprisoned. Yet the
women were still praying for them and following them. It
seems that they were too foolish.

Here we see two groups of people. The larger group was
the Jewish religionists. The smaller group was those who followed Peter and the other Galileans in a simple way. Both
groups were serving God, but whose service was under a
vision? I am afraid that we have never thought about this
matter. We need to see that not only was Peter's service under
a vision, but even the simple ones who followed him were
serving under a vision.

The Service of Paul and His Companions

In Acts 11 Barnabas took Paul along with him in his service and brought him to Antioch (vv. 25-26). This was something done according to the vision. In chapter 13 we find that one day the Holy Spirit spoke to those who were serving in Antioch, saying, "Set apart for Me now Barnabas and Saul for the work to which I have called them" (v. 2). Here the Scripture puts Barnabas first. This shows that he was the leader. In recording their journey, the Bible puts Barnabas's name first and Paul's name second. When they came to Pisidian Antioch, however, and the need arose for someone to speak in the synagogue on the Sabbath, Barnabas had nothing to say. At that time Saul, who was called Paul, stood up, motioned with his hand, and began to preach the gospel and pour out his speaking like a torrent (vv. 16-41). From that time onward, the Bible reverses the order of the two men; it begins to refer to them as "Paul and Barnabas." This shows that at that time the vision turned to Paul.

In Acts 15 after Paul and Barnabas returned from the conference in Jerusalem, they had the burden to revisit the cities in which they previously preached and to see the brothers again. At that juncture, Barnabas voiced his opinion; he wanted to bring Mark, his cousin, along with him. Paul disagreed, the two had a contention, and they separated from each other. Barnabas took Mark and went another way, while Paul took Silas with him (vv. 36-40). From that time onward, the book of Acts has no more record of Barnabas. We believe that though Barnabas was still serving, his service was no longer governed by the vision. From that time, the ones who were serving under the vision were Paul and Silas, the one Paul had chosen.

Serving by Following the Leadership of Those Who Have the Vision

The Example of Aquila and Priscilla

At the beginning of Acts 18, we are told that through his tentmaking Paul gained a couple, Aquila and Priscilla. Immediately they joined Paul in his vision and in his service.

Thereafter, there were meetings in this couple's house continually. When they were in Rome, the church in Rome met in their house. When they went to Ephesus, the church in Ephesus met in their house (Rom. 16:5a; 1 Cor. 16:19b). Paul praised them for risking their necks for his life (Rom. 16:4). Not only was Paul grateful to them, but all the churches in the Gentile world were thankful to them. The service of Aquila and Priscilla was a service that followed after Paul. Hence, their service was a service under the vision.

The Case of Apollos

At the end of Acts 18, there appeared a man named Apollos. Was Apollos's service under the vision? It is not safe to say that it was not, for "he was powerful in the Scriptures" (v. 24). He knew the Bible very well, but while he was ministering and working in Corinth, he created some problems. After he left, a division arose in the church in Corinth. Some said that they were of Apollos, and others said that they were of Cephas or of Paul. Another group of people thought that they were superior; they did not consider themselves as belonging to anyone. They claimed that they were of Christ (1 Cor. 1:12). Because of this problem, Paul said in 1 Corinthians 16:12, "Concerning our brother Apollos, I urged him many times to come to you with the brothers; yet it was not at all his desire to come now, but he will come when he has opportunity." This means that Paul wanted to go to Corinth, and he wanted Apollos to go with him to solve the problem of division in the church in Corinth. The strange thing is that although Paul "urged him many times," "it was not at all [Apollos's] desire to come now." The reason Apollos gave was that the opportunity was not there. This was why he would only come when he had "opportunity."

Today we all have to admit that Paul was a very spiritual man. Since such a spiritual person had said, "I urged him many times to come to you," we have to believe that his urging was not of the flesh but of the spirit. Perhaps some may ask, "Does this mean that Apollos was not spiritual?" Many would answer, "Of course, Apollos was spiritual. Otherwise, why would some in Corinth have claimed that they were

of Apollos?" The Bible clearly says that Apollos was powerful in the Scriptures and was an eloquent man. Even Paul
affirmed Apollos by saying that he planted, but Apollos
watered. It is difficult to say that the one who plants is under
the vision, but the one who waters is not under the vision.
Therefore, we can at most say that Paul was more spiritual
than Apollos. We cannot say that Apollos was not spiritual
and that he was not under the vision.

The Pattern of Timothy and Titus

Today in Christianity, many Christians claim that they
are spiritual, but they do not like to listen to others. Even if
Paul were here, they might not listen to him. This attitude
has found its way even to us. It seems that in a way we are
also "spiritual." Sometimes we have a feeling concerning a
certain matter, but we can only say to the brothers, "I urge
you to do this. Perhaps you can pray to the Lord concerning
it." Strictly speaking, this condition is not too normal. If we
study the book of Acts and the Epistles of Paul, we can see
that many times Paul pointedly told people to do certain things.
In 2 Timothy 4, Paul directed people to do a number of things.
He told Timothy, "Be diligent to come to me quickly...Take
Mark and bring him with you, for he is useful to me for the
ministry. But Tychicus I have sent to Ephesus. The cloak
which I left in Troas with Carpus, bring when you come...Be
diligent to come before winter" (vv. 9-13, 21). When Paul
charged Timothy in this way, Timothy did not say, "It is not at
all my desire to come now, because the weather is somewhat
cold, but I will come when I have opportunity." No, he acted
accordingly, following Paul's instruction.

In the same way, when Paul asked Titus to remain in
Crete, Titus remained. When he asked Titus to come to him at
Nicopolos, Titus obeyed. When he sent Titus to Corinth, Titus
went accordingly (Titus 1:5; 3:12; 2 Cor. 7:6-7). In 1 Timothy
1:3, Paul told Timothy, "Even as I exhorted you...to remain in
Ephesus." Paul told Timothy to stay behind in Ephesus, and
Timothy stayed behind. We cannot find a trace where Paul
exhorted Timothy in the way of saying, "Timothy, for the sake
of those who are teaching differently in Ephesus, I feel that

you should stay behind and consider the situation. Please pray to the Lord to see whether or not this is the Lord's will." Nor can we find Timothy answering, "Good, I will pray and see. If it is the Lord's will, I will stay behind." Acts 17:15 says, "Those who conducted Paul brought him as far as Athens; and receiving a command for Silas and Timothy to come to him as quickly as possible, they went off." Acts 18:5 says, "Both Silas and Timothy came down from Macedonia." They all obeyed immediately after they received Paul's command. No one said, "Sorry, I have to pray a little and see if this is the Lord's leading."

SERVING ACCORDING TO THOSE WHO HAVE THE VISION BEING TO SERVE UNDER THE VISION

We see clearly from the revelation of the New Testament that when the Lord Jesus was on earth, He was acting under the vision. Outside His leading there was no vision. Others might have been in tradition or knowledge. Gamaliel was very knowledgeable; he was very familiar with God's principles, but he was not under the vision. His speaking was not under the vision; it was a speaking that was merely words of knowledge. After the Lord's ascension, it was Peter and his co-workers who were under the vision. We are not saying that Peter had one vision and John, James, and the other apostles had another vision. There was only one vision, which was the vision of Peter. This vision became the vision of his followers. When Paul was raised up in his ministry, he received a vision that touched the heavens, the earth, and Paradise (2 Cor. 12:2-4). Although Paul had many co-workers, no one except him saw any other vision. They all had one vision, which was the vision that Paul saw.

There is great controversy in Christianity concerning the matter of one vision for one age. However, God's Word reveals to us clearly that in every age there is only one vision. At the time of Abel, Cain did not worship an idol and he did not build a shrine. He was doing the same thing that Abel was doing, offering a sacrifice to God. Under the vision, however, Abel offered a sacrifice that was acceptable to God, but Cain offered his sacrifice apart from the vision. If you were born in the age of Abel, you would have had to take the way of Abel; otherwise, you would have been off from the vision and in the way of Cain. At the time of Enosh, one man was under the vision, and he called on the name of the Lord. Other people might have feared God according to other ways, but such fear was not according to the vision. In the same way, at the time of Noah there were more than eight people who feared God; there might have been a hundred or even a thousand people who feared God. They might not have sinned as others did; they might even have been serving in some way. Yet their service was not governed by a vision. Noah's family of eight people, by serving according to Noah's pattern, became servants who served according to a vision. What Noah saw became what they saw.

The vision that Noah saw was the vision of the ark. To man this was very peculiar and unthinkable. How can a person give up everything that he is doing and spend all his time building an ark? The building took one hundred twenty years (Gen. 6:3). During those one hundred twenty years, Noah was, on the one hand, preaching the word of righteousness and, on the other hand, building the ark (2 Pet. 2:5). To others he was wasting his effort and his money; he was too foolish. When the one hundred twenty years were about to end, there was still no sign of any rain from heaven. Yet while men were saying "peace and security," and while they were eating and drinking, marrying and giving in marriage, the flood of destruction suddenly came, as birth pangs come suddenly to a woman with child (Matt. 24:38-39; 1 Thes. 5:3). In the end, only Noah's family entered the ark and was saved.

We find the same principle in the New Testament. God's work in the New Testament is to produce and build up the church. This vision was given to Paul. For this reason, once Paul came on the scene, Peter's ministry faded away. When Peter was old, he said, "Our beloved brother Paul, according to the wisdom given to him, wrote to you, as also in all his letters, speaking in them concerning these things, in which some things are hard to understand, which the unlearned and unstable twist, as also the rest of the Scriptures, to their own destruction" (2 Pet. 3:15-16). This means that even the aged

Peter had to submit to the vision of Paul. He acknowledged that Paul's word was as precious as the Old Testament Scriptures and that believers should take heed to it.

Based on this, the names of all those who did not join themselves to Paul's vision were eventually dropped from the record of the Bible. For example, Barnabas was the one who initiated Paul into the service, but because he contended with Paul, his name was eventually dropped from the Bible. Apollos was very capable at expounding the Bible, but 1 Corinthians 16 records that he told Paul that it was not at all his desire to go to Corinth and that he would go when he had opportunity. After this, the Bible no longer mentions anything concerning him. Barnabas was zealous in his service, and Apollos was capable in his exposition of the Bible, but God did not use them anymore because their service was no longer under the vision. This is a very sober matter.

TO SERVE UNDER THE VISION MEANING TO SERVE ACCORDING TO THE REVELATION OF THE BIBLE

The Bible shows clearly that in every age God gives only one vision to man. We cannot find in the Bible that there were two visions in any age. What about those men who came after the apostles' time? How did they serve God according to the proper vision? Today Paul is gone. If we are to serve God today, what is our vision? Today the inhabited world is much larger than at the time of Noah; there are more people today. There are more than one billion Christians all over the six continents of the world. They come from different denominations such as the Catholic Church and the Protestant churches. In the Protestant churches there are the Anglican Church, the Lutheran Church, the Methodist Church, the Baptist Church, and the Presbyterian Church. Among all these churches and all these Christians, who are the ones who are serving according to the vision? We can ask ourselves the same question: Are we those who are serving according to the vision, and if so, what is our vision?

Concerning this matter of following the vision, many Christians do not act according to the truth. Rather, they act according to their own taste and preferences. Some join our meetings because they think that the brothers and sisters here are very zealous, loving the Lord, and that the messages are good. This is the reason they join our meetings. Formerly, they only knew about attending "Sunday morning services." When they hear that we go to church meetings, they also change their terminology and talk about attending "church meetings." However, very few believers are clear concerning what it is to meet and serve according to the vision. All of you here are elders and co-workers. It is important that you consider this matter carefully. What is our vision? What is the vision that is governing our service? We cannot answer this question in a general way with only some spiritual terminology. Our answer must be based on a solid foundation.

The Completion of the Divine Revelation

At the time of Abel, not a single book of the Bible had been written. It was fourteen hundred years after Abel, at the time of Moses, that the Pentateuch was completed. However, even at the time of Moses, God's revelation was still in the process of development; it was not yet complete. The vision that Moses saw was not enough to completely govern those who came after him. When we come to the New Testament, we find Paul saying that he became a minister to the church according to the stewardship that God had entrusted to him for the completion of the word of God (Col. 1:25). Around A.D. 94, three decades after Paul's martyrdom, the apostle John was raised up to do a mending work. He wrote the Gospel of John, the Epistles of John, and the book of Revelation. After these books were written, the revelation of God was fully completed. For this reason, at the end of Revelation John said that if anyone adds to the words of the prophecy of this scroll, God will add to him the plagues which are written in this scroll (22:18). This means that the apostle John's book of Revelation completes the entire revelation of God. The book of Revelation is certainly the ultimate consummation of God's revelation because Paul did not mention anything about the new heavens and the new earth, and Peter mentioned them only briefly (2 Pet. 3:13). Only the book of Revelation speaks about them in detail. This shows clearly that by the time the

apostle John finished the book of Revelation, the biblical revelation had reached its ultimate consummation. This then
becomes the vision and basis of our service today.

From the time of the apostles until today, for two thousand
years, all the servants of the Lord who serve according to the
revelation of the Bible serve according to the vision. This is
the standard and the basis of our service. After the apostles
passed away, servants of the Lord were raised up in every age.
They argued, fought, and debated over whose service should
be considered the genuine and right service. The verdict on
such considerations should be based on the standard of the
revelation as revealed in the Bible.

The Example of the Lord Jesus

Today God's revelation is already put into writing. It is
recorded in the Bible and is no longer something abstract.
This is a very important matter. When the Lord Jesus spoke
on the earth, He would say, "As the Scripture said" (John
7:38). Even while He was being tempted and was arguing
with the devil, He said, "It is written" (Matt. 4:4, 7, 10). He
did not speak according to any personal feeling within Him.
This means that the divine revelation upon which He based
His speaking is veritable; it is written in black and white and
is not abstract at all. When He debated with the Pharisees,
He quoted the Old Testament Scriptures. On the Sabbath day,
when He took His disciples across the grainfields, the disciples picked ears of grain and ate. The Pharisees interrogated
Him, and He answered, saying, "Have you not read what
David did when he became hungry, and those who were with
him; how he entered into the house of God, and they ate the
bread of the Presence, which was not lawful for him to eat,
nor for those who were with him, except for the priests only?"
(12:3-4). During the final six days of His earthly journey,
when He went up to Jerusalem and was questioned by the
Pharisees, Sadducees, elders, and chief priests, He answered
with the words of the Bible: "It is written...Have you never
read?...Have you never read in the Scriptures?...Have you
not read that which was spoken to you by God?" (21:13, 16, 42;
22:31). This shows clearly that the Lord argued and justified

Himself according to the revelation that was written down at the time.

The Example of the Apostles

In the book of Acts, both the apostles Peter and Paul spoke in the way of a defense. The first message that Peter delivered on the day of Pentecost was a defense based extensively on the Scriptures. He quoted the prophet Joel and proclaimed that Jesus of Nazareth, whom the people had crucified on the cross, had been raised up by God. This was what David referred to in Psalm 16. Moreover, as David prophesied in Psalm 110, God had exalted this Jesus to His right hand. Paul also wrote his Epistle to the Romans in the way of an argument based on the Old Testament. Someone said once that in order to be a good lawyer, one has to study the book of Romans thoroughly because this book contains the most perfect reasonings and the highest arguments.

STUDYING AND SERVING ACCORDING TO THE REVELATION OF THE BIBLE

With the truth of the Bible as our guiding principle, we can study and examine all the denominations and sects that we find today. From this perspective, Catholicism is far off the mark. Surely Catholicism is not governed by the vision. The Anglican Church takes as its head the queen, who may not be saved at all. It considers all British citizens members of the Anglican Church by birth, whether or not they are believers and have been baptized. This clearly shows that the Anglican Church is not under the vision either. If we examine and compare all the other denominations, free groups, and charismatic organizations, we will see that none of them is serving fully according to the complete biblical revelation.

We should ask how high the standard of the revelation is which these groups hold. For example, we cannot say that Catholicism is a hundred percent contrary to the biblical revelation. At least it acknowledges one God, and it acknowledges that Jesus Christ is the Son of God. In the Catholic Church there are some truths, but their standard is too low. In the same way, we have to admit that many people in the

Protestant churches do expound the Bible. There are even Bible schools that teach people the truths of the Bible, but whether they see the revelation in the Bible and whether they are clear about God's vision are other questions altogether. We cannot say that as long as people have the Bible, they have the revelation or are acting according to the vision. It is very possible that they merely hold the Bible in their hands; they have not realized the vision and revelation contained in the Bible. Hence, we have to recognize some basic principles. First, we must be governed by the revelation contained in the Bible. Second, the standard of such revelation must be sufficiently high; it must be up to the standard of the divine revelation.

THE LORD'S RECOVERY BEING UNDER THE VISION OF THE DIVINE REVELATION

The knowledge and discovery of divine revelation develop and advance with the ages. Today we are not in the age of Martin Luther. We are not in the age of Zinzendorf or the age of John Wesley. At the time of the Reformation in the 1520s, when Luther was raised up, anyone who wanted to serve under a vision had to join himself to Luther. In the seventeenth century, anyone who wanted to serve under a vision had to join himself to Madame Guyon. In the eighteenth century, anyone who wanted to serve under a vision had to join himself to Zinzendorf. Even John Wesley received help from Zinzendorf. In the nineteenth century, J. N. Darby took the lead among the Brethren, and the vision was with him. In the twentieth century, the vision came to us.

I am not "selling" myself here, but I would like to make a declaration. I began my relationship with the Lord's recovery in 1925. I fully agreed with the Lord's recovery, but during the first seven and a half years I was not in the Lord's recovery but in the Brethren assembly. It was in 1932 that I officially joined the Lord's recovery. Now, fifty-four years have passed. During the past sixty years, according to my observation and based on my knowledge of the Bible, my experience as a Christian, and my study of Christianity's history and its present condition, I can say with full confidence that the Lord's recovery is serving under the vision. There is no doubt about this.

This is not all. During these fifty-four years that I have been in the Lord's recovery, I have seen many people both in the northern and southern parts of China who had high moral standards and a noble character, who had learned deep lessons in life, and whose spiritual condition was good. When they passed through the Lord's recovery or met with us for a few years and then left, invariably they found their spiritual service fading and faltering. This is an amazing thing. Those who have never touched the Lord's recovery can still somewhat go on, but those who have come and then left invariably find their end less than desirable. There is not one exception. This proves that the recovery bears the vision that the Lord has entrusted to this age.

At the time of Noah the vision was to build the ark. At that time anyone who was not building the ark was not serving according to the vision. At the time of Paul the vision was to preach the gospel and to build up the church. Anyone at that time who was not serving according to this vision was off the mark. This included such men as Apollos, who was capable at expounding the Bible, and Barnabas, who was zealous for his service. What is our vision today? Today in 1986, our vision is also to "build the ark." The way to build this ark is to preach the gospel, set up home meetings, teach the truth, and have everyone prophesy. All those who do not practice these four things are not serving according to the vision. Perhaps you expound the Bible, and perhaps you serve very zealously, but your service is not "building the ark." Such service will not be acceptable to God.

SERVING ACCORDING TO THE VISION
THAT THE LORD HAS GIVEN US TODAY

I hope that all the brothers and sisters attending the full-time training will read this chapter so that they will see this matter clearly. We are not trying to dictate to anyone, and we are not congratulating ourselves behind closed doors. We are saying this based on the movement of history and the pure revelation of the Bible. Look around at the entire situation of Christianity today. Where are the revelation and the vision? We have the same Bible in our hands, but some people have no light even after they have read it a hundred times. In the Lord's recovery, every page, every verse, every sentence, and even every word shine with revelation and light. I believe that outside the Lord's recovery it is difficult to hear a word about Apollos like the one that is recorded in this chapter. The reason for this is that there is no light.

If we study the letter of the Bible, we may conclude that Apollos was not too deficient. In 1 Corinthians 3 Paul said that Apollos watered, but in the same verse he told the Corinthians that he was the one who planted (v. 6). Whether or not there is a waterer is not that important, but the planter is indispensable (cf. Mark 4:26-28). Although Paul was humble in pointing out Apollos's distinction, in the same verse he added, "According to the grace of God given to me, as a wise master builder I have laid a foundation, and another builds upon it...For another foundation no one is able to lay besides that which is laid" (1 Cor. 3:10-11). This means that anyone who does not build upon Paul's foundation is not serving according to the vision. In the eyes of man, this is too presumptuous, but Paul was not apologetic at all. He said that he was a wise master builder. He had given everyone the blueprint of the building, and he was supervising the building work. The phrase *master builder* here is *architekton* in Greek. It denotes a person who has the blueprint and builds and supervises the building according to the blueprint. The anglicized form of this word is *architect*. We know that in construction, the only person whose word counts is the architect's. This was Paul's position. No one else's word counts; only Paul's word counts because he had the blueprint.

We see the same thing at the time of Moses. Moses received the pattern of the tabernacle from God, and he supervised the building work. Moses was the one who had the dimensions of the tabernacle and the ways to construct it with all the utensils. In the building of the tabernacle, only his word counted; no one else's word counted. If everyone would have had his say in that work, I am afraid there would have been a hundred or two hundred different kinds of tabernacles. This is the situation with Christianity today. There are thousands of churches. Every one of them is different, and every one of them wants to build up its own group. The Anglican Church builds up its own church. The Presbyterian Church builds up its own church. The Catholic Church builds up its own church, and the charismatics build up their own tongue-speaking churches. Where is there a church that is built according to the proper pattern? There is none. No one is building according to the blueprint that Paul received; no one is building according to the revelation of the Bible. Everyone is building according to his own desire.

There is only one blueprint and one master builder in the proper, correct building. The only master builder is the architect who has the blueprint in his hand. This is true in every age. The Lord issues the blueprint, the revelation, and the utterance, and through one man He supervises and completes the building work. All those who do not build, speak, or serve according to the blueprint released by the Lord through that man are void of light and revelation and are not serving according to the vision. Today in the Lord's recovery, some are preaching and publishing messages. The portions in their messages that impart light, revelation, and the life supply invariably derive their source from this ministry in the Lord's recovery. Other than those portions, there is no revelation or vision in their writings.

Some have criticized us for not reading anything by outsiders or the denominations. But I would ask, why do so many enjoy reading the messages put out by this ministry? This ministry produces nothing but gold and diamonds. You can compare and see. For this reason, my dear brothers and sisters, today we are fighting the good fight for the truth. We are bearing on our shoulders the commission of this age. This is our vision. We need to be clear about this, and we need to serve God according to this vision.

CHAPTER TWO

THE VISION OF A SERVING ONE

In the first chapter, entitled "Vision in God's Economy," we read how God's servants and the Lord's followers must see a vision. In this chapter we will continue with this burden by speaking about the vision of those who serve the Lord.

REVIEWING THE OLD TESTAMENT VISIONS

Adam's First Vision

According to the revelation of the entire Bible, the Lord began showing men a vision from the time of Adam. When Adam was first created, God showed him a clear yet relatively simple vision before he fell; he was placed in front of two trees in the garden of Eden and was told, "Of every tree of the garden you may eat freely, but of the tree of the knowledge of good and evil, of it you shall not eat; for in the day that you eat of it you shall surely die" (Gen. 2:16-17). This is the vision that God gave to Adam.

A vision is a scene that God unfolds to man. When God gave Adam the command in the garden of Eden concerning the tree of life and the tree of the knowledge of good and evil, Adam saw a scene. That was the vision that God wanted to show him. That vision indicates something; it shows that God's intention is for man to eat the tree of life and to reject the tree of the knowledge of good and evil. For man to receive the tree of life means that he is living under this vision. It also means that he is serving God according to this vision. However, the devil, Satan, disguised as the serpent, seduced Eve through his speaking and turned her eyes from the tree of life to the tree of the knowledge of good and evil, against which God had warned her. Had Eve's vision been clear and

had her heart closely followed the vision, she would have
ignored the serpent when he spoke to her about the tree of
the knowledge of good and evil and would not have talked
about it or gazed upon it. Genesis 3:6 says, "When the woman
saw that the tree..." The minute Eve looked, she was dis-
tracted from the vision that God had given to man in the
beginning.

The vision that God gave to Adam is the first vision in the
entire Bible. The last vision is the New Jerusalem in the last
two chapters of the book of Revelation. Between these two
ends, God gave vision after vision to man.

Adam's Second Vision

After the first vision, Adam saw a second vision. After he
and Eve fell, they knew that they were naked. As soon as they
heard God's voice, they hid themselves among the trees of the
garden to escape God's face. However, God did not give them
up. Rather, He looked for them and gave them a vision. He
said to the serpent, "I will put enmity / Between you and
the woman, / And between your seed and her seed; / He will
bruise you on the head, / But you will bruise him on the heel"
(Gen. 3:15). This means that the seed of the woman would
bruise the head of the serpent and would inflict upon him a
death blow. The serpent, on the other hand, would bruise the
heel of the seed of the woman and would frustrate His move.
After this, God prepared a sacrifice—possibly a lamb—and
made coats of skin to clothe Adam and Eve.

If we put all these acts of God together, we have a clear
vision. It shows that man is sinful and that there is an evil
one who is trying to hurt him, but the seed of woman will
come and will solve the problem of sin for him. He will bruise
the head of the evil one. This vision also shows that man
needs redemption; he needs the killing of the sacrifice and
the shedding of the blood. He needs coats of skin to clothe
him. This was the second vision that Adam saw. It is the
second vision that God gave to man.

From that time onward, Adam began to live by this vision.
He named his wife Eve (v. 20), which means "living." This
indicates that he had heard and received the gospel. The

judgment of death had passed over him, and he lived. Eve was also living by this vision, because when she bore a son, she called him Cain, which means "acquired." This indicates that in her concept, Cain was the acquired seed of the woman that God had promised. She believed in the seed and was waiting for the seed. We have to believe that Adam and Eve not only lived by the vision, but they also told their children about this vision.

Abel's Vision

According to the Scriptures, the children of Adam were of two kinds. Those who lived under their fathers' vision were the first kind, and those who did not live under their fathers' vision were the second; they took another way to serve and worship God. Abel belonged to the first kind; he lived under his father's vision, and his father's vision became his vision. Hence, he was serving God according to a vision. Cain belonged to the second kind. He did not take his father's vision, and he did not live by it. On the contrary, he invented another way of serving and worshipping God. He was absolutely not serving by a vision. By the second generation of mankind, it came to be that, although all men were serving and worshipping the same true God, only Abel's service was carried out according to a vision. Cain was not worshipping idols; he did not serve other deities. Yet his service was one that was detached from the vision. He did not oppose God. On the contrary, he was also making sacrifices to God and worshipping God. Yet his sacrifice and worship were done apart from the vision; he was serving without a vision. This is the reason Abel was accepted by God, but Cain was rejected by Him.

Enosh's Vision

The time of Enosh was the third generation of mankind. Here we see a further advance in vision. The fallen man discovered that he was a frail being, that he was nothing, could do nothing, and had nothing. He was as vain, frail, and empty as a puff of air. He needed reality, and reality is only God Himself. Hence, Enosh began to call on the name of Jehovah in hope of receiving reality from Him. In Exodus 3:15 God said to Moses, "Thus you shall say to the children of Israel, Jehovah, the God of your fathers, the God of Abraham, the God of Isaac, and the God of Jacob, has sent me to you. This is My name forever, and this is My memorial from generation to generation." This indicates that the name of Jehovah is the name of the Triune God. Therefore, for man to call on the name of Jehovah means to receive the Triune God into him to be his enjoyment and supply. For Enosh to call on the name of Jehovah means that he saw a greater vision. He realized that not only must the fallen man seek covering in God's righteousness through the shedding of the sacrificial blood, and not only must he trust in the coming One for the destruction of the enemy according to His revealed way, but this same fallen man must call on the name of Jehovah out of his vanity, nothingness, destitution, and impotence and live by the enjoyment of God's riches and supply. This indeed is a further advance in vision.

Enoch's Vision

Then came Enoch. He inherited Adam's vision, Abel's vision, and Enosh's vision, but he went on to see that he could not be separated from God. He needed to walk with God moment by moment. This is another vision. Enoch walked with God and did not see death (Heb. 11:5). He not only escaped the punishment of sin and the snare of transgressions but was spared of death itself. In other words, by walking with God he was walking with the tree of life and was able to enjoy the tree of life because God is the very tree of life. Hence, we see a further progression of vision in the case of Enoch.

Noah's Vision

We have to believe that Noah at his time inherited Adam's vision, Abel's vision, Enosh's vision, and Enoch's vision. In addition, he received a further vision himself. In Genesis 6, God showed him clearly that the age was altogether evil. God wanted to give up and destroy that generation, and He wanted Noah to build an ark. Noah was living not only under the visions of Adam, Abel, Enosh, and Enoch; he was not only the heir of all these visions but was living, working, and serving under a greater vision which he saw with his own eyes. For this reason, we can say that Noah's life, work, and service were totally governed by the vision.

We can believe that at the time of Noah, there were more than his family of eight people who were fearing God. Although the Bible does not say anything about this, we can deduce it from history. Surely there were other people who were worshipping God and serving Him. However, no matter how many people were worshipping God at that time, according to the record of the Bible, they were worshipping and serving apart from any vision. Only Noah and his family of eight were serving under a vision. This is very clear.

The Visions from Abraham to Joseph

At the time of Abraham, we see a more expansive and far-reaching vision. Abraham saw that one of his descendants would rise up and become a blessing to the nations. We can believe that Abraham did not drop the visions of Adam, Abel, Enosh, Enoch, and Noah. He inherited all these visions and was living under them. Yet he went on and saw a more expansive and far-reaching vision. After Abraham, we have Isaac. In Isaac we see a person who fully inherited Abraham's vision. Jacob was also an heir. After these three persons we have Joseph. In Joseph we have another vision. Through Egypt the entire earth was blessed. Joseph was a type of Christ. He was a descendant of Abraham, yet he became the chief minister who managed all the food supply in Egypt. During the seven years of famine over the whole world, everyone came to Egypt and to Joseph for food. Hence, in Joseph we see a person through whom the entire earth was blessed. This is a picture of Christ ministering to and blessing the whole earth.

From Moses to David

Moses also saw a vision. He saw the tabernacle and the ordinances regarding the offerings and other matters, which we cannot describe here in detail. Joshua inherited from Moses and saw something further in the way of a vision. He led the Israelites into Canaan and inherited the good land. During the time of the judges, there were visions after visions, until the time of Samuel. Samuel was also a man of vision, and he served according to the vision that he saw. Through him the age was changed from the confused age of the judges to the age of the kingdom. At the same time that Samuel was on earth, another person appeared on the scene—Saul. He was a king anointed by Samuel, yet he was not living by the vision. Another person who inherited from Samuel was David. He was a man living under the vision.

The Prophets

Beginning from the time of his reign, Solomon and his descendants gradually departed from all the visions. Nearly none of the kings during the age of the kings served according to a vision. Instead, they followed the custom of the nations. Under such circumstances God raised up the prophets. These prophets were not only living under a vision; they actually received visions. For this reason, the prophets were also called seers. Not only did they prophesy and speak for God; they saw vision after vision in a definite way and served according to these visions. At that time the kings had all departed from the visions that God had imparted to His people; as a result, the prophets were raised up to correct and adjust them. They turned the kings back from the things contrary to the visions to a service that was once again under the visions. This is the story of the kings in the age of the kings.

The Conclusion of the Old Testament

The last two books of the Old Testament are Zechariah and Malachi. Both have certain rich utterances concerning Christ. They are the conclusion of the revelation concerning Christ in the Old Testament. There are three ways by which the Old Testament speaks about Christ—clear declarations, types, and prophecies. All these revelations concerning Christ come to a conclusion in the books of Zechariah and Malachi. They conclude everything. These two books speak much concerning Christ. This is the conclusion of the Old Testament.

THE VISIONS IN THE NEW TESTAMENT

The Vision of John the Baptist

At the time the Old Testament era ended, the earthly system of service was still in place. In Jerusalem of Judea there was still the temple, and there were still priests offering sacrifices, worshipping, and serving God according to the God-ordained institutions. Then suddenly John the Baptist appeared. He was not in the temple, and he was not a priest. He did not wear a priestly garment but instead lived in the wilderness, eating locusts and wild honey and wearing camel's hair. He was serving the Lord totally apart from the traditional rituals and ordinances. Please tell me who was serving according to a vision at that time: Was it the priests who were abiding by the traditions, or was it John the Baptist who had dropped all the traditions? The Gospel of John shows clearly that the priests, the elders, the scribes, the Pharisees, and all the other Jewish religionists were serving God fully according to their religion, traditions, ordinances, knowledge, and doctrines. They were not under any vision. Only one man was serving under a vision—John the Baptist.

The Vision of the Lord Jesus and the Competition from John the Baptist

The ministry of John the Baptist was a kind of termination. It was for the purpose of ushering in a new beginning. The baptism of John the Baptist initiated the Lord Jesus into His office for the accomplishment of His ministry. John the Baptist clearly indicated that his ministry was a pioneering and initiating ministry (John 1:23, 28-30), but his disciples did not understand this. They thought that John was a great man and that his teaching was unique. This was why they followed him and his teachings. Unconsciously, they began to compete with the Lord's ministry. Beginning from Matthew 9, we see the disciples of John questioning the Lord Jesus. Their questioning put them in the same category as the Pharisees (v. 14). According to Luke 5:33 it was the Pharisees who questioned Him, but Mark 2:18 seems to say that it was the disciples of John and the Pharisees together who questioned

the Lord. Before this time, the Pharisees were the only questioning party. After Matthew 9, John's disciples became
another party.

At this point we see three parties: the Jewish religion,
John's religion, and the Lord Jesus. All of them were serving
God. Please tell me which of them were serving under a
vision. No doubt those who followed the Lord Jesus were the
only ones serving under a vision. Not only were the Jewish
religionists not under the vision; even the followers of John
the Baptist were not under the vision. God had set the Jewish
religion aside and had used John the Baptist to bring in a
new beginning, but when the Lord Jesus came, John's religion
still remained on the scene competing with the Lord. God was
forced by the situation to send John to prison. However, John
still sent his disciples from his prison to the Lord Jesus to ask
Him questions. On the one hand, the Lord commended John's
ministry. On the other hand, He encouraged John to take the
way that the Lord had ordained for him and to experience the
blessing in that way. Soon after this, John was martyred. In
this way God sovereignly ended the ministry of John.

However, John's religion did not stop with his death. In
Acts 18 and 19 this line reappeared and caused a problem.
Apollos only knew the baptism of John, and he preached this
when he went down to Ephesus (18:24-25; 19:3). This brought
in the decline of the church. In the seven churches in Revelation 2 and 3, Ephesus shows the beginning of the degradation
of the church. John's religion was the source of this problem,
and Apollos was the one who sowed the seed of this problem.

The Vision of the Followers of the Lord Jesus

While the Lord Jesus was fulfilling His ministry on the
earth, those who were following Him were the only ones who
had inherited the visions of the previous ages and who were
at the same time catching up with the vision that matched
that age. Not only had they inherited the visions that went
before them, but they were caught up with the vision of that
age when they followed the Lord Jesus. This group of people
consisted of men like Peter, James, and John. None among the
disciples was as foolish and uncouth as Peter. However, he

was not foolish in one thing. While the Lord Jesus was shining on him as a great light and calling him by the Sea of Galilee, he together with Andrew, James, and John responded to the light and was attracted by the Lord to drop everything to follow Him (Matt. 4:15-16, 18-22). Andrew was first a disciple of John the Baptist (John 1:35-40). Now he and Peter, James, and John forsook the Jewish religion and John's religion. They even forsook their fishing career, leaving behind their fathers and their nets, and followed the Lord single-heartedly.

Outwardly speaking, Peter was following blindly. He was blindly following for three and a half years. Every day he was speaking nonsense. However, once, and only once, he spoke a clear word. When the Lord took the disciples up to the region of Caesarea Philippi and asked them who the Son of Man was, Peter answered, "You are the Christ, the Son of the living God" (Matt. 16:16). This was a word full of revelation. Regrettably, he only spoke one clear word. After this, he spoke many foolish words again. When the Lord indicated to the disciples that He had to go to Jerusalem to suffer under the hands of the elders, the chief priests, and the scribes and would be killed and then resurrected after three days, Peter took Him aside and rebuked Him, saying, "God be merciful to You, Lord! This shall by no means happen to You!" (vv. 21-22). But the Lord turned and said to Peter, "Get behind Me, Satan!" (v. 23). This shows that Peter was indeed following blindly. He did not know what he was doing. He followed blindly but rightly. Sometimes when a person is too clear, he ends up doing the wrong thing. When he is a little foolish, he ends up in the right place. At that time all those who were following the Lord Jesus, male or female, including such ones as Mary, were all foolish. Today we may appear foolish, but we can follow the Lord faithfully.

From the Bible we can see that not too many who followed the Lord were clear. Even the Lord Jesus' own mother, Mary, was not so clear; she was somewhat muddled. She spoke some foolish words a few times and was rebuked. Although they were all foolish, they were foolish in the right direction. Men like Nicodemus who were so "clear" were not doing better in any way. Although they were clear that the Lord had the

vision, they were not absolute in following Him. They were following Him only in a halfhearted way. Actually, they were
only trailing behind Him and not following Him. I believe
that among those who were "following" the Lord, Nicodemus
was the clearest one, and Peter was the most foolish one. Yet
the one who was the most foolish was the one who followed
in the most genuine way. Although sometimes he failed, he
was the most absolute one in following. When the Lord told
the disciples that they would all be stumbled because of Him,
Peter responded by saying, "If all will be stumbled because of
You, I will never be stumbled." The Lord told him, "Truly I say
to you that in this night, before a rooster crows, you will deny
Me three times." Peter then said, "Even if I must die with You,
I will by no means deny You" (Matt. 26:31-35). Of course, he
did not keep his promise. On the contrary, he denied the Lord
three times as was foretold by Him. Although Peter was such
a person, he took the right path, and he followed the vision.

Peter's Vision

The One whom the disciples followed eventually brought
them to the cross. They were crucified with Him, died with Him,
were buried with Him, and resurrected and ascended with
Him (Eph. 2:6). On the day of Pentecost, Peter saw the vision.
Formerly, he only identified himself with the vision through
the Lord Jesus. Now at Pentecost, he saw the vision himself.
When he stood up to speak, he was no longer foolish. He was
very strong and clear in everything. In Acts 2 through 5, we
find him caring for nothing other than the Lord's ministry. He
did not even care for his own life. The vision did not find any
resistance or hindrance in him at all.

When we come to Acts 10, however, we find that his strong
Jewish background stood in the way and caused the vision to
suffer a setback. In Matthew 16 the Lord told Peter that He
would give him the keys to the kingdom. The keys are plural
in number, indicating that there are at least two keys. On the
day of Pentecost, Peter used one key to open the door for the
Jews to enter God's New Testament kingdom. At that time
the vision did not suffer any setback in him. However, by the
time God wanted to use him further to exercise the second

key to open the door to the Gentiles and to spread His New Testament economy among the Gentiles, Peter was lagging behind. This became a problem to God; He was forced to revert to the Old Testament means of visions and dreams. Peter saw a vessel like a great sheet descending from heaven to the earth. In it were all the four-footed animals and reptiles of the earth and birds of heaven. A voice came to him: "Rise up, Peter; slay and eat! But Peter said, By no means, Lord, for I have never eaten anything common and unclean. And a voice came to him again a second time: The things that God has cleansed, do not make common" (Acts 10:13-15). This went on three times. By this we can see that Peter had a problem in following the vision.

If we study Acts 10, Galatians 2, and Acts 15, we will find that, in those cases, Peter was no longer as absolute and strong in following the vision as he was in following the Lord during the first three and a half years. He became somewhat weak. The vision had come into conflict with his tradition, and he could not quite go along with it. He remained to a certain extent in that tradition. It frustrated him and hindered him from going on. We see a falling behind in his case with respect to the vision. We have to pay attention to this matter and be warned by it.

Paul's Vision

By the time of Acts 13, another person appeared on the scene. In Acts 7 through 9 he was Saul of Tarsus, a person who was in the Jewish religion and had received the highest education. He had also studied the best Greek culture and was an endeavoring man. At that time Judaism was under attack. The followers of Jesus Christ, the so-called "Nazarenes" (24:5), were getting stronger and stronger. Saul could not suffer to see his ancestors' religion being destroyed, and he became very zealous, being determined to wipe out the Nazarenes and to uphold his fathers' religion.

We cannot deny that Saul of Tarsus was serving God. After he was saved, he told the believers, "You have heard of my manner of life formerly in Judaism, that I persecuted the church of God excessively and ravaged it. And I advanced in

Judaism beyond many contemporaries in my race, being more abundantly a zealot for the traditions of my fathers" (Gal. 1:13-14). As to zeal, he was a persecutor of the church (Phil. 3:6). He was so zealous that he consented to Stephen's death (Acts 7:58—8:1a). He also put many believers into prison, cast votes to condemn them to death, and persecuted them even as far as foreign cities (26:9-11). Saul was indeed serving God, but he was serving without a vision. While he was being zealous for his fathers' traditions, who was serving God under a vision? It was Peter. Peter was under a vision, and those who were following him were also under the same vision. Saul, however, was not under the vision, yet one day on his way to Damascus the Lord met him and showed him the vision.

I truly believe that the vision Saul saw on the way to Damascus was more advanced than the one Peter saw. In the New Testament records concerning Peter and in his own Epistles, we do not see any mention of the Triune God working Himself into us to make us His duplication. We do not see anything about the believers being built up into the Body of Christ to be one with the Triune God as His organism. But on the way to Damascus, Paul saw a vision. The Lord said to him, "Saul, Saul, why are you persecuting Me?" (Acts 9:4). The "Me" here is a corporate Me; it includes the Lord Jesus and all His believers. Although the word *Me* is a small word, it speaks of a great vision. Paul in Galatians 1 says that "it pleased God...to reveal His Son in me" (vv. 15-16). In the Bible we do not find that Peter saw the same clear vision.

Paul's vision was indeed profound. At the beginning of Galatians, he refers to the Son of God (1:16). When we speak of the Son of God, we have to realize that this involves the Triune God. The Triune God was revealed to Paul, and Paul became one of His members. All the members together with Paul were constituted to become His Body and were joined to Him to become an enlarged "Me." Although the vision Paul saw at the beginning was so high and profound, he did not take up his ministry immediately. In Acts 13 a few prophets and teachers were serving the Lord and fasting together in Antioch. It was then that the Holy Spirit said, "Set apart for Me now Barnabas and Saul for the work to which I have called them" (v. 2). It was not until then that Paul became clear concerning the vision he had received earlier and was sent to fulfill the ministry which he had received.

Both Barnabas and Saul were Jews, yet they were sent to preach the gospel throughout the Gentile lands. This was not a small vision. In his own time Peter was only sent to make a brief contact with a Gentile and to visit his home. Here Paul received a serious commission: "Go, for I will send you forth far away to the Gentiles" (22:21). This means he was to go to the Gentile lands, nation by nation and city by city. This is a great vision: "That in Christ Jesus the Gentiles are fellow heirs and fellow members of the Body and fellow partakers of the promise through the gospel" (Eph. 3:6).

Many of us have been affected by Christianity; we read the Bible in a superficial way. We think that Paul was sent merely to preach the gospel and to save sinners from hell. In reading the book of Acts, many believers come away with the impression that the Lord's desire is to spread the gospel to the uttermost part of the earth. They see the great number of sinners in the Gentile world and consider that they cannot be saved unless the believers go out to preach the gospel to them. In their understanding, this was the reason Paul was sent on his evangelistic journey to preach the gospel. However, if we carefully study the book of Acts and Paul's Epistles, we will discover that this matter is not that simple or shallow. Paul was sent to preach to the Gentiles the unsearchable riches of Christ (Eph. 3:8) in order that the Triune God could be dispensed into them to transform them into the members of Christ for the building up of the Body of Christ. At this time, Paul's vision became fully clear.

Factors of Frustrations

The Problem of Judaism

Here we have to ask, while Paul was fulfilling his ministry, who on earth was clear about God's vision? At that time there were still many God-fearing people in the Jewish religion. For example, Gamaliel feared God; he understood the

Old Testament and was familiar with the teachings of the Old Testament, yet he was not in Paul's vision.

The Problem of the Church in Jerusalem

At that time Peter and John were in Jerusalem. There was also a very pious James. These were the leading ones in the church in Jerusalem (Gal. 2:9). At the time Paul was fulfilling his ministry, it seems that James and Peter were one with his vision. However, they were not one with it. The best we can say about them is that they did not oppose Paul. They were going along in a general way but were actually not in the same company. They received the same grace as Paul did, and they were apostles together. They should have belonged to the same group and the same company. Yet they were not of the same company, though they were of the same general group. Galatians 2:9 says that James, Peter, and John gave to Paul and Barnabas the right hand of fellowship that they should go to the Gentiles, and they would go to the circumcision. It seems as if they were shaking hands with Paul and saying to him, "Okay, Paul. Go to the Gentiles to fulfill your ministry, but we will not go with you. We are apostles to the Jews, and you are an apostle to the Gentiles."

The Problem of Barnabas

I do not believe that many Christians have detected this flavor when they read the Bible. Faced with this situation, Paul surely must not have had a sweet feeling. It was good that Barnabas was with him, but not long after this, the two had an argument. In the end Barnabas left. This shows that even Barnabas could not catch up with the vision of that age, the vision which Paul saw. Although he was the one who ushered Paul into the service, when Paul saw the up-to-date vision of the age, Barnabas was left behind.

The Problem of James

Not only were men like Gamaliel and Barnabas falling behind in the vision; even apostles such as Peter and James were in danger of missing out on the vision. They were of the same general group as Paul, but they were not co-working together. When Paul went up to Jerusalem for the last time, James said to him, "You observe, brother, how many thousands there are among the Jews who have believed; and all are zealous for the law" (Acts 21:20). Before this time, Paul had said clearly in Galatians that the law is over. But here, James, the leading apostle in Jerusalem, was exhorting him to keep the law. This shows that even a person as renowned in the church as James could be short in the vision. James did not walk according to the flesh; he was not a light person in any way. From history we know that he was quite a pious person. Yet he was not serving under the vision. We can say that even Peter did not catch up with the vision; even he was not in the vision.

The record of the Jerusalem conference in Acts 15 shows that the decision was full of Judaistic influence. James's word was saturated with a Jewish and Old Testament overtone. I do not believe that decision could have satisfied Paul. Yet in order to keep the peace, he tolerated the decision, for without such a decision, there would have been unceasing arguments between the Jewish and Gentile churches over the matter of circumcision, and the churches would forever be in turmoil. However, things did not turn out as he had hoped. That decision did not solve in a clear and accurate way the problem of the Old Testament law. This proves that the church in Jerusalem did not come up fully to the vision of the age; instead, it made a compromise.

The Problem of Apollos

In Acts 18 Apollos appeared on the scene. He was "powerful in the Scriptures" (v. 24b). We have to realize that the Scriptures here refer to the thirty-nine books of the Old Testament. Apollos was powerful in expounding the Old Testament, but he was not in Paul's vision. At that time, Aquila, Priscilla, and Timothy joined Paul's ministry one after another. No doubt they were in Paul's vision. They were walking with Paul and working together with him.

Paul worked throughout the Gentile world, but he never stayed in one place for as long as three years except in Ephesus. Acts 20:31 clearly shows that Paul stayed in Ephesus for three years. His preaching affected the entire region of Asia, of which Ephesus was the center. Paul was teaching there, and his teaching affected all those who were in Asia, but at the same time in Ephesus a negative seed was sown, and Apollos was the one who sowed it. This is one of the reasons that Paul had to work and minister in Ephesus for three years. In Acts 20, after Paul finished traveling to all the places to exhort the believers, he passed by Ephesus, called the elders together, and charged them, saying, "Take heed to yourselves and to all the flock...I know that after my departure fierce wolves will come in among you, not sparing the flock" (vv. 28-29).

After this Paul went up to Jerusalem, and soon he was bound and sent to prison. He was imprisoned in Caesarea for two years (24:27), after which he was sent to Rome. In Rome he was imprisoned for at least another two years (28:30). After he was released from prison, he wrote the first Epistle to Timothy, in which he began by saying, "Even as I exhorted you, when I was going into Macedonia, to remain in Ephesus in order that you might charge certain ones not to teach different things" (1:3). This word shows a trace of some kind of problem in Ephesus. A little more than a year after Paul was released from prison, Nero, the Roman emperor, began to persecute the church again, and Paul was sent back to prison. While he was in prison, he wrote the second Epistle to Timothy. In 1:15 he said, "All who are in Asia turned away from me." Among these churches who had turned away from Paul, Ephesus was the leading one. Hence, in Revelation, the first of the seven letters to the seven churches was to the church in Ephesus.

The seed that Apollos sowed in Ephesus eventually became the basic factor for the decline of the church. The reason that the church in Ephesus degraded was that it had taken the lead to depart from the teaching of the apostles. To depart from the apostles' teaching is to depart from the apostles' vision. With the departure of the apostles' teaching came the teaching of Balaam (Rev. 2:14), the teaching of the Nicolaitans (vv. 6, 15), and the teaching of Jezebel (v. 20). These three teachings represent the heresies in Christianity.

Paul tells us in Colossians that the ministry he received

from God was to complete the word of God (1:25). After Paul completed his ministry and finished his Epistles, the church in Ephesus took the lead to bring all the churches in Asia away from the teaching of the apostle Paul. By the time the book of Revelation was written, we find the apostle John continuing the Lord's commission and following Paul in fulfilling his ministry. John continued from where Paul had left off in his ministry. While Paul was on earth, he dealt with the problem of decline. The last church he dealt with was Ephesus in Asia. Thirty years later, at the beginning of the book of Revelation, in writing to the seven churches in Asia, the first church that was addressed was the church in Ephesus. John rebuked Ephesus for having left its first love. The reason it had left its first love is that it had left the apostles' teaching.

The Vision of the Apostle John—
the Ultimate Consummation of God's Visions

The book of Revelation, which the apostle John wrote, begins with the seven churches. It covers this age and extends to the coming of Christ, the judgment of the world, and the advent of the millennium, and it concludes with the New Jerusalem in the new heaven and new earth. This constitutes the ultimate consummation of the divine revelation. After this there is nothing left to be said or seen. Everything is said and everything is seen. This is the ultimate consummation of God's economy. Once the New Jerusalem appears, we have the final scene. For this reason, the end of Revelation says that nothing can be added to or deleted from this book (22:18-19). From that time onward, no one could add anything to the Bible. If anyone tries to add anything, his portion will be the punishment of the lake of fire. No one can delete anything. If anyone tries to cut off anything, he will be cut off from the blessing of the tree of life, the water of life, and the city of life. This shows that at the end of Revelation, God's vision is consummated. No one can see more, and those who see less will, of course, suffer loss.

SERVING GOD ACCORDING TO THE COMPLETE VISION

From the time the apostle John completed the book of

Revelation until today, nineteen centuries have passed. During the past nineteen hundred years, countless numbers of Christians have been serving God. Added to this great number of Christians serving God are the Jews, who also are serving God. Of course, the Jews serve only according to the vision of the Old Testament. Some Christians are serving according to the vision revealed in the New Testament Gospels, which has to do only with the earthly ministry of Jesus. Some serve without any vision at all. In order to serve God according to the up-to-date vision, we need to come up to the level of Paul's very last Epistles. In fact, we need to come up to the level of the epistles to the seven churches in Revelation as well as the revelation which covers all the ages, including the kingdom, the new heaven and new earth, and the ultimate consummation of the church—the New Jerusalem. Simply put, in order for us to serve God today, our vision must extend all the way from the first vision of Adam in Genesis to the ultimate vision of the manifestation of the church, the New Jerusalem. This and this alone is the complete vision. It is not until today that this vision has been fully opened to us.

In the National Palace Museum in Taipei, there is a painting on a long scroll called "The River Scene at Ching-Ming Festival." It describes in detail the culture, life, and way of the Chinese people at the time of the painting. It is not enough to see only the first few portions of that long scroll. One has to go all the way from one end to the other end before he can have a clear picture, or "vision," of the entire spectrum of life in China. In the same way, we have our own painting, our "River Scene at Ching-Ming," in our service to God. It begins from Adam's vision of the tree of life in the garden of Eden and extends all the way to the New Jerusalem with the tree of life. The New Jerusalem is the last scene of the vision. After that there is nothing more to be seen.

The problem today is, who has seen this complete vision, and who is living in this vision? During the past nineteen hundred years, many people have been serving the Lord, but how have they served? Can we say that five hundred years ago Martin Luther saw this vision and was serving according to this vision? Throughout the ages many people were serving the Lord only according to the first few scenes. I wish that all the brothers and sisters would have an enlarged and far-reaching view. I hope they will realize that all the books that we have put out cover the entire spectrum from the first scene to the last scene. We are not serving God based on the first few scenes alone. We are serving God according to the last scene which includes all the previous scenes.

Today many people have not seen what we have seen. They are merely serving according to the first few scenes, and they are even arguing with one another. The Jews are pious people; they are zealous in expounding the Scriptures from Genesis to Malachi, but they have only the Old Testament. Many Christians love the Lord and are zealous for the gospel. Yet they preach only the story of Jesus Christ. They have never progressed beyond the four Gospels. Some have seen only the vision of the book of Acts. Others have seen the vision of the Epistles. All these are fragmentary, but we should serve God according to the entire spectrum, from the first scene of Adam to the last scene in Revelation. It is for this reason that we face so much opposition. Many people say that we are wrong. They criticize us for "stealing sheep." It is not that they do not love the Lord or serve God; it is that they love the Lord and serve God only according to the vision which they themselves have seen. Today we must be clear about the standing that we take. The goal of all our services, including preaching the gospel and edifying the believers, must be ultimately consummated in the New Jerusalem. Only then will we be unshaken in the face of any criticism.

CLOSELY FOLLOWING
THE COMPLETED VISION OF THIS AGE

Since we have the up-to-date and ultimate vision, we should closely follow after it. We are absolutely not following a man; rather, we are following a vision. It is grossly wrong to say that we are following a certain person. We are following a vision that belongs to the present age. It is God's consummate vision.

The Lord's recovery was brought to us through our dear Brother Nee. Because of this he became a target of attack. In

1934 he was married in Hangchow. Some took this opportunity to stir up a storm. He became very sad, so one day I went to him to comfort him, saying, "Brother Nee, you know that between the two of us, there is no natural relationship. I do not take the way that you are taking or preach what you are preaching out of a natural friendship with you. The two of us are widely separated from one another. I am a northerner and you are a southerner. Today I am taking the same pathway not because I am following you as a person. I am following the way that you are taking. Brother Nee, I would like you to know that even if one day you do not take this way, I will still take this way." I said this because the storm affected some, and they decided not to take this way anymore. In other words, many people were following a man. When the man seemed to have changed, they turned away. But I told Brother Nee, "Even if one day you do not take this way, I will still take this way. I am not taking this way because of you, and I will not leave this way because of you. I have seen that this is the Lord's way. I have seen the vision."

Fifty-two years have passed. Today I do not regret at all what I have done. During the past fifty-two years, I have seen the same story repeat itself again and again. Some people came and left. One scene changed, and another scene came along. Since the beginning of our work in Taiwan, during the past three decades we have witnessed some major crises. Even brothers whom I led to salvation and who went through my own training have left the Lord's recovery. The vision has never changed, but the persons have indeed changed, and those who follow the vision also have changed. I would say a sober word to all of you from the bottom of my heart. By the Lord's mercy, I can stand here today to bring you this vision. I hope that you are not following me as a person; I hope that by the Lord's mercy you are following the vision that I have shown you.

I have no intention to be proud. America is the leading country in this world. It is also the top Christian country. There are many theological professors there. When I went there, I spoke boldly about the vision that I saw. At the beginning their ears were pricked, but by now, some are speaking what we have seen. Up until today, they are not able to put out a proper book to refute the truth that I have released. In order for them to write a book to refute me, they must first read my books, but once they read my books, they are convinced and subdued. They cannot refute anymore. Rather, they have to admit, "If you carefully and seriously read what this old Chinese man has written, you will discover that he has a solid basis for what he is saying. It is best not to challenge him in any matter. If you do, he can come back and ask you ten questions, none of which you can answer." They are very clear about this.

I would like to relate to you one fact. It is the Lord's mercy that He has revealed to me the vision. I advise you not to follow me but to follow this vision which Brother Nee and all the servants of the Lord throughout the ages have left to us and which I have handed to you. This is indeed the vision that extends from the first scene of Adam to the last scene of the New Jerusalem. More than fifty years have passed. I have seen with my own eyes that those who take the way of the Lord's recovery for a while and then leave do not come to a proper ending. There is only one way. All spiritual things are one. There is one God, one Lord, one Spirit, one church, one Body, one testimony, one way, one flow, and one work. If you do not take this way, you will have no way to take.

Some who left us once shouted and boldly declared that they had seen the vision. Today where is their vision? After so much shouting, the vision is lost. They have lost the way. To start a war one must have the proper cause. With a proper cause we have the boldness to say what we say. If we do not take this way today, what other way do we have? I speak this for myself also. What other cause can we take up? Between 1942 and 1948 there was a great storm, and Brother Nee was forced to discontinue his ministry for six years. At that time some saints who appreciated Brother Nee very much said, "Let us start another meeting." Brother Nee said, "You must never do this. The church is the church; if it agrees with me, it is the church. If it does not agree with me, it is still the church. We can never set up another meeting apart from the church."

Paul told Timothy, "All who are in Asia turned away from me" (2 Tim. 1:15), but Paul did not authorize Timothy to have another beginning. In the same way, at the time when almost everyone in China forsook Brother Nee, he did not try to make another beginning. This proves that even Paul and Brother Nee could not change the way they took. If they were to change the way, they would not have been able to go on.

This is my burden. I hope that you will clearly see the vision of the Lord's recovery and will follow this vision. You are not following me as a person. Sister Faith Chang can testify for me. She witnessed how I followed Brother Nee absolutely, yet I was not following the person; I was following the vision that he saw. In that age, the vision that came up to God's standard was the vision that Brother Nee saw. If you remained in that vision, you were serving according to the vision. If you did not remain in that vision, you were not serving according to the vision. Today Brother Nee has passed away. I have no intention to make a new beginning, but the Lord has commissioned me with this ministry. I can only take the lead willingly and obediently. The vision that I have brought to you today is God's vision for this age. If you remain in this vision, you are serving according to the vision. If you do not remain in this vision, you should be aware of what your end will be.

Therefore, you are not following a man; rather, you are standing with the Lord's ministry. You are following a vision, a vision that matches the age, a vision that inherits all that was in the past and a vision that is all-inclusive. It is up to date, and yet it builds on the past. If you remain in the book of Acts, you may have inherited everything prior to that time, but you are not up to date. Today as we stand here and ponder the revelations unveiled in the Lord's recovery, as we read the publications that are released among us, we can see that they cover everything from the church to God's economy to the New Jerusalem in the new heaven and new earth. This is a bountiful and all-sufficient vision. If you remain in this vision, you are serving according to the vision. If you are not in this vision, you could still be an Apollos, expounding the Scriptures in a powerful way; you could still be a Barnabas, visiting the churches; you could still be a James, serving piously; and you could even be a Peter, who served as the leading apostle. However, you would not be in the vision.

I believe this light is very clear among us. No one can argue with this. I hope that the young brothers and sisters will all be clear about this. From your youth, while you are serving the Lord, you should understand what we are doing here. This is not a personal thing. It is absolutely the Lord's ministry. He has unveiled the visions generation after generation to His children. All those who are in this vision now are serving according to God's vision.

THE GENUINE ONE ACCORD

Where there is no vision, the people cast off restraint, because there is no one accord. It is true that many people love the Lord and serve God, but everyone has his opinion and his own vision. As a result, there is no way to have the one accord. This is the reason that Christianity has become so weak. God's people are divided and split apart. There are divisions everywhere. Although everyone says that he loves the Lord, there is no clear vision, and men are "carried about by every wind" (Eph. 4:14). Some among us also doubt, saying, "Are we the only ones who are right? Do not others also preach the gospel? Do they not also bring men to the Lord and edify them? Consider the aged James. He was more pious than Paul or Brother Nee. How can we say that he did not have a vision?"

Recently while we were translating the New Testament Recovery Version, I used two Catholic translations among my references. In some expressions we felt that these Catholic translations are not bad. I joked with my helpers, saying, "In this sentence, let us follow the Catholic Church." My point is this: Although James was pious to the uttermost in Jerusalem, we cannot conclude from this that his pathway was the right one. We cannot conclude from this that he possessed the vision that matched the age. No, we must be clear what the genuine vision is.

I believe this word will answer many questions in your heart. Although we are far behind many people in their zeal for preaching the gospel, although many people are more zealous and more burning in spirit than we are, and although we are poor, the vision is still with us. I truly hope that the young workers among us and the trainees would exercise themselves unto godliness. It does not mean that once we have the vision, we do not need to have godliness anymore, yet I hope that you would remember that godliness alone cannot match the vision. We certainly need to exercise ourselves unto godliness; we should not be loose, and our personality and character, should be noble. But this does not mean that once we have a noble character, we are in the vision. In other words, our vision should be one that matches the age. It should also be one that includes everything that has gone before us. It should include the godliness of the Jews, the zeal of the evangelicals, and the genuine service. Only then will we be able to practice an all-inclusive church life, the church life Paul revealed to us (Rom. 14). We are not divided into sects, and we do not impose any special practice on anyone. We only live an all-inclusive church life. If we do this, we will have the genuine one accord.

Today we can be in one accord because we have only one vision and one view. We are all in this up-to-date, all-inheriting vision. We have only one viewpoint. We speak the same thing with one heart, one mouth, one voice, and one tone, serving the Lord together. The result is a power that will become our strong morale and our impact. This is our strength. Once the Lord's recovery possesses this power, there will be the glory of increase and multiplication. Today our situation is not yet to that point; it is not yet at the peak. Although we do not have many major contentions, we do have some small complaints and criticisms. These things lower our morale.

When I returned to Taiwan in 1984, there was no morale at all because the one accord was gone. The goal was gone, and the vision had become blurred. At the present time we hope that the Lord would be merciful to us. We want to recover our morale, beginning from Taiwan. We want to recover our vision. We want to have the one accord, and we want to see clearly that there is only this one way. The churches in the Lord's recovery should have the Lord's testimony and a definite standing. Today there is still much ground for us to cover in the spreading of the Lord's churches. We have to preach the gospel everywhere, build up the small groups, and teach the truth. With this goal in view, we should have no arguments and no different opinions. We should speak the same thing, think the same thing, and press on in one accord. Not only should the churches in Taiwan do this, but all the churches in all the continents throughout the earth should do this. If we do this, the power will be great. The Lord will surely grant us an open door because this is the way that the Lord wants to take today.

CHAPTER THREE

THE PRESENT VISION AND PRACTICE IN THE LORD'S RECOVERY

Paul writes in 1 Timothy 1:3, "I exhorted you, when I was going into Macedonia, to remain in Ephesus in order that you might charge certain ones not to teach different things." This verse shows that Paul was inwardly clear that there were some in Ephesus who were teaching differently. For this reason, he charged one of his closest co-workers, Timothy, to remain in Ephesus to help the Ephesian believers and even charge them not to teach different doctrines or teachings. This proves that the matter of different teachings is a serious matter.

THE HEALTHY TEACHING

In 6:3 Paul writes again, "If anyone teaches different things and does not consent to healthy words, those of our Lord Jesus Christ, and the teaching which is according to godliness." This is one of Paul's final words in this book, which reminds us of his opening word. What is it to teach differently? It is to not consent to healthy words. These healthy words are the words of our Lord Jesus Christ. We need to realize that those who were teaching differently were teaching the words of the Old Testament. Although the Old Testament words are part of the Scriptures, they are not the "healthy words." Unhealthy words are words that do not minister or supply life to others. What then are the "healthy words"? They are the words of the Lord Jesus in the New Testament age and the teaching that is according to godliness.

First Timothy 3:15-16 says, "The house of God, which is the church of the living God, the pillar and base of the truth. And confessedly, great is the mystery of godliness: He who was manifested in the flesh..." If we put all the above verses together we can see that the healthy teaching includes two parts. The first part is the words that the Lord Jesus Himself spoke. The other part is the words that the apostles spoke on earth after the Lord resurrected and ascended. These words are "the teaching which is according to godliness." The teaching which is according to godliness concerns God becoming flesh, passing through human living, dying, and resurrecting to produce the church, which is God manifested in the flesh. What the church supports and upholds is the teaching according to godliness, which is God manifesting Himself in the flesh through the church. In reality, the healthy teaching covers the entire New Testament; it is constituted with the Lord Jesus' words of life and the preaching of the apostles, which is the word of the mystery of godliness, that is, of God becoming flesh to produce the church. It extends all the way from Matthew to Revelation.

Paul's burden in his first Epistle to Timothy was to instruct him to remain in Ephesus to charge the dissenters not to teach anything outside the New Testament teaching. If anyone teaches anything apart from the New Testament teaching, he is teaching differently, and he does not consent to healthy words. If we study this book carefully, we will see that at that time there were some Judaistic Christians who were spreading such things as Old Testament knowledge and genealogies, not only among Jewish believers in Jerusalem but among the churches in all the Gentile lands. Although their speaking was in accordance with the Old Testament, it was not the healthy words. Consider the case of circumcision. According to the record of Genesis 17, God established circumcision with Abraham as a sign of an eternally immutable covenant. The Jewish Christians argued that even in the New Testament age, God's people, that is, His children, were not exempt from circumcision. Superficially, such a teaching sounds scriptural. Actually, it is absolutely contrary to God's New Testament economy, which the apostles preached.

Moreover, these preachings which were superficially scriptural did not give life to men. They did not afford men any life supply. On the contrary, they led some to become shipwrecked regarding the faith (1 Tim. 1:19). Therefore, they were unhealthy teachings. Healthy words are those that are not only scriptural, but those that consent to the revelation of the Lord Jesus. They cover the speakings concerning His birth, death, and resurrection. They also cover the words which the apostles continued to speak after His ascension concerning God becoming flesh and passing through death and resurrection to release God's life and to produce the church to be the corporate manifestation of God in the flesh. These words according to the mystery of godliness are the consistent and overall revelation of God in the New Testament.

THE BACKGROUND OF THE FIRST EPISTLE TO TIMOTHY

In order to understand 1 Timothy, we must first understand the background behind the writing of this book. In Acts 20 we find Paul sending for the elders of the church in Ephesus while he was on his way to Jerusalem. He spoke a solemn and crucial word to them. He reminded them how for three years he was in their midst, not shrinking from declaring to them all the counsel of God (vv. 20, 27, 31). This means that Paul fully and thoroughly explained to them God's revelation in the New Testament. Then he said, "I know that after my departure fierce wolves will come in among you, not sparing the flock" (v. 29). The wolves here refer to the Judaistic believers. They were doing an unhealthy work in the church, speaking unhealthy words. Unhealthy words are poisonous words, killing words. Those who were speaking these unhealthy words destroyed men and poisoned them rather than supplying them. In this sense, they were like wolves. In John 10 the Lord said that He is the good Shepherd and that He came to lay down His life that men may receive life (vv. 10-11). He also said that the wolf comes not to give life but to snatch and scatter (v. 12). Hence, everyone who causes harm and destruction in the church is a wolf. Outwardly, those who teach differently are God's people, but the different teaching that they are teaching is the unhealthy teaching. To be unhealthy means to not supply men with life. This is to harm and destroy. This may be compared to the food that we eat: if it is not healthy, it is harmful. If we eat unhealthy food, not only will it not benefit us, but it will actually harm our body and threaten our physical life.

Paul's Burden

The Bible is written like a jigsaw puzzle. It is not written in a systematic way. Rather, it says a little here and a little there. We must spend the time to put all the pieces together. In Acts 20 Paul knew that the church in Ephesus had a problem. He was very concerned about the situation, and he sent for the elders to come to him. He charged them repeatedly to be watchful and sober and on the alert. After this, he left for Jerusalem. Once he arrived in Jerusalem, problems arose. The Christians there were deeply into the practice of keeping the law. James and the elders came to see Paul and said to him, "You observe, brother, how many thousands there are among the Jews who have believed; and all are zealous for the law" (21:20). Not only were they keeping the law; they were even vowing the Nazarite vow and purifying themselves (vv. 23b-24; Num. 6:2-5). This indicates that the Jewish believers in Jerusalem were still keeping the law of Moses and remaining in the Old Testament age. Under the strong influence of Judaism, they mixed God's New Testament economy with the out-of-date Old Testament economy.

Being Entangled in James's Snare

However, James thought that this mixture was good. He even told Paul, "They have been informed concerning you that you are teaching all the Jews throughout the nations apostasy from Moses...What then is to be done? They will certainly hear that you have come" (Acts 21:21-22). James was saying that there were tens of thousands of believers in Jerusalem who could not accept what Paul had done. As a result, Paul had an evil name. What should he do? James advised him, saying, "Therefore do this that we tell you: We have four men who have a vow on themselves; take these and be purified with them, and pay their expenses that they may shave their heads. And all will know that there is nothing to the things that they have been informed of concerning you, but that you yourself also walk orderly, keeping the law" (vv. 23-24). The four had vowed a Nazarite vow. In order for a Nazarite to complete his vow, he had to pay a sum for the sacrifice (Num. 6:13-17). It was a substantial sum of money; therefore, according to the Jewish tradition, those who paid on behalf of a poor Nazarite were not only considered pious but actually became partakers of the Nazarite vow.

Paul writes strongly in the books of Romans and Galatians that the law is over. Since that is the case, why would Paul concede to James's proposal when he was in Jerusalem and go back to the law? Perhaps Paul was thinking, "Although I have written the books of Romans and Galatians, I have also written the book of 1 Corinthians. There I said that to the Jews I became as a Jew that I might gain the Jews (9:20). Since all the people here in Jerusalem are Jews, I can only be a Jew." To put it in a nice way, Paul did this in order to not be different from others. To put it in a not-so-nice way, Paul was compromising.

God's Sovereign Rescue
for the Sake of His New Testament Economy

Although Paul tried to become as a Jew to the Jews and as a Gentile to the Gentiles, the Lord did not allow him to compromise. It was a serious thing for him to participate in that vow. It jeopardized God's New Testament economy to the uttermost. This is the reason that after Paul stayed with the four men in the temple for six days, while waiting for the priests to come on the seventh day as the Nazarite vow was concluding, a riot suddenly broke out. Some Jews from Asia saw Paul in the temple, and they stirred up the crowd to seize him (Acts 21:27-30). Outwardly, it was the rioters who seized Paul. Actually, in God's eyes, it was a rescue to Paul.

I believe that while Paul was staying in the temple for nearly seven consecutive days, he was both ashamed and disgusted with the whole affair, yet he dared not express himself. He did not know what to do. It is very possible that he prayed desperately: "Lord, save me from this troubling situation. I have told others in the books of Romans and Galatians that Christ is the end of the law and that I have died to the law and have nothing to do with it anymore. I have said this so clearly. Even the ink of my writing may still be wet. How can I now go back to offer a sacrifice and keep the law? It is true that I have determined to become as a Jew among the Jews, but I will not remain in the Jewish land for long. I have to go to the Gentile lands to work. By then the news will have spread to these Gentile lands. The Gentile believers will ask me, 'Paul, what have you done? What happened to you? Your action did not match your word! We have been reading your Epistles. How are you going to explain to us what you have done? Why did you go back to Jerusalem to keep the ordinances of the law? How are you going to justify yourself?'" It is very possible that Paul prayed, "Lord, rescue me out of this troubling situation!" The Lord used the riot and rescued him in this way.

To the Jews, the reason for the riot was to kill Paul, but God in His sovereignty protected him. The news of the riot reached the commander of the cohort (v. 31). Immediately he brought soldiers to rescue Paul out of the hand of the Jews and keep him in custody. This was a big protection to Paul. It not only saved his life from the persecuting hands of the Jews, but it saved him from the peril of tearing down God's New Testament economy. In the end, Paul did not complete the Nazarite vow. This spared the church completely from the havoc of Judaism, but at the same time it also terminated the first part of Paul's ministry.

We have already covered this matter in detail in the *Life-study of Acts* (see Messages 56 to 59). The events in Jerusalem eventually brought Paul to Caesarea. There he was kept for about two years. No doubt those two years were a very profitable and excellent time for Paul. They afforded him the peace to reconsider everything. In his prison he was separated from all the hindrances, distractions, frustrations, and influences. He surely would have realized that his going up to Jerusalem was a big mistake. Such pondering must have brought him under an open sky.

Actually, after the conference in Jerusalem in Acts 15, Paul's spirit was already quite troubled. He was not at peace concerning the situation in the church in Jerusalem. He must have been clear that the church in Jerusalem was in an ambiguous situation. It was not absolute for God's New Testament economy, and it contained a strong mixture of Old Testament elements. Jewish and Christian influences were all mixed up together. He could not have been at peace regarding it. Because his burden was so heavy, he was not able to forget about Jerusalem even during the third journey of his ministry. This must be the reason that in 19:21 Paul purposed in his spirit to go to Jerusalem. I believe he had a strong desire to go to fellowship with James and to deal with the matter of the mixture. Little did he realize that not only would he not be able to fellowship much with James, but he would be forced into an embarrassing situation by James and the elders in Jerusalem. In the end he was subdued by James and fell into his trap.

However, God did not allow the situation to continue this way. His hand came in to intervene. First, He rescued Paul out of the mixture of the church in Jerusalem. At the same time, He rescued him out of the hands of the Jews who sought to kill him. In the end, Paul was kept in custody under the hands of the Romans and was isolated from the disturbance and riot. He remained in prison in Caesarea for two years. This afforded him a period of quiet reflection. It prepared him to write the last few Epistles, especially the Epistle to the Ephesians. Two years later, he appealed to Caesar. This brought him to Rome, where he remained in prison for another two years. During that period he wrote the Epistles to the Ephesians, Philippians, and Colossians. The thought in these three books is very deep. Such a thought had not been in him before he was put into prison. Neither had he ever written anything concerning it before this time. In these three books he unveiled God's economy, which concerns God's dispensing of Himself in His Divine Trinity into His chosen people in order that they may gain Christ, who is the Triune God Himself, for the producing of the members of Christ, to be constituted as the organic Body of Christ to be the church of the living God to manifest Him.

Paul's Concern for the Church in Ephesus

From the time of Acts 20 Paul was very concerned regarding

the condition of the church in Ephesus. This is the reason that he wrote to the church in Ephesus even while he was in prison, revealing to them God's economy, which is God's working Himself through His Divine Trinity into man, in order that man would enjoy the riches of Christ to become His members and be constituted into the Body of Christ for the manifestation of the Triune God. This is the central vision of God in the entire Bible. It is the consummating vision in both the Old and New Testaments. Later Paul was released from the Roman prison. He passed through Macedonia and wrote the first Epistle to Timothy, telling Timothy that some in Ephesus had a problem. He told Timothy to remain in Ephesus to charge them not to teach anything different from God's economy. This is the entire background of the writing of the first Epistle to Timothy.

THE BACKGROUND
OF THE SECOND EPISTLE TO TIMOTHY

A little more than a year after Paul was released from prison, Nero, the Roman Caesar, began to persecute the Christians. He put leaders such as Peter and Paul into prison. After Paul went into prison again, he wrote the second Epistle to Timothy. Before his second imprisonment, there were many Jews among the churches in the Gentile lands who were beginning to teach Old Testament things different from the New Testament teaching. By the time Paul went into prison, the Judaizing Christians had become even more aggressive. Perhaps they told others, "See? Paul is in prison. If his teachings were right, why would God have allowed him to end up in prison?" Paul's imprisonment gave the Judaizing Christians and those who taught differently a strong ground to speak. This is the reason Paul wrote the second Epistle to Timothy.

The two Epistles to Timothy were written approximately two years apart. Therefore, Timothy did not remain in Ephesus for a long time. In 2 Timothy 1:13 Paul said, "Hold a pattern of the healthy words that you have heard from me, in the faith and love which are in Christ Jesus." Paul reminded Timothy to hold "the healthy words." He had already spoken concerning this in 1 Timothy 6. As we have already seen, these healthy words are the words of the Lord Jesus in the New Testament and the preaching of the Lord's apostles concerning such things as God becoming flesh and the mystery of godliness. Paul charged Timothy to hold these words. This proves that at that time some believers were already not holding these words. This is a very serious matter.

Second Timothy 1:14 says, "Guard the good deposit through the Holy Spirit who dwells in us." This is the Lord's commission to the apostles. It is also the apostles' charge to the believers. We need to deposit the Lord's healthy words, including the riches of life in the Lord's words, into our being, like we deposit money in the bank. Verse 15 says, "This you know, that all who are in Asia turned away from me." Paul was sitting in his prison in Rome. How could believers far away in the province of Asia have turned away from him? This proves that what the Asian believers were turning away from was not Paul's person but his ministry. The "me" here does not refer to Paul's person. It refers to his teaching. When we come to Revelation 2 and 3, we find the Lord writing to the seven churches in Asia, and the first letter was to the church in Ephesus. This proves that it was the church in Ephesus that took the lead to forsake Paul's ministry and teaching. This is the background of the writing of the second Epistle to Timothy.

THE PRESENT VISION AND PRACTICE

The burden in this chapter is not to expound the Epistles to Timothy but to continue from the previous chapter to speak on our present vision and practice.

The Problem Created by the Ministry of Spirituality in the West

First, let us fellowship a little concerning our history. In 1955 Brother T. Austin-Sparks was invited for the first time to come to Taiwan. In 1957 he came for the second time. During the second time, he raised a crucial issue. He thought that the way we were taking was good in every matter except one. The one thing he considered to be seriously wrong and absolutely intolerable was the ground of the church. In other words, it was the practice of the church. While he was alive, he was the only one on the whole earth who could echo what we saw concerning spiritual life principles. He echoed what we saw, and we responded to what he saw. At that time the rejection he faced in the West was more severe than the rejection we faced in the East. In the entire Western world he was the only one who saw the principles of life, and he was the only one who spoke on the deeper truths of life. Almost no one accepted his teaching. In the East we also spoke on these deep matters. Hence, on the side of life principles, we held the same view, but on the side of church practice and church ground, we could not fellowship with each other. At that time we saw that the church ground cannot be separated from church practice. Without the ground there can be no practice. In order to have the practice, there must be the ground. However, he did not agree with the matter of the church ground, and he did not agree with that kind of church practice.

From 1937 to 1938 Brother Watchman Nee visited a number of countries in Europe and stayed there for more than a year and a half. Most of the time he stayed in London with Brother T. Austin-Sparks. After he returned to China, he cabled me immediately to join him in Shanghai. At that time he called together a special fellowship meeting and reported to us in detail his fellowship with Brother Austin-Sparks in London. At the end he said that in almost every aspect they were in harmony with each other and echoed each other. The only exception was the practice of the church, which they could not get through in their fellowship. Brother Nee was somewhat sympathetic regarding the matter. He felt that in England the Brethren had spoiled the matter of church practice for more than a hundred years. Because of this, most seekers of the Lord were unwilling to speak concerning the subject. Brother Nee sympathized with their frustrations and spoke to us in this way, but he also pointed out that this was exactly where the problem between Brother T. Austin-Sparks and us lay.

Inviting the Ministry of Spirituality from the West

After we heard Brother Nee's fellowship, we asked why we should not invite Brother Austin-Sparks to come and visit us, since Brother Nee spoke so highly of him. Brother Nee answered in a wise way: "The time has not come." At that time we did not quite understand what he meant. About fifteen years later, in 1954, our work in Taiwan was very much blessed by the Lord. At that time a brother visited England and America and met with Brother Austin-Sparks. After his visit, he wrote three letters, one to Manila, one to Hong Kong, and one to Taipei, highly promoting Brother Austin-Sparks. He said that Brother Austin-Sparks was a spiritual giant and that he had a strong burden to come to the Far East to witness for the Lord.

In the first part of 1955, I was conducting the life-study training in Taipei. Brothers Chang Yu-lan and Chang Wu-cheng took the letter and showed it to me. After I read the letter, I considered a little. Then I told them that for many years we had learned a certain thing before the Lord: In knowing a person we should not look at the big matters but at the small matters. It is not very easy for a person to expose his flaws in the big things; the problems are always with the small things. Brother Austin-Sparks published a bimonthly magazine called *A Witness and a Testimony*. In the January 1955 issue there was a column acknowledging the Christmas cards that he had received from readers. His magazine was altogether on spiritual subjects, yet there was such an acknowledgment. This was a small point. By the Lord's leading, we had completely dropped the celebration of Christmas, but Brother Austin-Sparks, whom we had always respected so much, published an acknowledgment thanking his readers for Christmas cards. From this small matter I could tell that there must still be some distance between him and us. If we were to invite him to come, it would be hard to guarantee that there would be no friction between us; perhaps the better thing to do would be to keep our distance and remain cordial to each other.

At that time the two elders agreed with what I said, but two weeks later, they said, "Brother Lee, we feel that on the spiritual side, we still need the spiritual help from Brother Austin-Sparks." The phrase *spiritual help* made it difficult for me to say no to them. Since the brothers had felt that the small differences did not matter and that they needed spiritual help, how could I insist on not inviting him? I then suggested that if we were to invite him, it would be better not to bring up the subject of church practice, because Brother Nee had discussed this matter in detail with Brother Austin-Sparks already and had not been able to get through. The two Brothers Chang agreed and said, "We will only receive the spiritual help from him." I then drafted the letter in English myself. The Taipei brothers signed it and sent it to Hong Kong and Manila for their signatures. In this way, Brother Austin-Sparks came.

The Problem Brought About by the Practice

At the end of 1955 Brother Austin-Sparks came for the first time. He restricted his speakings to spiritual subjects. The messages helped many people. Everyone was happy and decided to invite him to come again. In the spring of 1957 he came again at our invitation, but this time it was different. He told us clearly regarding his feelings. After visiting for about a month, one morning we asked him to have a time of fellowship with the hundred or more co-workers that we had. One brother among us took the lead to ask, "Brother Austin-Sparks, you have been staying with us for some time, and you have observed our situation. What is your feeling concerning us?" As soon as I heard this, I knew at once that this brother had dissenting thoughts within him. It turned out that my feeling was correct. Right after this brother asked the question, Brother Austin-Sparks replied, "The last time I came, I did have some feelings, but I was determined not to say anything. I was waiting for another opportunity to come again to speak regarding them." Later I found out that this dissenting one was echoing Brother Austin-Sparks. He took the initiative to ask that question in order to provide Brother Austin-Sparks the opportunity to speak what he had prepared.

The first thing that Brother Austin-Sparks disagreed with was the way we conducted the bread-breaking meeting. He thought that our bread-breaking meeting was too disorderly. There was no proper order. One person could call a hymn, and another could pray. I did not say much regarding this because

I was the translator. However, I will speak in detail regarding the second matter with which he did not agree. We need to realize that if one's vision is not clear, he can be very spiritual, but he can become quite confused in certain matters. The second thing that Brother Austin-Sparks mentioned shows that he was somewhat confused. He said, "Please tell me why the brothers among you who are in the military service put on their uniform cap even before they leave the meeting hall?" At that time we had many brothers among us who were in the military. They all came to the meetings dressed in military uniforms. After the meetings they would put on their caps and fellowship with the brothers and sisters in the meeting hall. When Brother Austin-Sparks saw this, he began to criticize.

At the time this happened, one brother answered Brother Austin-Sparks, saying, "According to the Chinese tradition, a soldier does not take off his cap when he is standing up, whether or not he is inside a building. These brothers remove their caps when they sit down for the meetings in accordance with the biblical teaching concerning not covering their head, but when an announcement is made that the meeting is dismissed, they put their caps back on." When Brother Austin-Sparks heard this, immediately his countenance changed. He asked, "Are you here to keep the tradition, or are you here to keep the Bible?" When I heard this, I was not too happy inside. I realized that he was wrong. It was he who was following the Western tradition and not we who were disobeying the Bible. The Bible says that when a man prays or teaches, he should not cover his head (1 Cor. 11:4, 7), but it does not say that a man cannot put on his cap inside a building. To take off the cap inside a building is a Western tradition. Brother Austin-Sparks was imposing on us a tradition that Western unbelievers keep.

I did not have any prejudice against Brother Austin-Sparks. Before that day, I supported that elderly brother almost completely. He did render us quite an amount of help, and he also received some help from us. For a long time we communicated with one another and fellowshipped with one another, but from that day onward, I became alarmed. First of all, for him to say such a word lowered his spiritual ministry. Why did he need to touch such outward matters? At his invitation I went to London in 1958 and met with his group for four weeks. Their bread-breaking meeting lasted for an hour. During that whole time Brother Austin-Sparks took the lead. At the beginning he took the lead to pray, to call a hymn, and to speak. Afterward everyone prayed for about ten minutes. At a certain point, he would break the bread and give it to the congregation. He would first give it to the seven deacons; then the seven deacons would distribute it to the others. After everyone had the bread in his hand, Brother Austin-Sparks would say, "Now we can eat." Only after he had announced this, was anyone allowed to eat. After the eating, they did the same with the distribution and drinking of the cup. At the end he stepped in and monopolized the meeting again by announcing, "Now the time for public worship is over," which meant that no one could do anything anymore. This was his way. It is no wonder that he considered our bread-breaking meeting to be somewhat disorganized.

Brother Austin-Sparks came to our meetings and started questioning such practices among us as the breaking of bread. He even touched on such insignificant matters as the donning of military caps. Was it not too much for him to touch such matters? These were traces that gave us a hint that his way and our way could not be reconciled because what we saw was different.

Defending the Ground of the Church

Recently I have felt the importance of the one accord. As long as we have different views on a minor point, we cannot have the one accord. This is the reason that in this training, right from the beginning, I spoke concerning the vision in the Lord's recovery. I believe all the brothers and sisters love the Lord, and all of us want to be in one accord, but if our vision is not up to date, it is impossible for us to be one. Concerning Brother Austin-Sparks, I could never have dreamed that a spiritual ministry as high as his would touch upon and even seriously meddle with minor things. It was actually not worth it. I kept all these things in my heart and did not tell anyone, because I did not want to ruin the atmosphere there. At that time more than five hundred co-workers from all over the island were together. Every morning we were under the training and his ministry. I needed to maintain a good situation.

One evening we had another fellowship with Brother Austin-Sparks. The atmosphere was a little tense, and no one knew what to say. We thought perhaps we would fellowship a little concerning something related to spiritual principles. Suddenly a brother asked, "Brother Austin-Sparks, suppose here in Taipei there are five assemblies that meet in the Lord's name. Please tell us which one is right and which one is wrong, or are they all wrong?" As soon as I heard this, something jumped up in alarm within me. I knew that this would lead to trouble. Yet I had to translate what he said. Brother Austin-Sparks was well prepared for such a question. He said, "None is right and none is wrong; everything is relative." Another brother was quite stirred up, and he and the first brother together asked, "Relative to what?" Brother Austin-Sparks immediately answered, "Relative to the measure of Christ. Those who have a greater measure of Christ are more right, those who have a lesser measure of Christ are less right, and those who do not have any measure of Christ are not right." All the brothers became very agitated. I was the translator, but I had to somewhat calm them down.

The third time we gathered together with Brother Austin-Sparks, we were still on this subject. In the previous two meetings, I remained quite neutral and served only as the translator. This time I felt that I could not be neutral anymore. No one was speaking then, and I opened my mouth. I said, "For the last few times we were together we have been speaking of the matter of the church and the church ground. Brother Austin-Sparks has told us that none is absolutely right, and none is absolutely wrong; how much one is right depends on the measure of Christ he has." I did not appear to be stirred up, but I turned to a brother from Denmark and said to him in a calm voice, "Brother, let me ask you a question. God ordained that the children of Israel would be taken captive in Babylon for seventy years, after which they would return to their homeland and would rebuild the temple upon its original foundation. Suppose a very influential prophet would rise up at that time and tell the people that it did not matter whether or not one returned to Jerusalem. Suppose he would say, 'See? Daniel is such a spiritual person, but he did not return to Jerusalem. Therefore, it does not matter whether or not one returns, as long as he is spiritual.' I would ask all of you here if this is right or wrong." Brother Austin-Sparks was an intelligent man. He knew that I was reacting to his word concerning the spiritual measure. I explained further: "Daniel had the greatest spiritual measure of his time; in today's terms, we would say that his measure of Christ was the highest. The reason that he did not return was that the time had not come for him to go. Around the time the Israelites were returning, he died. He could not go while he was living, yet his heart was toward Jerusalem. He knelt down three times a day and prayed with an open window toward Jerusalem. During his time with us here, at least a few times our Brother Austin-Sparks has highly recommended Dr. F. B. Meyer. I have read Dr. Meyer's books and have received some help from him. But all of us know that Brother Meyer is still in the denominations, that is, in the so-called 'organized Christianity' that our Brother Austin-Sparks condemns in his messages. Since Dr. Meyer still remains in organized Christianity, the very organization which Brother Austin-Sparks condemns, can we say that he is right in the matter of the church merely because his spiritual stature is high?"

I continued, "For more than three hundred years, all those who have sought after the inner life have received help from Madame Guyon. She should be regarded as a person with a great measure of Christ. As far as the spiritual stature of Christ is concerned, probably none among us can match hers. But Madame Guyon, a person with such a spiritual stature of Christ, still remained in Catholicism. Today any Christian who is enlightened at all would condemn Catholicism, yet Madame Guyon, whom we respect so much, never left the Catholic Church. We cannot say that simply because her spiritual stature was high that she was right in the matter of the church."

Finally I said, "These examples prove to us that it is one thing to be spiritual, and it is another thing to have the proper

ground of the church. Spirituality has to do with our personal
condition. The ground of the church, on the other hand, is a
corporate ground; it is the corporate standing that we take.
Not everyone who left Babylon to return to Jerusalem was
a spiritual person. Neither was everyone who remained in
Babylon necessarily unspiritual. In fact, among those who
returned, we find many who were not that spiritual, because
some had married Gentile wives. However, as far as their
ground was concerned, they were approved by God. With such
a ground they could build the temple. No matter how poor
their situation was, their ground was still the right ground.
When the temple was built, God's glory filled the house."

I then made the following conclusion: "Today in pursuing
the Lord, we must take care of both aspects. Spirituality has
to do with our condition, and the ground has to do with our
stand. A man cannot be right only in his condition; he must
also be right in his stand and position. Whether or not a
person has a justifiable position is based not so much on his
condition as on the ground he takes. On one hand, no matter
how spiritual a person was, if he remained in Babylon and
stood on the ground of captivity, he was wrong. On the other
hand, no matter how poor and confused the returned captives
were, they stood on the proper ground which God had
ordained for them and which their forefathers had left to
them. Their approval was based on their ground and not on
their personal condition. Of course, their confused situation
did not please the Lord. It is for this reason that God raised
up Ezra to teach them the law to enlighten and rebuke them;
as a result, they wept, repented, and confessed their sins. At
any rate, we cannot despise the returned captives' ground
simply because their spiritual condition was poor. Nor can
we justify the ground of those remaining in Babylon simply
because they were spiritual."

OUR VISION NEEDING TO MATCH THE AGE

In the previous chapter we said that God gave men a vision
even in the Old Testament age. We cannot say that those who
remain in the Old Testament visions do not have any vision
at all. Yet their visions are not up to date; they do not match

the age. In the New Testament, after the four Gospels we have the book of Acts. After Acts we have the early letters of Paul. Paul went into prison, was released, was imprisoned again, and then was martyred. By that time, he had written his Epistles. All of them concerned God's visions. About thirty years after his martyrdom, around A.D. 90, the aged John wrote the book of Revelation. It was also a book of visions. We can say that the entire Bible from Genesis to Revelation is a record of visions. Throughout the ages there were many saints who loved the Lord and who feared the Lord, but we cannot say that they all had the vision that matched their age. Some, like Gamaliel, were still stuck in the Old Testament age. I believe Apollos somewhat belongs to this category of people, because Acts 18 says that he was powerful in expounding the Scriptures (v. 24). He knew the Old Testament well, but he did not know the four Gospels; he only knew the baptism of John (v. 25b). His vision only went that far. He did not see any further vision after John the Baptist.

The Case of James

In Acts 15 we find James becoming the leading brother among those in the church in Jerusalem. Although he was a man in the New Testament, he had one foot in the New Testament and the other foot in the Old Testament. His two feet were standing on two "boats," and his two hands were holding on to two "oars." He was very pious, and he feared God very much. History tells us that he was so pious that the skin of his knees grew coarser than an elephant's skin from kneeling. It was his piety that attracted many to the Lord. It was also his piety that made him the chief apostle among those in the church in Jerusalem. However, although he was spiritual, he did not have an adequate vision. History tells us that the Pharisees and priests thought that James was for Judaism. They even gathered together the Jews and the Christians around Jerusalem and asked James to speak to them. However, James feared the Lord very much, and he spoke concerning the New Testament on that occasion. This upset the Jews, and they killed him on the spot. This is how James was martyred. It is difficult to say whether James's martyrdom was something pleasing to the Lord. How could God reward him for his ambiguous condition? All we can say is, "Only the Lord knows." Although James was much more advanced than Gamaliel, he also did not have the vision that matched the age.

The Case of Barnabas

Then there was Barnabas. He was the one who ushered Paul into his apostolic ministry (Acts 11:25-26). In Acts 13, when the Holy Spirit commissioned him and Paul to the ministry, he was the leader between the two. Halfway through their journey, however, there was a turn in the ministry. When the crucial time came for someone to speak for God, Barnabas had nothing to say, and Paul took his place. From that day onward, Paul became the leader. In other words, the vision and the revelation shifted to Paul; they were no longer with Barnabas. At the end of chapter 15, the two of them contended, and they parted from each other. From that time onward, the Bible does not mention anything further concerning Barnabas's fellowship and work. This means that Barnabas disappeared from the stage of God's move at that time. He no longer played a role on that stage. Although he was still in the New Testament, the vision he saw was not adequate.

The Case of Apollos

In Acts 18 Apollos appeared on the scene. He was a person partly in the Old Testament and partly in the New Testament. As we have seen, he went to Ephesus, and the church in Ephesus first received help from him. In the end, Apollos's work dominated Ephesus by virtue of its early arrival. Once Apollos's seed took root in the church in Ephesus, it was difficult to eradicate it. We can detect through various hints that the cause of Ephesus's decline was its failure to rid itself of Apollos's seed. From the standpoint of the New Testament, that teaching was a different teaching; it was a different doctrine. The work of Apollos left a lasting mark of different teachings on the church in Ephesus. For this reason, Paul was always concerned about the church in Ephesus, as evidenced by Acts 20.

THE CHURCHES' DECLINE
THROUGH FORSAKING THE APOSTLES' TEACHING

From the time of Paul's first imprisonment to the time he was imprisoned again was a period of about three years. During that period he charged Timothy to remain in Ephesus to take care of the church because there was a problem there. Some were teaching differently. During Paul's second imprisonment, he wrote the second Epistle to Timothy to tell him that all the churches in Asia had forsaken his ministry. Here we can trace the source of the churches' decline. The cause for the churches' decline was the forsaking of the apostles' teaching; they forsook the apostles' ministry. Because of this forsaking, the teaching of Balaam, the teaching of the Nicolaitans, and the teaching of Jezebel (Rev. 2—3) crept into the church one by one. These three kinds of teachings represent the heresies. When the church departs from the apostles' teaching, all kinds of doctrines invade the church. This is very clear.

THE ULTIMATE CONSUMMATION
OF THE DIVINE REVELATION

About thirty years later, the aged John wrote the book of Revelation. After he finished writing concerning the New Jerusalem in the new heaven and new earth, God's visions were complete. At the end of Revelation, which is the end of the entire Bible, there is the warning against any further addition or deletion. All the visions of God have been completed. After the book of Revelation was completed, three hundred years went by until in A.D. 397, at the Council of Carthage, the authority of the entire canon of the holy writings, including the books of Revelation and Hebrews, was recognized. In A.D. 325 when Emperor Constantine convened the Council of Nicaea, the books of Revelation and Hebrews still had not been recognized as part of the canon. These two books occupy a pivotal position in the vision concerning God's New Testament economy. Hence, the creed produced at the Council of Nicaea did not include the revelation revealed in these two books. Today many Protestant and Catholic groups recite the Nicene Creed every Sunday in their services. While I was in the West fighting for the truth concerning the Triune God, I told people, "The creed that you hold is defective, for it does not say anything regarding the seven Spirits." They had nothing to say in response.

THE BASIS OF THE ONE ACCORD

By A.D. 397, the entire Bible was recognized. Today this holy Word before us is full of visions. Whether or not we can come up to the standard of these visions depends entirely on our understanding of the visions contained in these sixty-six books. During the first sixteen hundred years of church history, countless numbers of lovers of the Lord were raised up. Regrettably, all these lovers of the Lord, all these servants of God, were not able to be in one accord. The reason for this is that the visions they saw were all different. Some saw only the vision of the four Gospels. They liked it, and they faithfully adhered to that vision, but they did not advance any further. Some advanced a little and saw the vision of Acts. Spontaneously they became different from the first group, and they discovered that they could not fellowship with the first group. Other people advanced to the different visions recorded in the different Epistles, and similarly they held different views from the previous groups. Throughout the last sixteen centuries, many lovers of the Lord were raised up, yet they were not able to be in one accord. The reason is not that there was sin or evil among them, but that the vision each held was different in degree. Each remained in the degree to which they saw the various visions. Because the degree of the visions they saw was different, spontaneously there was no one accord.

In the nineteenth century, Hudson Taylor saw a vision. He felt that he should go to China to preach the gospel. We cannot say that his vision was wrong. We can only say that his vision was not up to the standard of the age. During the past three decades, we lost the one accord a number of times in Taiwan. The case with Brother Austin-Sparks was one example of such a time. Can we say that he did not love the Lord or that he was not spiritual? Even today I still recommend his books. Some of them are certainly worthwhile reading. However, he did not see what Brother Nee led us to see in the Lord's recovery. Needless to say, all our differences were not caused by the flesh but by the difference in our visions. In 1958, there were some aspiring and promising young people who were saved and perfected through my ministry. I entrusted to them the crucial works on the island of Taiwan, including hall three of the church in Taipei and the churches in Taichung, Chiayi, Tainan, and Kaoshung. They became proud, and through Brother Austin-Spark's influence, they decided to no longer speak concerning the ground of the church but to speak regarding only the fullness of Christ, the full Christ. They boldly proclaimed that they had seen a vision. At that time, the one accord was truly lost.

Although Brother Austin-Sparks was spiritual, he limited himself to the scope of his vision. His problem was that he was unwilling to see more. Moreover, he considered all those who saw something different to be wrong. He tried all he could to annul the "ground," which was recovered among us. He told me personally in a meeting that he had been speaking for decades, but in his whole life he had not found one place with such a good audience. He also discussed with me the possibility of moving to Taiwan to set up a ministry station. In the end, however, he and we were still not the same. The reason for this is that our visions were different.

THE PRESENT VISION
OF THE LORD'S RECOVERY

What then is our vision? A young brother once said, "Brother Nee used to speak of the cross, but we do not speak concerning it anymore." This is a shortsighted remark. Who says that we no longer speak concerning the dealing of the cross? By reading the messages on the New Jerusalem, we can see that in order to become the gates of pearl we must pass through the Lord's death. We need to enjoy the secretion of the Lord's resurrection life through His death. Only then can we become the pearls. Furthermore, every one of the nineteen items in the book *The Experience of Life* involves dealings that are related to the cross. We need to speak regarding the dealing of the cross, but we should not make this truth our limitation or our issue. In the West some people emphasize tongue-speaking. We do not oppose tongue-speaking, but if someone emphasizes tongue-speaking to the point of strongly promoting it, it becomes a great damage. One may do this out of harmless zeal, but if his listeners receive his speaking and enlarge upon it, it will bring a problem into the church. We must remember that the vision we have received does not concern itself with such small matters. This is not the focus of our vision.

What is our vision? Our vision is that God so loved the world that He gave His Son to die for us to redeem us, the sinners, in order that we can have the life of Christ and be regenerated by Him to be God's children, enjoying the riches of the Triune God to become the Body of Christ. In practice, the Body is expressed as the local churches in various localities, practicing the Body life in a practical and proper way. This Body, the church of God, is the focus of God's economy.

In the theology of the early church fathers there was such a term as *economy*, but in the Lord's recovery, during the period when we were in mainland China, we did not use this term. It was twenty years ago that I first picked up this term in Taiwan, but it was only two years ago that we saw the entire New Testament economy of God. At the same time, we saw the mingling of God and man and the divine dispensing, which is the Triune God dispensing all His riches in Christ as the Spirit into us to constitute us the Body of Christ. This is God's economy.

During the past few centuries, no one saw God's economy. Even if some did see it, no one spoke concerning it. No one spoke of the mingling of God and man, and no one spoke of the divine dispensing. Some spoke regarding sanctification, but that speaking was somewhat ambiguous. From the Bible we see that sanctification is of three stages. There is separating sanctification, positional sanctification, and dispositional sanctification. Dispositional sanctification is transformation, and transformation includes the dealing and breaking of the cross. But even the inner-life Christians, including those attending the Keswick conferences and the many spiritual giants who have written on the subject of the spiritual life, did not clearly explain what transformation is. The teaching of transformation is an item which is characteristic to the Lord's recovery.

The vision that the Lord has given to His recovery is an all-inclusive one. It includes the economy of God, the mingling of God and man, the dispensing of the Divine Trinity, and the believers' salvation in Christ, including God's selection, calling, regeneration, sanctification, renewing, transformation, conformation, and glorification. In the history of the development of Christian doctrine, this entire set of truths finds its full recovery only among us. Such truths as selection, calling, regeneration, sanctification, renewing, transformation, conformation, and glorification were not recovered much before us, and the recovery of these truths will not increase much after us. This set of truths has found its full recovery among us.

THE PROBLEM AND DANGER OF A VISION NOT MATCHING THE AGE

The problem among us is that some are bound by the little experience and vision that they have. Some have said that Brother Lee is now different from Brother Nee. This is a remark made not only by those outside the Lord's recovery or by some who have left us but by some who are still among us. Actually, if there is anyone on this earth who knows Brother Nee, I must be that one. He fellowshipped with me all that he had seen, and I received tremendous help from him. If anyone says that my work is different from Brother Nee's, he is an outsider with regard to the vision. Of course, because of the lack of opportunity on his part, Brother Nee did not develop the vision as far as I have. We may use the Recovery Version of the New Testament as an example. I spent twelve years day after day writing the footnotes, yet what I wrote was nothing more than what Brother Nee had sown earlier. I can only say that the seed has sprouted and grown, although, of course, it has not grown to the fullest. I ask the Lord to give me more years so that I can develop this seed within me. If the Lord would give me another twelve years to rewrite the Life-study messages, I will have another set of Life-studies. It will not be different, but it will be new. If anyone thinks that I am different from Brother Nee, it is because such a person has not come up to the standard of the vision of the age!

I would like the co-workers, the elders, and all the churches in the Lord's recovery to realize that today we have not changed. If we are different in any way from others, it is because we hold to all the visions of the Bible, from the first vision of Adam in Genesis to the ultimate, consummate one in Revelation. If anyone sees only a part of this entire vision and condemns us for being different, it is not merely because we are different from them; it is because they do not have the vision that matches the age.

We cannot blame those whose vision does not match the age for doing what they are doing. James was very pious. We cannot criticize him for his piety, yet he did not have the vision that matched the age. In the end he not only destroyed himself, but he destroyed the work of God and brought trouble to all the saints in the land of Judea. Because of his inertia and reluctance, the Roman prince Titus marched with his army in A.D. 70 and ransacked Jerusalem. The temple was destroyed, and not one stone was left on top of another. Josephus the historian told us the tragedy of the whole story. Many Christians were killed. Even children were murdered. Who would have wished that the whole matter end this way? However, God was forced to do this. If God had not done this, the result would have been even more unmanageable. Christianity would have become entirely mixed with Judaism. Faced with such a murky situation, God had to step in to clear the atmosphere. The fact that Jerusalem was burned to the ground and that thousands of people were killed was altogether James's fault. This is not a small thing. This is what the Chinese mean by "off by a fraction of an inch, missed by a thousand miles." One faulty step resulted in the loss of tens of thousands of lives. History bears a tragic testimony to this.

Today the Lord has been merciful to His recovery. Within a short period of sixty years, He has brought us to the ultimate consummation of all the visions. I hope that all of us will seriously study the messages that we have published, especially those in the *Elders' Training* and *Truth Lessons* series. If we study them thoroughly, we will have the full view; we will see the vision that the Lord has given us in His recovery, and we will realize what is the ultimate consummation of all the visions—the New Jerusalem. Within this ultimate consummation everything is included, such as gospel preaching, loving the Lord, the dealing and breaking of the cross, the resurrection life, and the outpouring of the Holy Spirit.

Regrettably, today on the earth, when believers see a little revelation in the New Testament, they begin to think quite highly of themselves. They become very zealous concerning that one point that they see. So naturally they think that our actions and words are too extreme. There is no doubt that many Christian groups are very busy on the earth today, but not only are they not able to be one with us; they are not able to be one with each other. They cannot be one mainly because they have different visions; they see different things. This difference is a difference in degree, although the basis is still the same. We have the same Bible, the same God, and the same Savior, and we have received the same Spirit and the same salvation. We all believe in the blood of the Lord, and we all share the same faith, but any further advance beyond this basis ends in differences. Some advance only a few steps and then stop; others advance a few steps more; and some advance even further. We thank the Lord for giving us the same basis. We are all saved, and we all have God's life and nature. We all have the same standing. However, while the Holy Spirit is moving on, we may remain where we are. The minute the Holy Spirit moves on, some decide to follow, but others decide to stay. The more the Holy Spirit moves on, the fewer there are who follow Him. In the end, we are the only ones left who have followed Him all the way.

ANSWERING THE LORD'S CALL AND FOLLOWING THE PRESENT VISION TO BE THE OVERCOMERS

Faced with such a situation, what should we do? Thank the Lord that at the end of the Bible there is the call to the overcomers. Although the seven churches in Revelation 2 and 3 had degraded and their condition was poor, the Lord still recognized them as churches. The Lord did not call the overcomers to leave the seven churches. Why? Because their ground was still the right ground. They were not meeting as many churches in one locality but as one church in each locality. Although the condition of Thyatira was poor, it was still one church in one locality. Its ground was still the right ground. It was corrupt, and its condition was poor, but its ground was still the right ground. This can be compared to a member of a family. Whether the family is a good one or a poor one, that person still belongs to the family. If he separates himself to begin another family and changes his name, he is splitting up the family. According to his condition, he may be very good, moral, and educated. However, as for his standing, his ground, he has caused a division. In the same way, we can say that Thyatira was poor beyond measure, yet the Lord did not ask anyone to leave the church in Thyatira, because it was still standing on the proper ground. The Lord instead called some to be overcomers in the midst of that situation.

Today's situation is the same. Many have seen the initial vision, and they are satisfied with what they have seen, but they should not stop there. We must follow the Holy Spirit, and we must go on, but the more we go on, the fewer there will be who follow. Hence, it is not true that we refuse to be one with others. The truth of the matter is that they will not follow. We are not only following, but we are practicing what we have seen and what we follow, which is the dispensing of the Triune God, the mingling of God and man, to become the Body of Christ to be the manifestation of the Triune God. In the process of becoming this, we experience regeneration, sanctification, renewing, transformation, conformation, and glorification.

THE PRESENT PRACTICE IN THE LORD'S RECOVERY— PREACHING THE GOSPEL, NOURISHING THE NEW ONES, TEACHING THE TRUTH, AND BUILDING UP THE CHURCH

In our practice we must take care of the increase. First we need to spread the high gospel and bring people to salvation. Next we need to build up the home meetings and nourish the new ones. Then we need to build up the small groups and teach the truth. Finally we must edify and perfect the new ones to be the same as we are, practicing the Body life in all the local churches for the Lord to gain a full-grown, mature Body. These are the four things that we need to attain in our practice. If we all see this clearly, we will be in one accord. We cannot stay in the past; there is no future in that kind of standing. That vision and that practice are short. With only that vision there is no preaching of the gospel and no teaching of the truth; there is only the bearing of the cross, the dealing and breaking of the cross. What kind of future will this narrow view afford us? I am very clear concerning the responsibility that the Lord has given me. More or less I am a leading one, and I must bear great responsibility for the things I say and do, because they affect hundreds, even tens of thousands of people. In the future I must give an account to the Lord. For this very reason I have observed the situation very much. Some emphasize the preaching of the cross, but there is not much practice with them. When they want to lose their temper, they still lose their temper. They do not preach the gospel, they do not nourish and perfect others, and they do not pursue after the truth. The cross is merely a doctrine to them. We do not care for mere doctrines. We need to see the vision. As we have seen, the vision that matches the age is the vision that extends all the way from Genesis to Revelation.

Now we need to consider the proper practice. Matthew 24:14 says, "This gospel of the kingdom will be preached in the whole inhabited earth for a testimony to all the nations, and then the end will come." This means that we must do everything we can today to spread the gospel. We should spend every cent and every drop of our sweat, tears, and blood on the gospel. Only this will satisfy the Lord and take care of His gospel. The little island of Taiwan has twenty million people, but there are only five hundred thousand Christians. Are we sitting still, not willing to be on fire for the gospel? If we are, how can we give an account to the Lord? I believe one day, when we stand before the judgment seat of the Lord, He will ask us, "You have been in Taiwan for so long. What was your attitude toward My gospel?" He will tell us that He was not a hard Master, that He had given us a talent. But how did we use it, and how much did we use it? How many people did we bring to the Lord? How many people did we nourish and care for? How many people did we teach? In the future we will need to answer these questions one by one.

Matthew 24 and 25 show that one day we will have to stand before the Lord and give an account item by item. I admit that my responsibility is greater than yours. I also will have to stand before Him to give an account of myself, but I cannot give an account on your behalf. Today you have risen up and have responded to my leading, and I thank and praise the Lord for this. I worship the Lord for you, but you need to be clear that you are not following me. You are following this ultimate and completed vision, and you are spreading the gospel according to the Lord's commandment. No one can say that he does not know how to preach the gospel. Matthew 28:19 says, "Go therefore and disciple all the nations." This commandment is to all the believers. The Bible has never said that some are exempt from preaching the gospel. If we are faithful to the Lord in the matter of the gospel, and if we are diligent, the number of believers in the churches will greatly increase in a country as densely populated as Taiwan, but if we do not do anything, we will have nothing to say when we face the Lord.

Those who are sitting here today are either co-workers, elders, or full-timers who are learning to serve the Lord. Please consider calmly: If we cannot save one or two people within a year in an island as populous as Taiwan, how are we going to give an account to the Lord when we see Him? If each of us brings one to the Lord in a year, in a short time we will reach the goal of gospelizing Taiwan, but if we all hold back our energy, how can we gospelize this country? In the parable of Matthew 20, the householder went out and said to the idle workmen, "Why have you been standing here all the day idle?" (v. 6). All those who do not participate in the gospel move, even if they are pursuing "spirituality" and are knowledgeable in the truth, are idle in the eyes of the Lord. Today when we speak concerning the one accord, we are not speaking concerning a certain method that we must practice. We are saying that we should be attuned to the Lord's heart. The Lord's heart is that we enter the vineyard and labor for His gospel. If we are attuned to the Lord's heart, and if we dispense the Triune God to others, imparting to them the Lord's life so that they become His members and are constituted to be His Body as His full expression, then spontaneously we will be in one accord.

THE PRESENT NEED—BEING IN ONE ACCORD AND BEING FAITHFUL IN COORDINATION

The preaching of the gospel is the first step in the spreading. Following this we need to have home meetings and the nourishing of the new believers. We also need to build up the small groups and teach the truth. Finally, we need to have the practical manifestation of the Body life. These four things must become the "family tradition" among the churches in the Lord's recovery. In order to develop this "tradition," we must have the same view and the one accord. This is reason that I have presented to you the matter of the ultimate and completed vision. Today we should no longer emphasize different ways. We should not have any different leadings. We are all in the Lord's recovery, and we have all seen today's concluded vision. Even if some cannot follow and do not see clearly, they should not say anything. As long as they follow, they will obtain the blessing. The sons of Noah did not see the vision that he saw, yet they were in one accord with their father. They closely followed him, and they were saved in the same way that their father was saved. Peter was also one who blindly followed the Lord. He did not know anything. He only knew that the vision was with the Lord, and he followed. In the end he received the blessing.

If we have different emphases and different ways of doing things, our energy will be dissipated, and our faith will be weakened. We will lose the one accord, and our morale will be gone. However, if we are in one accord and we preach the gospel desperately, we will become hotter and hotter; our mutual burning will heighten our determination. Even the new ones will be brought into the proper function. We will have an invincible morale, and we will march over all obstacles. Wherever we go, we will more than conquer. This is what we must have today.

Do not ask why we did not do this ten years ago. Ten years

ago we were not as clear as we are today regarding the way of the work. Thank the Lord that His leading is always progressive. If a child does not grow in ten years, he must be sick with some terrible illness. If I am still teaching the same thing as I did ten years ago, you may think that I have not grown. We are not changing our way. During the past twenty-three years that I was in America, I did not change my tone. Faced with all the opposition and attacks, I stood firm on the truth. However, we are advancing and spreading. Today our work has to advance because the vision that the Lord has given us has advanced.

CHAPTER FOUR

SOME DEFINITE STEPS TO CARRY OUT THE PRESENT PRACTICE IN THE LORD'S RECOVERY

In the previous three chapters, we saw clearly the vision in the Lord's recovery, the vision in the New Testament, the ultimate consummation of the visions, and the vision that matches the age. Today we are taking the same way, doing the same work, entering the same flow, and speaking the same thing in this ultimate, consummate, and up-to-date vision. This can never be accomplished without the proper vision.

ONE ACCORD FOR THE PRACTICE OF THE NEW WAY

Needless to say, in mainland China, with its vast differences between the north and the south, it was difficult to practice the one accord. Even in the little island of Taiwan we have many differences. There are the "locals," the southern Fukienese, and the Hakka people. There is no way for us to be one. Yet as children of God, we know that God's desire is that we be one. Ephesians 4 tells us that we have seven "ones" as our base. There is one Body, one Spirit, one hope, one Lord, one faith, one baptism, and one God and Father of all.

In the Gospels the Lord did not speak much about the matter of the one accord. In Acts after the Lord resurrected and ascended, He left the disciples on earth to continue His ministry and to carry out His commission. It is at that juncture, at the beginning of Acts, that the crucial matter of the "one accord" is mentioned (1:14).

The first of the Epistles is Romans. In that book, after writing concerning many important truths, Paul says in 15:5 and 6, "Now the God of endurance and encouragement grant you to be of the same mind toward one another according to Christ Jesus, that with one accord you may with one mouth glorify the God and Father of our Lord Jesus Christ." In the original language, the phrase *one accord* means having the same mind, will, and goal. This means that as our whole inward being is one, our outward speaking also becomes one. When we are in one accord, we speak the same thing with one mouth.

Following Romans we have 1 Corinthians. In 1:10 Paul says, "Now I beseech you, brothers, through the name of our Lord Jesus Christ, that you all speak the same thing and that there be no divisions among you, but that you be attuned in the same mind and in the same opinion." The reason Paul said this was that some in the church in Corinth said that they were of Paul, because Paul had brought them to the Lord. Others said that they were of Apollos, because Apollos was powerful in expounding the Scriptures. Still others said that they were of Cephas, because he was the most prominent apostle. Then there were those who claimed that they were more superior than others; they said that they were of Christ. These four groups of people appreciated different things, and they all argued with one another. It is because there were these four schools that Paul exhorted them to speak the same thing. Unless these four groups of people saw the same vision, it would be impossible for them to speak the same thing.

This is the reason that Proverbs 29:18 says, "Where there is no vision, the people cast off restraint." A vision controls men and heads them up. Ephesians 1 says that God's eternal economy in the fullness of the times is to head up not merely the believers but all things (v. 10). In the millennium there will be a miniature heading up. When the new heaven and new earth come, God will head up all things, including all men, under Christ the Head. Today is the time of preparation. In eternity we will taste the true oneness. Not only will we speak the same thing; all creation will speak the same thing.

Isaiah 11:6-9a says, "The wolf will dwell with the lamb; / And the leopard will lie down with the kid, / And the calf and the young lion and the fatling together; / And a young boy will lead them about. / The cow and the bear will graze; / Their young will lie down together; / And the lion will eat straw like the ox. / The nursing child will play by the cobra's hole, / And upon the viper's den / The weaned child will stretch his hand. / They will not harm nor destroy / In all My holy mountain." This is a picture of the millennium. Today the cobra preys on the mouse, and the lion preys on the cow, but in the millennium neither the cobra nor the lion will harm or destroy anyone. When the new heaven and new earth come, the same will be true to a greater extent. One day God will restore everything to this state. As God's children, we can have a foretaste of this today. By God's grace we are qualified and can be saved to the extent that we speak the same thing. No matter what nationality and race we belong to, and no matter what language we speak, we can speak the same thing. This oneness comes from the one vision we hold in common.

The reason Christianity is divided is that it has different teachings. The different teachings come from different visions. Every denomination has its own beliefs, which become its own tenets of faith. The source of these tenets can be traced to the founders of the different denominations. They saw a certain portion of the truth in the Bible, and this truth became their "vision." Based on these "visions," they devised a set of tenets of faith, and based on these tenets, a denomination was founded. The result is that many grounds are claimed by many different kinds of Christians, and the end is a multitude of divisions.

In looking back over the history of the Lord's recovery during the past sixty years, we can see some who came but later were troubled and left. The reason they were troubled is that there was a difference between their vision and ours. Thank the Lord that the co-workers, the elders, and the young full-time workers among us here today have all seen the ultimate and consummate vision. There is no difference of visions. However, we cannot stop here. We also must be the same in our footsteps and our tone. Not only must we speak the same thing, but we must do the same work, which is to preach the gospel, build up the small groups, and teach the truth. It is not an easy task to accomplish these three things, and there is a real need for us to be in one accord.

PRACTICAL STEPS TO IMPLEMENT
THE PRESENT PRACTICE

In October of 1984, when I returned to Taiwan to study how to change the system, I emphasized repeatedly the need to discard the old things and adopt the new things. In particular, I focused on the way we met and the methods with which we worked. At that time I "blew the trumpet" in a clear and loud way. The proclamation was clear, and the explanation was plain. I also pointed out that since the practice of the new way was in its experimental stage, we were not clear about the way ahead of us. We had never taken such a way before, and we needed to study it thoroughly. For this reason, none of our ways was set. Even our co-workers had to try out different ways to meet. Now that a year and a half has passed, we should be able to do a little evaluation.

The Slowness of the Process
of Changing the System

First, we must realize that the process of changing the system is very slow. This is the reason that we are having this training at this time. I believe every saint agrees with our proposal to change the system. In practice, however, do we all agree that we need to spread the gospel, meet in the homes, build up the small groups, and teach the truth? I believe all of us would readily agree that we need to beget, nourish, and teach. To spread the gospel is to beget. To build up the small groups is to nourish, and to impart the truth is to teach. We are not forced to do the work of begetting, nourishing, and teaching. As long as we are men, and as long as we have a family, live in a society, and have a nation, we need to beget, nourish, and teach. In order to be a man, we need to beget; in order to have a family, we need to nourish; and in order to have a healthy society and a strong nation, we need to teach. These are clear and reasonable things that we must do.

We may agree with the new way, and we may agree to the change of our system. However, in practice we may still hold on to the habit of the old way and abide by the old system. In my hometown, four years after the Chinese Revolution, the people still kept their pigtail hairstyle. Some had a difficult struggle before they would give up their pigtail. I tell you this to show you that it is not an easy thing to drop the oldness and pick up the new things. At the end of the Ching Dynasty, the Chinese leader Sun Yat-sen promoted the revolution. He had to struggle for a few decades before the revolution finally succeeded. Actually, the revolution only changed the form of government and ousted the imperial dynasty; there was no real change in politics and society as a whole. Later, men like Yuan Shih-kai and Chang Shun rose up and attempted to restore the imperial dynasty. China went through a civil war for a few decades. Countless numbers of people appeared and disappeared from the political scene, but the real revolution was still not realized. The common Chinese people still held on to their oldness. It is difficult to change bad habits.

I hope that the brothers and sisters will see that since we have made up our mind to change the system and have resolved to be renewed, we must change all our ways and be renewed thoroughly. We cannot carry on business as usual and follow the old rules. Unless we make a strong resolution and abandon everything old, we cannot succeed in changing the system. When I was young, my brother and I went to study in an American school. Some students already had adopted Western-style clothing, but we were still wearing the Chinese long blue gown and cloth shoes. Although we were studying in a Western-style school and were learning English, we dared not speak English at home for fear that we would be accused of being influenced by the West. We were even afraid to speak in proper Mandarin, preferring instead to use the local dialect and native colloquialisms. The more unsophisticated we acted, the safer we felt. Although we had studied diligently and learned much, and although a bright future awaited us, the strong tradition still tenaciously held to us. This shows that it is not an easy thing to adopt something new.

Now we have all seen the vision, and we are all clear about the practice, which is to spread the gospel, build up the small groups, and teach the truth. However, we cannot merely shout slogans. We must have the determination to carry things through to the end. Of course, at the beginning we may not do a good job. It always takes a period of time to study and improve before we can succeed in adopting anything new. When the Chinese first immigrated to the United States, they did not speak English well, but as long as they were willing to improve, they eventually picked up the language. Here, in the previous weeks I visited three places. In some places I saw much improvement, but in other places people were still holding on to the old things. This proves that after a year and a half we are still not that absolute in adopting the new system.

Recently the church purchased a piece of land in Lin-ko. Our plan is to build a big meeting hall there. The news spread to all the countries, and in the United States more than two hundred fifty people have applied to come see that land and observe our meetings. When I was in the United States, I learned that even some from the churches in Europe wanted to visit us. After some fellowship, I agreed to give them a quota of four people. Those from the United States are not allowed to come at all. On the surface I told them that we wanted to be spared the trouble of hospitality and of taking care of the differences in habit and food of foreigners. Acts 6:1-6 does speak about this inconvenience. Actually, I have other reasons for refusing them. I know that they all want to come to observe how we are changing the system and adopting the new way. However, we are still groping with the proper way to meet in the small groups. We still do not know how to teach the truth. What do we have to show them? All the churches think that Taipei is in the third heaven. Actually, we are hardly a few feet off the ground, and we can easily fall back to the ground at this point in time. This is the reason I do not want them to come. I say this as an exhortation. We must be absolute in our endeavor. Since we have decided that we will change the system, and since we have put this matter into practice, we should be thorough and absolute in our work. Surely at the beginning it will be somewhat messy and not so proper, but in the end we will succeed.

The Benefits of Changing the System

As far as the outward façade is concerned, the big meetings are wonderful. A large meeting with fourteen thousand attendants surely draws much admiration, but the wonderful feeling does not last long. Once the excitement is over, what change has resulted in the saints when they return to their daily routine? What change has been brought about in the church? Is the Lord satisfied with us? In hall one of the church in Taipei, every Lord's Day there are at least three hundred fifty people meeting. The atmosphere is proper, a well-dressed person with a suit and tie conducts the meeting, the speaker is eloquent, the singing is accompanied by a grand and sonorous piano, and the meeting's atmosphere is uplifted. Many saints like to invite people to such a gathering. They like to tell their friends, "This is our church." It seems as if they come to the meeting with the sole purpose of making such a display to people. When we speak of the small groups, however, who wants to bring their friends and relatives to such a meeting? The attendants are all unorganized, and everyone comes late.

We need to understand that the element of nonuniformity is the very characteristic of the small groups. This is a very distinctive feature of the small groups. It means that the small groups are able to take care of every saint in the group. This is the reason we say that the small groups are the life pulse of the church. Without such an element of nonuniformity, a small group is not able to be a proper small group. I have attended some very uniform small groups, and I like them and appreciate them, but I appreciate even more the disorganized small groups. They may meet from seven to eleven o'clock at night. The saints may be constantly coming and going, and there may be much excitement. One brother testified that when his small group meeting began, no one showed up; as a result, he decided to go out and visit some people. By nine o'clock at night, however, everyone arrived, and there were more than twenty people meeting. At the beginning the scene may be discouraging, but those who endure to the end will be saved and will prevail.

We have had too much experience with the big meetings. During the past twenty years, how many people have we brought in through the "props" of the big meetings? In the United States Billy Graham also organizes large gospel campaigns. His campaigns often are attended by hundreds of thousands of people. Countless numbers of people come forward to commit their names, but in the end, it is difficult to tell where they have gone. This can be compared to scooping up water from a pond with a woven basket; eventually, the water leaks back into the same pond. The small groups may not seem that great, but if we look at the statistics, the results are astounding. If each small group brings in one new one per month, from the four hundred small groups in Taipei there will be four thousand eight hundred new ones added to the church in a year. The individual numbers are not that impressive, but the total is staggering.

We have pointed out that one of the goals of the small groups is to recover the dormant saints. Until now, however, we still have not seen this carried out. If we practice this matter conscientiously, we can recover one dormant saint in a year, even if we cannot bring in any new people; in a year we will recover four thousand eight hundred dormant saints. If from the beginning we had set our mind to labor in this way, we would have recovered seven thousand five hundred dormant saints during the past one and a half years. This is the reason I say that our new practice is something that is on paper only; there is no reality to it yet. The reason there is no reality is that we have not practiced properly and conscientiously.

I am not rebuking anyone. If I were an elder, I also would be happy to see a large gathering. If the hall or church under my administration were made up of small unorganized groups, I also would be unhappy. Still, we need to realize that it is this "unorganized" element that brings in new ones. Romans 8:25 says, "If we hope for what we do not see, we eagerly await it through endurance." If we are clear about our situation, we will exercise much endurance. We will not be afraid of the so-called "unorganized" element in the small groups. Once the small groups become uniform, the requirements increase, and it becomes difficult to bring in the new ones. The fact that the small groups are somewhat disorganized is proof that the new ones are being brought in. In order to care for everyone's condition, each one can come as early or as late as he pleases.

My hope is that the elders would pick up this burden to do

their best to promote the small groups in all the meeting halls and all the churches. Tell the saints about the benefits of the small groups. The government of Taiwan has produced an overabundance of food, and the domestic consumption cannot catch up. The government is now on a promotional campaign to teach everyone how to best utilize the excess rice. In contrast, I am afraid that the elders have accepted the new practice merely as a doctrine or a theory; in practice they have not promoted it but have left the whole matter to run its own course. Of course, when they take this attitude, the saints do not pick up a taste for the small groups.

The primary task of the elders is to promote the small groups. If I were an elder, I would surely speak concerning the small groups every day. In every meeting I would take the opportunity to promote them. I would work on the saints until every one of them is in a small group and enjoys the small groups. After this I would dig out the records of all the saints and make a list of those who are dormant or who seldom come to the meetings. I would distribute the names to the small groups who meet in close proximity to them, and encourage the saints in the small groups to visit them and recover them. The elders may think that though this exercise is good, it will not increase the number in the big meetings. Perhaps at the beginning, the number in the big meetings will not increase, but in the end it will increase. We are here to pay attention not only to the number in the big church meetings but to the number attending the small group meetings. I hope that one day the church in Taipei will have two hundred thousand saints meeting in the small groups. The number will increase, but the meeting halls will remain the same. Of course, when that happens, the big meetings will not be that important anymore.

The New System Taking Care
of Every Aspect of the Church Life

Our new system is not a one-sided arrangement; it takes care of every aspect of the church life. First, we still keep the big Lord's Day morning meeting. This is to take care of those who come for the bread-breaking meeting and to listen to a message. We are not dropping the big meetings. We want to be proper and not go to an extreme. The elders need to take care of the Lord's Day morning meeting. They need to prepare a good message, and the subject needs to be appropriate. We can speak concerning the burden of the small group meetings in any meeting except the Lord's Day morning meeting. In that meeting we cannot speak concerning the small group meetings, and we cannot have the truth lessons. We use the Lord's Day morning meeting to keep the people who come only to listen to a message. Gradually, as their church life becomes more normal and they begin to know the saints more, we will transfer them to the small groups and the truth lesson meetings. As long as there are people sitting in the big meetings on the Lord's Day morning, we must take care of their needs.

Second, the elders must work and labor diligently on the ones who come only to the big Lord's Day morning meeting and not to the small group meetings. The elders cannot force them to do anything, but they must exercise wisdom to visit them, nourish them, and stir up the hunger in their inner being. In this way they can lead them into the small groups. We need to work on the small groups in this way, and we need to work on the truth lesson meetings in the same way. This is to be faithful to the new system, and this is what it means to continue steadfastly in it.

Although this is a training, I want to study the matter together with you. After we have studied it, we can bring the result of our study back to our church to practice it in an absolute way. On the one hand, we must do our best to promote the small groups. On the other hand, we cannot give up the big Lord's Day morning meeting. That meeting more or less helps some people. The big meetings also must be proper. They should not be like the small group meetings. Neither should they follow the format of the truth lesson meetings. We need to deliver a solid message, a proper preaching. Some meeting halls use the big Lord's Day morning meetings to conduct the truth classes. This is like teaching mathematics in a history class; it is a little of everything but almost nothing in actuality.

One and a half years ago, I removed all the co-workers from the meeting halls. I was hoping that the meeting halls would not degenerate into a region for the work but that the elders would do the work of management, perfection, and care themselves. However, in order to strengthen the speaking in the big Lord's Day morning meetings, we have asked a few co-workers to return to the meeting halls to help the halls and to support a good preaching. Still, I am very concerned that once the co-workers return to the meeting halls, they will immediately pick up the work again. This is wrong. The meeting halls must be managed and cared for strictly by the elders. The co-workers do not need to busy themselves with the work there, but their help in sustaining a good preaching is needed.

We may take hall one of the church in Taipei as an example. There are sixty to seventy saints who need to listen to a message when they come on the Lord's Day. If we turn that meeting into a truth class, they will not come. Every meeting hall has a group of people who are like this. If they stop coming to the meeting, our attendance will immediately drop by one thousand. This is a serious matter. This is the reason that I deliberately said that it is improper to conduct the Lord's Day morning meeting like a truth class. Whatever we do, we must do properly. If we want a Lord's Day morning meeting, we must conduct one properly. Otherwise, it is better not to have one at all. Even if there are only a few dozen people who come to listen to a message, we must still deliver a proper message. At the same time, our truth classes need to be absolutely proper according to the standard of the truth classes. The small groups also must be proper according to the standard of the small groups. Although the small group meetings are somewhat unorganized, we must still encourage everyone to practice them. Do not forget our slogan: "Heaven and earth may pass away, but the small group meetings and the truth lessons must never be forsaken."

Our practice will take care of all aspects of the meetings. Since the church is a family, it has to take care of the needs of all kinds of people. Suppose a family has a two-month-old baby, some teenagers, and some old persons. It will not work for everyone to eat the same kind of food. Different kinds of people must have different kinds of food. We need to prepare many different kinds of food for many different kinds of people. We must take care of each group of people properly. We cannot serve one kind of communal cooking to everyone. This is the reason we have different kinds of meetings. In addition to the big Lord's Day morning meeting, which takes care of those who come for a message, we have the bread-breaking meeting, the prayer meeting, the small group meeting, and the truth classes.

We have pointed out in the past that we need a life message after the bread-breaking meeting or the prayer meeting. Some meeting halls, however, do not practice this. Some do practice this, but the messages they use are not the right ones. Perhaps it is too much of a burden to prepare the messages in each meeting hall. They may not be able to do a good job. Perhaps the church in Taipei as a whole should pick up this burden and prepare the messages for the various meeting halls as well as make them available to the other churches. The various meeting halls and churches do not necessarily need to use these messages. They can consider their local situation and use them accordingly. If the elders are flexible and apply these messages in an organic way, the small groups will become vital.

One advantage to reading the messages is that in the sharing time the saints will not ramble in their speaking. The weakness in our meeting lies in the fact that those who have something do not share, but those who have nothing show up at every meeting, open their mouths in every meeting, and speak too long every time they open their mouths. Some people are all right when they are silent, but once they open their mouths, they turn others away. Although everyone knows that some stand up and speak every time, no one stops them from their rambling. Instead, everyone holds back his function and refuses to share the portion that perfects the saints and benefits the church.

The elders must exercise wisdom in managing the church. There is a time to exercise control. After the message, when the time comes for everyone to share, the elders need to exercise control. The minute they observe that there is some improper or vain sharing, they should stop this speaking and ask others who have something to share to speak instead. If there is no control, the meeting will flow "where the wind blows"; it will not move according to the leading of the Holy Spirit. If we have life messages, we can choose a few passages to read together. In this way we can save the meeting from rambling, and we will afford the attendants a solid supply. This can be more beneficial to the saints than listening to a message in the big meetings.

The Small Group Meetings and the Truth Lessons

There is one important principle that we must keep in the small group meetings and the truth classes: Everyone must speak, but no one should preach from *Truth Lessons*. In the truth classes we do not need to expand or supplement *Truth Lessons*. In the small group meetings we should encourage everyone to speak. In all the places that are practicing the truth classes, some are doing it rightly, but others are doing it wrongly. Every lesson of *Truth Lessons* is a good message. The main points, the lines of thought, and the material presented are very rich; they are more than what an ordinary believer can absorb. You must trust me that everything that should be included was included when we compiled *Truth Lessons,* and everything that should not be there was excluded. I do not believe that anyone, myself included, can give another message as good as the printed lessons. The subject matter is well organized, and the content is concise. For this reason, the teachers do not need to expand, expound, or supplement these lessons with anything. Sometimes a short passage contains a tremendous amount of material. I am afraid that some brothers have been elders for many years, but they still do not understand the material contained in the lessons. In teaching the truth classes, the first ones we should teach are ourselves. There is no need to preach the lessons. All we must do is study and memorize them. There is no need to engage in a long discourse regarding them. All we must do is help everyone to absorb the points and remember them. There is no need to add or delete anything.

The outstanding point about *Truth Lessons* is that it presents to the reader the truths in the Lord's recovery level by level, from the most simple to the most advanced. We have been in the Lord's recovery for many years, but many of us still do not quite understand the truth. Our understanding is very general. We know something, but we do not know it in depth. Since we are saved and by the Lord's mercy we are in His recovery, we should receive some basic education in the truth. For example, all of us need to know the origin and functions of the Bible. These are all found in *Truth Lessons*. All we need to do is study and memorize them, and then teach the saints to "repeat-read," "emphasize-read," "pray-read," and "vitalize-read" them.

If the saints can continue steadfastly in this matter, and if they go through one lesson a week, in four years all of them will become "scholars." They will be rooted in the truth. This will fill up the lack we have had in the past. In the past some of you listened to messages for more than twenty years, but you still did not know the origin and the functions of the Bible, and you still did not know that Satan is both an enemy and an adversary. All you knew were such terms as bearing the cross, loving the Lord, and the resurrection life. This is like some who teach arithmetic for years but teach only simple counting; they do not advance to addition, subtraction, multiplication, and division. Now we must overturn our past. We must not repeat the past. Consider the educational system in our society. A man does not receive a good education by listening to famous speakers every day. Rather, he learns by going to school day by day. If he merely listens to lectures day by day, he will not graduate from school, and he will not learn anything solid. This will greatly affect his family, society, and nation as a whole. The teaching of the truth lessons may appear dull, but in four years it will lay a firm foundation in the truth.

Today in Taiwan we have intercollegiate college entrance examinations. If all our schools did not teach according to the syllabus, and if every class went according to the way it pleased, how could students pass these entrance examinations? Today among us we do not have any examinations; we do not know how much truth the saints know and how much experience they have in their daily lives. If we test everyone on matters such as the cross, resurrection, and the functions of the Bible, I wonder how many would pass. This is a great lack among us. I only wish that I could overturn all our practices. Now that *Truth Lessons* is printed, I hope that this situation will change.

In education, the first thing to take care of is the students. If we are teaching in a primary school, we need to use a primary school curriculum. We cannot teach with the material we use in a doctorate degree seminar. This is the reason that I need to repeat what I have said, that in teaching the truth we must not enter into a lengthy discourse. All we need to do is read, ask some questions, and repeat a little when we come to the crucial points. We may have a "doctor" among us, but we must remember that we are teaching the truth; we are not training people to become "doctors." We do not need to use our own material to teach. Rather, teach according to the *Truth Lessons*.

At the same time, you need to encourage the saints to attend the small group meetings, and you need to make everyone speak. In particular, those who do not usually speak must open their mouths. Those who always speak should be advised in private to speak less and to give more opportunity for others to speak. They may be full of words, but in order for others to be perfected, they should be advised to exercise some restraint. Encourage those who speak little or who do not speak at all to speak more, and the small group meetings will become living.

PUTTING INTO PRACTICE
THE NEW SYSTEM IN AN ABSOLUTE WAY

On the spiritual side, we have all seen a vision, and we know what we are doing here. Under the same vision we are speaking the same thing, we have the same view, and we think the same thing. I have spoken much today, but not for the sake of forcing others to follow me. Since I dropped my job in 1933 to serve the Lord full-time, I have been serving in the church life for fifty-three years. I have observed the situation in Christianity and have studied the history of Christianity. In order to consider how to change the system I have even studied the present condition of society in general. Throughout the ages, many groups and organizations have risen up, and many have fallen down. There are reasons for the ups and downs. The conclusion I drew from my studying is what I have fellowshipped with you during the past one and a half years. I am not forcing you to take the burden of my fellowship. I am imploring you. If you want to hold on to the old traditions, you are on a dead-end street. If you try to find another way, you are wasting your time. Here I am presenting to you a practical way. I hope all of you will follow and practice this in a simple way.

Our present practice is to spread the gospel, build up the small groups, and teach the truth. If we can do these three things, the church will surely be strong; it will surely multiply and spread. Our failure in the past was because of the lack of these three things. We trusted only in the big meetings, and the result was a downward slide. Today we are not dropping the big meetings. Rather, we are practicing and building up these three things in addition to the big meetings. If we practice them, the church will multiply. This requires every elder to do his best to work in a disciplined and serious way. Simply giving verbal consent will not work.

The way to take care of the dormant saints is to compile a list of names and pass it on to the serving ones in all the districts, charging them to visit these ones in a suitable way. They may not be able to visit them every day, but they can at least invite them for a meal once a month. I believe if they will do this continuously for half a year, the dormant ones will be recovered. Human hearts are made of flesh; they are soft. Everyone has feelings, and everyone knows who is actually helping him. At the beginning this may require some labor, and it may not show results immediately, but after half a year or a year, the results will be obvious. In the past we wanted quick and great results, but we ended up dropping everything. The only thing that was left was a façade. Today we do not want to have a façade. We want to gain people.

I hope that the brothers and sisters will receive my fellowship in this message. I include sisters because I hope that even the sisters will understand what we are doing and will help to practice this matter in all the halls and churches. It is too early to ask the saints from foreign countries to come and see anything at this point in time. I have told them that the new way has not taken full shape yet. We are still adjusting and improving. I ask them to be patient. They all want to receive news and the messages that you are receiving here, but I told them that after they hear something, they may not understand it at all. This is because they do not know the context of what they are hearing. It is useless for them to imitate according to the letter. My hope is that a model, a miniature, would be built up here in the church in Taipei. If that is built up, we will have something to show the saints and to fellowship about when they come to visit us.

I beg you once again to practice these two things: the truth has to be taught in a proper, living, and matter-of-fact way; there is no need to preach too much. We must also continue steadfastly in the small group meetings. We considered much at the time we compiled *Truth Lessons*. I am convinced that after a believer goes through the one hundred ninety-two lessons in four years, he will have a "Masters of Theology." As far as the small group practice is concerned, we must continue to exhort the saints to learn to nourish others, to warm their hearts, to care for them, to fellowship with them, and to bring them to the small group meetings. We must also tell the saints not to expect the small group meetings to be too orderly. We should rather take care of the condition of all the people. It is more attractive when it is not so orderly. The atmosphere should not be too tense, and everyone should have the opportunity to know everyone else, but of course, we should never drift into worldly conversations. There should always be a message for nourishment and teaching. If we practice this consistently for a long time, we will see great results.

A QUESTION AND ANSWER

Question: How should the teachers prepare themselves in order to make the truth lessons attractive, and how can they avoid preaching and expounding?

Answer: In reality, your preparation does not have that

much to do with the material; it has to do with your spirit. Of course, you need to read the lesson through a few times. You need to find out the crucial points and practice repeat-reading, emphasize-reading, pray-reading, and vitalize-reading. Then you should exercise to do the same in the meetings. If some saints do not understand a point, you do not need to expound too much. Simply read the points a few more times until they remember the points. I beg you not to prepare something to preach. Whatever is in you will come out of you. "Out of the abundance of the heart the mouth speaks" (Matt. 12:34). If you prepare too much, you will have too much deposit within you, and it will be difficult for you not to preach. Therefore, do not prepare too much. Simply open the book and teach. It is not difficult to teach. All you need to do is repeat-read, emphasize-read, pray-read, and vitalize-read. You must prepare yourselves for this, but you do not need to prepare the lessons too much.

At the time we compiled *Truth Lessons,* my helpers asked me if we should list some reference books at the end of each lesson. I told them that the lesson itself has enough material for the saints to digest; there is no need to provide any reference material. When we compiled *Truth Lessons,* we considered all these. Please forget about preaching. There is no need to preach anymore. Simply teach, which means, simply read. If we do this, our teaching of the truth will be a success.

CHAPTER FIVE

THE PRACTICE OF CHANGING THE SYSTEM

Prayer: Lord, our heart is filled with praises toward the throne. We worship You for calling and gathering us out of this busy age. We treasure this time—You called and gathered us here to meet in Your name. Lord, we ask You to visit us and bring us into Your heart's desire that we may have thorough fellowship in You. Lord, open Yourself to us, open the heavens to us, reveal Your word to us, unveil Your economy to us, and show us what You intend to do today. We also ask You to shine on us that we would not have anything hidden, any covering, or any shadow, but that we would be absolutely in the light and under an open sky to have open fellowship with one another through Your open word.

Lord, we ask You again to open Your will to us that we may see the way You want to take today. Give us an open mind and an open spirit; even more, give us an open word. We truly long to have open fellowship. We pray that You would save us. We desire to be delivered from this age, this religious world, and to come forward to live to You. Lord, may You have mercy on us. Amen.

THE REASON FOR CHANGING THE SYSTEM

In this chapter we will continue our fellowship concerning the practice of changing the system. I would like to mention again, brothers and sisters, the purpose of changing the system. On the negative side, changing the system will deliver us from traditional religion, and on the positive side, restore the living and organic function of every member of the Body so that Christ and His Body can spread. Although we use the expression *change the system,* we are not merely changing a

method or a system; rather, our purpose is to spread the Lord
and His Body in His recovery in the present age. In order to
reach this goal, we must first be delivered from the religion
that binds us.

Christianity Killing the Organic Function
of the Believers

Some brothers in America recently gathered some statistics. In the past we always thought that Christianity was the
most powerful religion, the most widespread, persuasive, and
capable of gaining people. But I was shocked when I saw the
statistics. According to the statistics, in the past fifty years
Islam had a five hundred percent increase, Hinduism a hundred seventeen percent increase, and Buddhism a sixty-seven
percent increase, but Christianity had only a forty-seven percent
increase. Christianity has a low rate of increase because it
has become a religion that binds people, that kills the organic
function of the believers.

The Catholic Church has the largest membership in Christianity; almost one-fourth of the world's population today are
Catholics. Among them, however, it is difficult to find one out
of a thousand or even ten thousand who functions organically.
Concerning the Protestant churches, we can use Taiwan as an
example. The Presbyterian church came to Taiwan from Scot-
land about a century ago. Now after more than one hundred
years, it has fewer than 100,000 members on the whole island
of Taiwan. According to the statistics of Taiwan, which I saw a
few years ago, the Presbyterian church has the largest membership, but still it has only about 80,000 Christians. Next
is the Lord's recovery with about 47,000 members. The third is
the True Jesus Church with about 20,000 members, most of
whom are aborigines. Today Taiwan has a population of about
twenty million, but the number of Christians is fewer than
500,000. The total number of believers from the three biggest
groups is only about 150,000. This deserves our consideration.

The reason for such a situation is that, on the one hand,
Christianity preaches the gospel and teaches the truth; on the
other hand, it binds people with its system. It saves people on

the one hand, but it binds them on the other. It enlivens people, but it also kills them. We may say that baptisms in Christianity are truly burials. When people are baptized, their organic function is altogether buried; very few can escape from this. This proves that the practice of Christianity is a "dead end" street; it is a terrible way. What about us? We have been in Taiwan for almost forty years. We began our work in Taiwan thirty-seven years ago, but we still have not been able to gospelize the small island of Taiwan.

The Early Practice in Taiwan

I had said that when we first came to Taiwan, we tried our best to rid ourselves of the old ways and endeavored to preach the gospel. At that time the population of Taipei was fewer than 500,000. First, we decided to print gospel tracts. We determined that the number of the gospel tracts that we would print would be equal to the number of residents in Taipei, because we wanted the gospel to enter every home in the city. Using a map, we divided the city into many small districts and gave the gospel tracts to the saints, asking them to go to every street and alley in each district to put a gospel tract in the mailbox of every house. Within a week, almost every household in Taipei had received a gospel tract from us. Second, we sent out gospel teams to march on the street to spread the atmosphere of the gospel. We went to every street and alley in all the different districts, not only on the Lord's Day afternoons but also during the week. We went in large teams and in small teams, holding lanterns, beating drums, and marching on the streets to preach the gospel. Third, we printed many banners such as: "Believe in Jesus to receive eternal life," "God loves the world," "Prepare to meet your God," and "Christ Jesus came into the world to save sinners." We posted them at train stations, bus stations, intersections, and on the door of every saint so that the banners could be seen everywhere in the city. Fourth, every Lord's Day afternoon we preached the gospel in the New Park where the amphitheatre could hold three thousand people. We would receive at least four to five hundred gospel information cards every Lord's Day. The following day, on Monday evening, the brothers and sisters would gather together to receive lists of names grouped according to their addresses. Then the saints would go to visit them as soon as possible.

Through these four practices, we gained tens of thousands of people. At that time, we also determined not to contact those who were in Christianity. In the practice of our church life, we would not reject any of them who would come to us, but we would not take the initiative to contact them. Instead, we went only to the unbelievers. This was the reason for our success. Later, under the influence of the traditions of Christianity, we slowed down and made little advance. Hence, our changing the system today is primarily a change of concept and practice.

The Result of Adopting
the Custom of the Nations

The Lord highly regarded and blessed our early practice. In fewer than six years, the number of saints in Taiwan increased from 400 to 40,000. This was a hundredfold increase. Islam had a fivefold increase in fifty years, but we had a hundredfold increase in fewer than six years. This was truly the Lord's blessing. When I went to America in 1961, there were 22,000 information cards of the saints in the church in Taipei. If this rate of increase had continued until today, Taiwan would have been gospelized twice already. However, instead of practicing this way faithfully, we went backward to adopt the custom of the nations, and we took the old way of Christianity; hence, we ended up in the awkward situation we are in today.

I am not forcing you all to follow me to change the system, but I would like to reason with you. If I do not present both sides of this matter, it will be difficult for us to change our concept. Today I am crying out, Do we want to live in religion? If we do not want to live in religion, we need to indicate it plainly and not stay in a neutral position. To put it bluntly, it seems as if I have been a "mean" person for one and a half years, rebuking and making demands. But if we understand the history of the Lord's recovery, we will realize that when we first arrived in Taiwan the atmosphere and practice among us were not like what we see today. The saints at that time were all burning in spirit, functioning, and spreading the gospel in one accord. This is the reason that our numbers increased from 400 to 40,000. Many of us here were saved at that time. Among the ones saved in those days, quite a number later became elders in different localities.

When people in the denominations saw this situation, they started a rumor out of jealousy, saying, "They simply drag people in and hastily baptize them." I replied that if this were the case, they should try to drag in forty thousand people and baptize them in a period of six years. Sadly, these good circumstances did not last long. We turned unknowingly from being living fish to dead wood that simply drifts in a slow stream. Eventually, we drifted into Christianity and became the same as Christianity. We completely lost the "family tradition" we had brought to Taiwan in the beginning and turned instead to take the custom of the nations. This causes my heart to ache.

I hope we all can see that the religious way of Christianity buries the new ones and kills their organic function. As for us, over the past twenty years, beginning from 1962, we have been gradually going downhill. Even though the slope may not be steep, if we are off by a fraction of an inch we may end up missing the mark by a thousand miles. Today we are already seeing the consequences.

THE DIFFICULTY IN CHANGING THE SYSTEM

It has been a year and a half since I came back to push our changing the system, but not many of us have been moved yet. Apparently, we have a number of activities, but actually, the new way does not depend on how many activities we have but on whether or not we have cleared away everything that is old and picked up what is new. We were active for more than twenty years, going to meetings not only once a week but three or four times a week. Yet in the end we went downhill. Thank the Lord that in this year and a half we have all agreed and are willing to change the system. In terms of action, however, only a few of us have discarded the old things and have made a turn to practice the new way.

EXAMINING OUR CHANGING OF THE SYSTEM

Keeping the Big Meetings

Perhaps it seems that I am speaking too much and that I am demanding perfection. Let us speak about some specific practices as a way of examining the change of system. First, we have clearly said that no matter how much we change the system, we still should keep the big meeting on the Lord's Day morning to take care of those who like only to listen to messages and do not want to attend small group meetings.

The Lord Jesus kept the same principle while He was ministering on earth. Every Sabbath He went into the synagogue and preached there. He did not go there to keep the Sabbath, nor did He have the intention to worship God there. Rather, He took advantage of the custom in those days to preach the word of God. Not only did the Lord Jesus do this, the apostles also did this. When Paul preached the gospel in the Gentile lands, wherever he went, the first place he visited was the synagogue; moreover, it was always on the Sabbath. If the apostles were asked to return on the following Sabbath, they would go again (Acts 13:42-44). Surely Paul did not go to keep the Sabbath, but he utilized the custom practiced by the Jews who were scattered among the Gentiles. Thus, when the Jews were gathered in the synagogues to study the Scriptures on the Sabbath, Paul went to preach to them the New Testament gospel.

Today nearly everywhere in the world people have a day off on the Lord's Day; they do not go to work, nor do they go to school. Most people have the concept that Christians should attend "Sunday service" every Lord's Day. Among us there is also a group of saints who are used to this custom; for this reason, we must take care of them. We need to use this opportunity and take the time to give them a message. We should help them to have a gradual turn and should never give up on them. However, based on my observation, we have not done enough in this matter. In some meeting halls this matter has not been done properly. As a result, the Lord's Day morning meeting looks like a big meeting, and it also looks like a class that teaches truth lessons. Whatever we do will be ineffective if it is not done appropriately. If we must do something, we should do it properly and seriously. Since we have a Lord's Day morning meeting, even if only ten people come, we must be serious and speak a message to them.

When we began changing the system one and a half years ago, we set the basic principle of transferring all the co-workers out of the various meeting halls. Based upon the revelation in the New Testament, we left the church under the management of the elders of the respective meetings halls, not under the management of the co-workers. The management of the church by the co-workers is not a principle revealed in the Bible; it is a traditional practice in religion. However, in order to have a strong speaking of the messages in the Lord's Day morning meeting, there is a need for a few co-workers who are gifted to go to the various meeting halls to help the meeting. But I am concerned that if the co-workers go back to the meeting halls, they will again be involved with the administration of the church. The elders in a certain meeting hall may also feel that it is good for the co-workers to help in the administration of their meeting hall. Consequently, we may go back to the situation we were in before we began to change the system. Nevertheless, our present arrangement of preparing a message, in order to take care of the saints who come to the big Lord's Day morning meeting, is very considerate. We must carry this out according to what has been fellowshipped so that we can avoid creating problems.

The Importance of the Small Group Meetings

Apart from the big Lord's Day morning meetings, there are a few meetings that allow the saints to function organically; one of them is the small group meeting. In a small group the saints have many opportunities to carry out their function organically. Functions such as preaching the gospel, expounding the truth, teaching the Bible, loving others, helping others, taking care of others, and sympathizing with others can be manifested and are necessary. But because we are still accustomed to the old religion, once we see the loose situation in the small groups, we become disheartened. Eventually, we also become loose. Therefore, we do not consider the small groups to be important because we feel that they are not proper meetings. Nevertheless, the life pulse of the church is maintained by the small groups.

Please give me the grace to speak a frank word. We have been practicing the small group meetings for eighteen months. How do the co-workers and elders feel about this matter? Perhaps we would say that we do not have time to pay attention to these groups because we are very busy. Speaking of being busy, I do not believe any of you could be busier than I am. I have put out so many books, and I also review almost every one of them. Now in Taipei, I have been going here and there to observe the situation of various meeting halls. For the sake of the Lord's work and the changing of the system, I have visited many places. To say that we are so busy that we do not have time to go to the small group meeting proves that we have not seen the importance of changing the system.

The small group meeting is the life pulse of the Lord's recovery and the key to the survival of our "family." If we are willing to sacrifice our future and consecrate everything to the Lord, and if we see that this is the way the Lord's recovery should take, we would give ourselves even to the point of neglecting our sleep and meals and put all our effort into taking this way and making it a success. In this year and a half, I have said at least four to five times that we should have the spirit of devoting ourselves to the task until our death. I am translating the Recovery Version of the New Testament into Chinese with such a spirit. I work at least eight to nine hours a day, revising the drafts to the extent that my eyes become blurry. I know that it is risky for me to labor in this way. As a man more than eighty years old, I am risking my life by doing this, but I have the burden.

Brothers, we owe not only the Lord and the brothers and sisters, we even have an obligation to our consecration. If we do not have such a spirit, we are wasting our time here. We must make our consecration worthwhile. We have consecrated our future and spent our everything for the Lord in order to do something for Him. Now the matter of having small groups has been set before us. If we would not take them seriously and endeavor to work them out, we are being unfaithful to the Lord's commission and to our own consecration.

My most intimate brothers and sisters, the saints serving in the bookroom, can testify concerning the way I lead them. In the past when I was not here, they were muddling along. At this time I have not pushed them, but I have taken the lead to work with them. Now they are almost neglecting their sleep and meals, and as a result their translation work has greatly improved and has undergone a big change. In our translation of the Recovery Version of the New Testament into Chinese, beginning with the first word of the first verse of the first chapter of Matthew, we have considered every word carefully according to the Greek. When we first began our work, the progress was very slow. But now, to a certain degree, the serving ones have all learned how to carefully consider the words. In the past they had the ability, but they were not willing to learn or make the effort.

In Christianity today there are at least four versions of the Bible in Chinese. If our version were the same as the others, it would be unnecessary. Since we want to put out a new translation, we must produce a work of the highest standard. Even if it is not exactly according to the Greek, in comparison with the other versions, it should at least be commended and appraised as the best.

Today we have all rejected the earthly bribes. The world is a busy place; especially in Taiwan, everyone is under stress, and many hold more than one job. Yet all of us are here not for money or entertainment but for the Lord. We all know that as human beings, we must believe in the Lord; as believers in the Lord, we must love the Lord; and as lovers of the Lord, we must take the way of the Lord's recovery. There is no other way. Matthew 24 and 25 tell us that one day we will stand before the Lord and give Him an account. I am not speaking this word merely to all the saints; I am speaking to myself as well. Day by day I hold this kind of attitude: "O Lord, I hope that one day when You come back, I will be able to give You an acceptable account." The Lord will come back, and we will need to give an account before Him. Since this is the case, we should not have a slothful attitude. If we believe that one day we will stand before the judgment seat of the Lord, we should be very serious today. For example, if the brothers and sisters serving in the bookroom are serious, they will do at least eighty percent of the work, and I will not need to labor over every single word.

The co-workers and elders have a great responsibility for the improvement of the situation of the small groups. We must try our best to promote the small groups. I still remember the meeting in which I first mentioned the matter of the small groups; it was as if we were in heaven, and the atmosphere was very positive. But what has happened since? It seems as if we have all gone back to where we began, without taking any action. I do not mean to make things difficult, but I hope that we all will be awakened. I am not threatening anyone with the matter of reward and punishment, but I am speaking the truth. I hope that everyone will be serious to carry out the small groups and see that this is our life pulse; we must work it out.

SOME SPECIFIC PRACTICES IN CHANGING THE SYSTEM

Not Focusing on the Façade

Now we will fellowship further on how to seriously carry out the change of system. The way of religion is to have a Sunday service that is mainly a façade, but our way is to have all the saints functioning organically. Once there is a façade, the organic function of the believers is put aside, and the believers are killed. We must drop the concept of putting on a show. We do not care for the façade; we care only for the fulfilling of our organic function. In the spiritual service, any kind of façade kills people. This is true even in our daily life. A normal living should be without any façade. For example, in a family the husband wipes the windows, the wife cooks the three meals, the daughters wash the dishes, one of the sons sweeps the floor and dusts the furniture, another one cleans the restroom, and the youngest one mops the floor. Is there any façade? No, rather, every one of them is functioning. It is when they invite guests that a façade is put on for people to see. Once they have a façade, no one has to do anything, nor can anyone do anything. Therefore, no family can put on a façade every day. If a family puts on a façade every day, it would no longer be a family but a restaurant, and all the members would be "choked to death."

Today our changing the system is to remove the façade and recover the true condition of our daily life. I implore the co-workers and elders to have a change in concept. We should never think that our meeting hall is so big that there is therefore the need for a façade. If an elder in hall one puts on a façade, hall one will be killed. Therefore, never put on a façade.

This does not mean that we ignore the need of the actual situation. We truly understand the ideas of the people in our society. The majority of people who want to join Christianity desire to attend Sunday services and hear good sermons. This is the reason that I stress that we need to have a meeting on the Lord's Day where a proper message can be given. Besides this, we need to have a "home life," which is our small group meeting, with no façade. Hence, do not be bothered by the "dragging" situation in the small group; rather, welcome it, because it shows that we care for all the members.

Whether or not we can have a successful small group hinges on the co-workers and elders. If we are not willing to labor on this matter, the small groups will eventually be "dragged" into Hades and will become nothing. Hence, I beseech the elders and co-workers to labor diligently. We must have the determination to labor on this and to be persistent to the end. In this way, the "dragging" of the small group will be the "singing of the songs of ascents"; the more it is "dragged," the higher it goes.

At present there are four hundred small groups in Taipei. If every small group can bring in a new one each week, we will bring in 1,600 in a month, and almost 20,000 in a year. This could never be achieved through the big meetings. Moreover, the new ones are not strangers invited off the street; rather, they are all related to the members of the small groups. Because they are their friends, relatives, and neighbors, it is more likely that they will remain. Furthermore, since all the members function organically, they spontaneously will have a love for the new ones. For example, a sister may not know how to love and take care of children when she is single, but after she is married and has children, she spontaneously loves and takes care of her children.

Furthermore, in a small group the conversation is more intimate. The small group lends itself to the mutual shepherding and caring. No one puts on a façade. The small group has so many advantages. There is no façade but much supply. Without a façade and without rituals, religion is knocked down and the functions of the members are manifested.

The Elders Taking the Lead
to Promote the Small Groups

The elders must promote the small groups in every meeting hall. Ask the saints to set a time and place to have small group meetings and to let their friends, relatives, and neighbors know about the meetings. The meeting time should be flexible. It can be from 7:00 P.M. to midnight. Everyone needs to be in a meeting once a week. We want the saints to function organically to take care of people and shepherd them. Even if some people work late and come home at 10:00 or 11:00 P.M., they should still be able to come to eat, drink tea, and meet. Some may have something to do late at night, but they should still be able to meet with the group and then go and take care of their business. We do not even need to be so legal in the matter of having snacks. We do not need to begin with singing hymns and reading the Bible, and then serve snacks after the meeting is over. It does not need to be this way. We must simply make sure that every week we have a small group meeting. Even though this kind of meeting requires more work, it helps all the members to develop their organic function, to take care of one another, and to incite one another to love.

There is no façade in the group meeting, and there is no opportunity for people to show off. Instead, there are many advantages. This is the life pulse in the Lord's recovery. The best way to gain people for the Lord is to open all of our homes to contact, nourish, and cherish people. Do not rely on the way of holding big gospel meetings. That way does not work. Once we have a podium, there is the appearance of a law court, the putting on of a façade; this is religion, and it kills people. We do not trust in the big gospel campaigns but in the homes of the brothers and sisters.

Encouraging the Members of the Small Groups to Function Organically

In 1965 I visited Brazil for the first time to see the situation of Christianity there. The brothers told me that Catholicism is the principal religion in Brazil, yet it is altogether dead, empty, without content, and full of superstitions. As for Protestantism, it was mainly the Pentecostal movement that was there. It was "booming" for a time, but eventually it withered like flowers and vanished like the lightning. The only Christian group that lasted is called *Congregaçaon* in Portuguese, equivalent to *congregation* in English. This group spread to Brazil in 1915. After more than fifty years in Brazil, at the time of my visit in 1965, it had more than three hundred thousand saints. In São Paulo alone there were thirty thousand saints, and more than one hundred small meeting places. They did not have any speakers or preachers, and they required the believers to read the Bible purely.

For this reason I went to visit them, meet with them, and fellowship with their leading ones. They showed me everything. I found out that many of their practices are scriptural. Later the brothers asked me if we should meet with them. I told them that there was a certain matter with which we could not get through in our fellowship; they do not receive all genuinely saved believers but only those who were baptized in their way. This is the practice of a sect. In other matters many of their practices are scriptural. For example, they do not have preachers and ministers; instead, all the brothers and sisters function in the meetings. In their big meetings they put two microphones out, one for the brothers and one for the sisters, for testimonies. They meet from 10:00 A.M. to 2:00 or 3:00 P.M. From their practice, we drew the conclusion that the most effective way to meet is to forsake the religious rituals and meet in small groups in the believers' homes. The small group meeting should be held once a week, either in the morning or in the evening, and we should make it known to our friends, relatives, and neighbors.

The Small Groups Being the Life Pulse in the Propagation of the Church

If we all practice with diligence, what do you think the result will be? It will create "job opportunities" for the saints and bring out their organic function. If we have only big meetings, who will dare to function? All the one-talented ones will be buried because they dare not, cannot, and do not have the opportunity to function. But once we practice the small groups, we create opportunities for the saints. Moreover, is there another way that is more effective in spreading the testimony of the Lord's recovery? A great evangelist in America attracted one million people to his gospel campaigns, of which three hundred thousand people committed to Christ. But from 1948 until today, where is the result of his work of thirty-eight years? If he had begun to work on the home meetings and small group meetings thirty-eight years ago, I believe that the society of the United States today would have been turned around. With his great power and influence, he could gain at least a hundred thousand in a year. How many would he have gained in the past thirty-eight years? However, because he took the way of big meetings, there is hardly any result today.

In the past two decades, since I came to the United States, the number of Christians has been decreasing steadily. Christians are killed by the religious Sunday service. The evangelist also found out the reason for the decline in the number of Christians. When I first came to the United States, I heard him crying out to the believers, telling them to have small Bible studies and prayer meetings in the homes. He also knew that sending the saved ones to the denominations could be compared to putting them into a freezer; this way only leads to death. Hence, small-scale meetings were the trend in the United States about twenty years ago. There were more than one thousand different small meetings in Southern California alone. Therefore, I hope that the brothers and sisters will change their view. If we want the Lord's recovery to have a way, you and I must bear the responsibility of changing our views and concepts; we need to begin with ourselves.

In this year and a half, eighty elders have been newly appointed in Taipei to bear the burden of leading and taking care of the twenty-one meeting halls. Now the practice of the new way is clear and definite. The elders in every meeting hall must take this matter of the small group seriously and endeavor to carry it out. In summary, first, there must be a big meeting on the Lord's Day morning, with a certain brother responsible to release a message in a proper way. If one person cannot bear this burden, two or three can bear it together. These two or three should have fellowship once a week to see who is the appropriate one to release the message. The responsibility should fall on the most suitable one. If we can do this in a proper way, our Lord's Day morning meeting will be able to bring in people. Since the content of our message is weighty and full of light, the saints will spread the news around. Thus, those who like to listen to messages will come. This is something that is worth doing. However, we should not stop here. The big meeting is but an entrance. Those who are brought in should be given to and taken care of by the small groups. This is the proper practice.

Recovering the Dormant Saints

Moreover, the elders of the various meeting halls should check the information cards of the saints and find out who is meeting regularly and who is not. For those who are meeting regularly, we need to find out their present condition, and for those who are not meeting regularly, we need to find out the reason and look into their present condition. We should study every case in detail. Then we should make a copy of each card and distribute the copies to different small groups according to the addresses. The small groups will then be responsible to visit the saints who are not meeting regularly. They may invite them for meals or have some simple fellowship with them. When they go out to visit these ones, they must keep in mind the principle of not being quick to give up after the first visit; rather, they should go in a persistent way. They may need to invite a certain one for a meal once a month for six months before he is willing to come to a meeting. It may seem that the result is too slow, but they need to believe that "fine products come from slow work." Do not worry about being slow, but be wary of standing still. Those who have not been meeting for a while may fear a big crowd. But if they are invited to join the small group meeting in someone's home, they will feel more comfortable. Once they come to the small group and have some contact with the saints, their heart will gradually be warmed, their spirit will be supplied, and then they will remain. Hence, whether or not the small groups are successful hinges on whether we have the heart to carry this out.

Preparing Life Messages

The elders also need to study how to make the small groups attractive to people. The most important thing is to spend much time in prayer and study. We can then arrange message after message from the ministry publications to lead the small groups in pursuing the truth, fellowshipping, and reading in a living way. Even though the characteristic of the small group is "dragging," you should have a life message to supply people. If the saints are not fully fed, they should at least be half fed; do not let them go home with an empty stomach. Do not wait until the last minute to prepare such a message. Because some people are lazy in preparing dinner, they merely open a can of food or buy a loaf of bread. But we cannot do this in the small groups. We must plan everything ahead of time. The small group meets only once a week. We should be well prepared. There is not a lack of rich messages among us. Hence, whether a small group has a life supply depends on whether or not the serving ones are enlivened and prepared. Today we have the meeting place, the meeting ones, and the truth. The question is whether or not we are willing to labor. Promoting merely by words does not work. Only when we carry it out earnestly will there be a result.

The Way of Propagation

In order to propagate the small groups, we need to subdivide the groups. Once there are twelve people meeting in a small group, we must prepare to be subdivided into two groups. Some may think that it has taken them awhile to reach this number and that once they divide, their group will be finished. For this reason, they are not willing to be divided. At the beginning a group may seem weak after dividing, but gradually the group will be enlivened. After a group of twelve is subdivided into two groups of about five to six people, gradually, each group will increase to twelve. We need to remember that the small group is for the Lord's increase and not merely for our own enjoyment.

THE IMPORTANCE OF THE ONE ACCORD

The practice of the new way requires our coordination in one accord. Having the same goal, we can study the definite steps to practice. If we merely talk or sit on the fence without any progress, we will waste our time. We will not gain anything, the church will not gain anything, and the Lord will not gain anything. Our goal is to gospelize Taiwan in five years. One and a half years have already passed, and the remaining three and a half years will pass by quickly. I hope that we all can see this goal clearly and share this burden.

A FURTHER WORD ON TEACHING *TRUTH LESSONS*

In the previous chapter I pointed out that the key to teaching *Truth Lessons* is not to preach. Now I repeat: we should not try to expound *Truth Lessons;* we should simply teach them. Take mathematics as an example. The principle of addition, subtraction, multiplication, and division can only be taught, not explained. One plus one is two; one plus two is three. This can only be taught but not explained. The content of *Truth Lessons* is very solid, and some lessons may require two sessions. Some lessons may be very difficult. If we try to expound these lessons, we may not be able to finish them in several years. Hence, do not explain. Simply teach the saints to read livingly, to read with repetition, to read with emphasis, and to pray-read. We may not understand what we read at the beginning, but later we will understand. This can be compared to the ancient Chinese teachers teaching the *Three-character Classic*. At the beginning, the students recited the book, and no explanation was given to them. Later, they gradually received an understanding. In order to enter into the truths of the Bible, we first must recite them. As our growth in life reaches a certain degree, we will spontaneously understand the meaning. Therefore, the purpose of *Truth Lessons* is to show the saints that there are certain truths in the Bible that we should know. As we reach a certain degree in our growth in life, we will spontaneously receive understanding.

For example, in Taiwan we have intercollegiate entrance examinations. The content of the examination is not what the teachers have explained but what is written in the teaching materials. A good teacher must be able to teach and convey everything that is in the teaching materials to the students. In this way, the students will know how to answer the test questions. I hope that the whole church can teach *Truth Lessons* and impart the truths into the saints. Perhaps we also need an examination with rewards in order to encourage the saints to study diligently. In this way, even if a "famous professor" has his own way of teaching, we still must teach based on the teaching material. This way is worth practicing.

THE SMALL GROUP BEING THE LIFE PULSE OF THE CHURCH LIFE

The small group is the life pulse of the present practice of the church life. In the past year and a half, the number of saints in the church has in fact increased, but the rate of increase is not that encouraging. The reason for this low rate is that the small groups have not yet been worked out and are not strong enough. If our small groups are strong, we will surely have a great increase in number. I hope that the saints will change their concept to see that the content of the church life is based mainly on small group meetings and not on big meetings. Then in our daily life the small groups can function in mutuality to care for and visit the saints. If we mainly have big meetings, we will be unable to take care of the aspect of our daily life. This would be regrettable. I hope that the brothers and sisters will clearly see that only by the small groups can the church life be extended to and realized in our daily living.

EVERY MEMBER OF THE SMALL GROUP
BEING A "CORE MEMBER"

Question: If there are not enough core members in a small group, but the number of people exceeds twelve, should we still divide into two groups?

Answer: I regret mentioning the term *core member.* I have already said that there are no "leading" ones, and there should not be any in a small group. Everyone is a leading one. Hence, when we speak of core members, we are referring to every member in the small group. We should not consider that some are core members and others are not; rather, we should all labor together.

A change in system is always difficult. At first we may think that every small group must have some so-called "core members" to bear the responsibility. However, if this is our thought, the small group will collapse once these "core members" are not doing well. On the other hand, if all the saints are willing to bear the responsibility, everyone will be a core member. When we divide the group, making the number smaller, each group will be strong and propagating, even if it is weak temporarily.

To bring up the matter of "core members" shows that this religious concept is still in our blood. We cannot give our flesh any opportunity. Once we give a little ground to our flesh, religion will immediately come forth. Whoever thinks that only a few saints are "core members" is religious. If the church has a "perfecting training for core members," who would be the candidates? Every saint would be a candidate! We all are core members.

I truly hope that there will be a small group meeting in every saint's home. If we would do this, there will be a great revival of the church, and Taiwan will be gospelized.

EVERY SAINT HAVING A SMALL GROUP MEETING
AT HOME EVERY WEEK

In principle, after a Christian is saved, he should have a home meeting at least once a week. This is a reasonable thing. Based on the patterns shown in the Bible, we see that if anyone is willing to open his home every week and afford his friends, relatives, and neighbors the opportunity to hear the gospel, the gospel will spread into his whole family, saving his household from sin and temper, while at the same time, bringing in much of the Lord's blessing and shining. Husbands and wives are prone to quarrel and argue. But the weekly home meeting will save the couple from quarreling. Sometimes we may be weak, and we may not have read the Bible for the whole week. But we will at least read the Bible once a week in the small group. Reading the Bible fifty-two times a year is also a great thing.

I beseech the elders to take this matter seriously. We need to know that in order to make the meeting hall or church where we are prosperous and fruitful, we must labor on the small groups. This is the only way. We must do it successfully. Do not establish small group meetings merely in the homes of strong believers; rather, ask every saint to open his home for the small group meeting. If every home is opened for the Lord once a week, the Lord will pour out His blessing beyond measure.

OPENING EVERY HOME RESULTING IN A REVIVAL OF THE CHURCH

Our love for the Lord should not be only in word but in deed and faith. To open our homes for the Lord is the greatest expression of our love for the Lord. This will not only bring us the blessing but also a revival from God. We must see this fact clearly. We have this saying among us, "Heaven and earth may pass away, but the small group meetings must never be forsaken." We have labored on big meetings for more than twenty years, and we have delayed much of the Lord's work. Now we must be awakened to work on the small groups and allow the Lord to have a way.

CHAPTER SIX

THE PRACTICE OF THE HOME MEETINGS

Prayer: Lord, we thank You that we can be here to seek Your leading. You know that our inner being is in fear and trembling; we are afraid of losing Your presence and of either walking ahead of You or behind You. Lord, be in our midst and give us a deep impression so that we may clearly touch, and carry out as well, all that You want us to do. Save us from vanity and mistakes. Lord, may we not regret what we are doing today; instead, may it be of eternal value.

Lord, cleanse all of us that we may exercise our spirit to receive Your leading. We do not want to receive man's teaching or leading, we want to receive Your leading. Lord, You are the Head of the church. We pray that You would visit Your church, Your Body. We are members one of another, and we desperately need Your operating. Lord, we confess that we are weak, empty, and useless, and many of our activities, views, and feelings have become veils to us and restrictions, hindrances, to You. Lord, deliver us in these matters that we may enter into You to touch Your heart's intent.

Lord, give us the words and the utterance. As we speak and fellowship, make Your intention known to us so that we may touch the desire of Your heart, and be the testimony of Your heart's desire in this age. Lord, cleanse us and cover us with Your prevailing blood; draw the limit for us and do not allow Your enemy to overstep. Day by day spread a table before us in the presence of our adversaries. Amen.

PRACTICAL STEPS FOR THE HOME MEETINGS

In this chapter we will fellowship about the home meetings. First, Acts 2 says that immediately after the three thousand were saved on the day of Pentecost, they had meetings from house to house. They did not meet as small groups but met from house to house. Second, when we speak of meeting in a group, it seems as if the group can be either large or small, depending on our preference. But when we speak of meeting in a house, in a family, no one can increase or decrease the size of a house, a family, at will. Third, a home is the smallest corporate unit. If our promoting of a certain matter can reach the homes, we would have done a thorough job. Therefore, we are not subdividing merely into small groups; we are subdividing with the home as a unit. A year and a half ago I said that we needed to work to the point that there is a meeting in every saint's home. It should not be that only those who are strong and aggressive have meetings in their homes, whereas those who are weak, backslidden, and attend meetings infrequently do not. We hope that every home will have a meeting, including the homes of the weak and inactive ones.

Delivering Meetings to the Homes

Someone may ask, "If a certain saint has stopped meeting, how can we have a meeting in his home?" It is because he has stopped meeting that we need to establish a meeting in his home, to "deliver" the meeting to his home. He has stopped meeting because he does not have a meeting at home. If there is a meeting in his home, naturally he will meet. For most of the saints, as long as a meeting is established in their homes, it will not be a problem for them to meet. Hence, the best way to recover a saint who has stopped meeting is to deliver the meeting to his home instead of asking him to come to a meeting. We need only to meet in his home once, and he will begin meeting again. Therefore, the problem with non-meeting saints is that we do not deliver the meetings to their homes. We bear the responsibility. I hope we will all have a change in concept. Instead of dragging the saints and forcing them to come to a meeting, we should bring the meeting to their homes. Suppose we invite someone to our home for a meal. If he cannot come, we should deliver the food to him so that he can at least taste the food. I cannot guarantee that the non-meeting saints will be revived immediately, but if the brothers and sisters are willing to coordinate with one another to deliver the meeting to the homes, at least there is a great possibility for them to begin meeting again. We must carry this out.

Another advantage of delivering meetings to the homes is that it solves family disputes. Perhaps a saint has stopped meeting for no reason other than family disputes. The longer he stays away from the meetings, the more serious the quarrels between him and his wife become, and the more he loses his heart to meet. A wife who has stopped meeting for eighteen years might have been crying out for help the entire time but has been unable to find any help. Suppose one day some of the saints bring the meeting to her home; as a result of their singing and praying with her, she is nourished and filled with joy. Then she might pray, "Lord, have mercy on us, and have mercy on my husband so that he could also enjoy You as I do." Moreover, if this sister has not been meeting for eighteen years, her children must not have been meeting as well. Now through our bringing the meeting to her home, the children also are joyful to receive salvation. In this way we reap several benefits with a single action.

Twenty-five years ago the medical field in Taiwan practiced making house calls to give injections; now we need to practice to deliver meetings to the homes. If we deliver the meeting to the homes, not only will the inactive saints be recovered, but their friends and relatives will also be given a great opportunity to receive the gospel of the Lord's salvation. If we are willing to practice this delivery of meetings to ten homes per week, I believe that at least five homes will be raised up. At present there are at least six thousand non-meeting saints in about one thousand five hundred to two thousand homes, with at least one to two saved ones in each home. If in three months we visit these two thousand homes three to five times, at least one thousand homes will be raised up. This is truly the best way, and it is worthwhile to endeavor in this matter. Hence, we need to encourage the saints to practice this change in the system; moreover, we must find a definite way to effectively gain the increase.

Subdividing the Groups to Produce Increase

In the past month the number of saints meeting in the

small groups, that is, in the home meetings, has increased by one thousand. I have said that once a small group has more than twelve people, it should be subdivided into two groups. At this time some groups have exceeded twenty-four people, yet they are still reluctant to be divided. I understand this feeling, because I too am human. A certain hall has a very good small group that has brought in more than a hundred people. I attended their meeting once, and it was bustling with people. The saints in that small group told me that they did not want to be subdivided because they like that small group. I dared not touch them lest some would stop meeting. They are like plants in a green house that would die if they are moved. Furthermore, human beings are sociable by nature. When a group of people are always together, they build up a feeling for one another and like to be close and intimate with one another. However, we must see that if we do not subdivide the groups and the homes, the increase will stop, and the edification of the brothers and sisters will be greatly limited. This is the reason that the group we mentioned earlier has stopped increasing and is now at a standstill. We see this situation in other places as well.

The biological principle is that it is difficult for anything old to bear fruit. The spiritual principle is the same. Suppose a family migrates to a new place to spread the Lord's gospel and preach God's truth. Within a year this family may be able to bring in fifteen people, and then they may increase to thirty or fifty. Once they reach fifty, however, their rate of increase will slow down. This is similar to an old person being unable to bear children and an old tree not bearing fruit. For a tree to bear fruit, it must have new branches. If these fifty people want to bear fruit, they must be subdivided into different homes and into small groups. However, this may be difficult for them emotionally. Moreover, people usually love crowds. It is truly enjoyable to have many gathered together to sing and pray when the content and speaking of the meeting is very good. If they are subdivided into different homes, they are concerned about losing this kind of enjoyment. If they remain together, however, it will be difficult for them to gain an increase. For instance, when planting trees and grass, if we do not scatter the seeds, they will end up clustered together. If we scatter the seeds, they may initially appear uncomely, but a year or even half a year later they will spread all over the land and look beautiful. I hope that the elders will change their concept to see that subdividing the small groups is a tremendous matter and that they need to work on this carefully.

If there are presently six people in a home meeting, there would be one thousand small groups in the church in Taipei. These small groups might be very weak, but as long as the elders are willing to take the lead and aggressively take care of the saints, eventually the small groups will be strong, and the numbers will increase. It is not a matter of whether the small groups will be weak or strong; it is a matter of whether or not the elders are willing to take the lead. If the elders are willing to take the lead, there will certainly be a result. In the past month the number of saints meeting in the small groups in Taipei increased by one thousand. This is the result of the labor and endeavor of the elders. This also proves that as long as the elders are willing to take the lead, the saints will follow.

Our brothers and sisters have many relatives, friends, neighbors, classmates, and colleagues. If the elders are aggressive to take the lead, it will not be difficult for every home to gain one person a month. If every home gains a person each month, the church in Taipei will gain a thousand people in a month and twelve thousand in a year. This is a twofold increase. Moreover, the new ones gained in this way are more likely to be remaining fruit, because they were not compelled to come from off the streets and be saved and baptized; neither were they invited through gospel tracts or telephone calls. Rather, they are the relatives and intimate friends of the saints. Hence, it will be easy for them to be kept and to receive edification. This kind of increase is the most effective and practical.

These are the two steps, or two ways, to practice the changing of the system. The first step is to recover the non-meeting saints by delivering meetings to their homes. If we cannot do it once a week, we can at least do it once every two weeks. Moreover, we need to be steadfast. The second step is to subdivide the small groups. Once a small group has over twelve people, it should be subdivided into two groups. This will stir up the spirit of the saints to spread the gospel among their relatives, friends, neighbors, classmates, and colleagues.

BEING ABSOLUTE AND SERIOUS IN PRACTICING THE NEW WAY

Serving Faithfully and Diligently

We are those who belong to the Lord. If the Lord in whom we believe is not false, and if He is worthy of our believing in Him, we need to be serious, absolute, and faithful to Him. We have seven days in a week. Besides the Lord's Day, which we set apart for the Lord, we should consecrate at least one evening to the Lord. The practice of the new way does not require the brothers and sisters to give a whole day to the Lord; it requires only one evening from 7:00 to 11:00 P.M. Moreover, this is a demonstration of our service to the Lord. In this way our friends, relatives, neighbors, classmates, and colleagues will know that every week we have a definite evening, from 7:00 to 11:00, when we meet in a small group to preach the gospel and study the Bible. This period of time should be very free. People can come at any time and stay as long as they want. They can come to have a meal, drink some tea, or eat some fruit. In this way, the door of grace will be wide open for the spreading of the gospel and the genuine edification and exercise of the saints.

The Benefit of Practicing the New Way

Practicing the new way is more than our obligation; this practice brings us countless benefits. First, our "delivering" the meetings to the homes can be compared to sending people "charcoal during a blizzard." Suppose a certain family has been very cold toward the Lord; it has been difficult to make the members of that family burning for the Lord. Now by sending "charcoal" to their house, we light up the "fireplace" of this family. This will not only stir up their spirit, it will also burn away all their family disputes. In the past the couple always quarreled, and as a result, they would not speak to each other. But now they can ignore each other for only six days at the most, because on the day of the home meeting they need to read the Bible, pray, and sing together. In this way, they have no way but to be reconciled. This will be a big rescue.

At the same time, the children of this family will be greatly influenced. We all know that it is difficult to deal with our own children. No one can boast concerning his own children. However, the home meeting every week will provide our children the best opportunity to receive spiritual nourishing and edification. It will also leave them with a good pattern. The hidden benefit is truly great.

There are apartment buildings throughout the city of Taipei. In one apartment building there are dozens of families. If one of the families has a meeting in its home, over a period of time people will know that in this apartment building there is a family who speaks of the Lord Jesus one evening a week. Then when people suffer afflictions, when they are deeply distressed and discouraged, and want to find comfort, sympathy, and help, they will spontaneously look for those who believe in Jesus. In the past those people may have thought of a chapel, but now they think of the home where there is a meeting in which the Lord Jesus is preached every week. This will also affect our neighbors, colleagues, friends, and relatives because we not only preach the Lord Jesus at home, but we also testify for the Lord at work. If we continue steadfastly in prayer for our friends, relatives, and colleagues, though they may not come within a year, they will eventually come within three years. This long-term practice will certainly bring in the increase.

Home meetings can also stir up the organic function of the saints. Today in the Lord's recovery, there are still many saints who say they do not know how to speak for the Lord Jesus or preach Him. Some elderly brothers and sisters migrated to America; however, they did not know even the English alphabet. But after listening to the English language for a period of time, they were able to speak a few simple sentences. Consequently, it is not that we cannot speak but that we will not speak. When we deliver the meetings to the saints' homes, the saints may not know how to speak at the beginning. But in the meeting they will be supported and even forced to speak; eventually, they will learn to speak. Furthermore, it is easy for the saints to speak in a home meeting. It is as easy as chatting about domestic matters. The home meeting does not require eloquence, gift, or a sequence as the big meetings do. As long as one is willing to speak, this is good enough.

Therefore, a home meeting requires neither orderliness, good appearance, nor eloquence; these are the requirements of being in an army. What a home needs is warmth, empathy, and love; only these can keep people.

Being Steadfast in Practicing the Home Meetings

We should not carry out the home meetings sporadically; rather, we should do it steadily and continually, fifty-two times a year. Even though there may be conferences, trainings, and joint meetings, we should try not to interrupt the time of our home meeting. If one thousand homes in the church in Taipei maintain such a practice, the long-term impact and benefit will be immeasurable. I hope the elders will have a clear vision.

A SPECIFIC TESTIMONY

I have been very encouraged by the few small groups I attended in the past two weeks. Last Saturday I joined an "outlying" group. Initially, I was slightly worried that since this group was called an outlying group, there might be only a handful of people present, and the meeting might drag. When I arrived there, I was surprised to find that it was not an outlying group at all; rather, it was a "central" group. The home was filled with saints, including a sister who traveled thousands of miles from Hong Kong because she heard that I was in Taiwan. This sister is a widow, and she and her household are newly saved. She likes to read our books and was determined to see me in person. After she found out that I was going to the outlying group, she came with her whole family to the meeting. In the small group every member was a core member. Their prayers were strong, and they all functioned organically. After the meeting everyone came out of the house to say good-bye to one another; it was so warm and touching. They all love the Lord and the brothers and sisters. They are truly a good pattern.

This small group proves that the church in Taipei is wealthy. There are five families in this small group, and every family is qualified to establish its own group. They all love the Lord, their prayers are strong and clear, and their pursuit of the Life-study messages is excellent. They are able to read the sections clearly with spirit and life. If each of these five families opened their home for meetings, they will definitely bring in more people.

MAIN POINTS THAT
REQUIRE OUR ATTENTION IN PRACTICE

Those who promote any kind of movement or activity in society know that if they want to promote an activity, they must do so at the grass-roots; they cannot merely gain the husband of a household and not have any regard for his wife and children. If they have no regard for the entire household, the movement or activity will not succeed. But if they gain the wife and children as well, the promotion will be easy. Likewise, the goal of carrying out the home meeting is to gain the wife and children of the family. The result will be that the entire family will become the Lord's good soldiers who work for the Lord to preach the gospel.

Furthermore, Acts 1:8 tells us that we need to spread from our "Jerusalem." Those whom we bring to salvation will follow us in what we do. If we bring our relatives and friends to the Lord, our relatives and friends will also bring their relatives and friends to salvation. In this way, the cycle will continue endlessly. We would no longer need to rely on big gospel meetings or any great work. Our number will increase speedily and spontaneously. I hope the elders will have this foresight.

A SCRIPTURAL PRACTICE

What we have fellowshipped is a scriptural practice. This is the way shown in Acts and in the Epistles. When the Lord Jesus was on the earth, He also took this way. Rather than holding gospel campaigns, He preached everywhere He went—by the shore, on the mountain, or in people's homes. He deliberately went to Samaria to bring the meeting to a Samaritan woman, and in so doing He brought salvation to her (John 4). After the Samaritan woman was saved, she went back to her city and testified for the Lord. This resulted in the entire city being shaken and receiving great benefit.

Today we are influenced by the tradition of Christianity to the extent that we are tied down by its rules and formalities. We like to hold gospel meetings at the meeting halls with a set time and topic. In the end, even though we spend much time and energy, we hardly gain anyone. Even if we have gained some, only a handful remain and the rest are lost. Therefore, we should not continue in this wasteful way.

In the previous chapter I said that in a period of thirty-eight years, from 1948 to 1986, a world-renowned evangelist held big gospel meetings wherever he went. At every gospel meeting several thousand were in the audience, many of whom left their names. He was a talented, learned, and influential person. If he had spent his effort on the home meetings for those thirty-eight years, I believe that he could have stirred up at least several million homes. If there were three million active homes in the fifty states of America, the whole of America would have been turned upside down.

I am fellowshipping these matters to help us change our view so that we would no longer focus on big meetings and good messages. If we emphasize the big meetings and good messages, our work will be killed immediately. Today we are not only few in number; those who function among us are even fewer. Hence, when we have a slight increase, we feel over-whelmed and do not know how to nourish the new ones. The big meetings have become a bondage to us. For this reason, I hope that all the churches will accept this fellowship to no longer rely on the big meetings and good messages but to rely on the home meetings. Co-workers and elders, the only thing that we need to work on is the home meetings. As long as we succeed in carrying out the home meetings, the church in our locality will be living, and the number will increase.

THE CONTENT OF THE HOME MEETINGS

The content of the home meetings is the truth in the Lord's recovery. This truth is concerning God's New Testament economy, the gospel of the kingdom. When the Lord Jesus was on the earth, He preached this truth. When the apostles went out to labor, they preached this truth. We also should preach this truth. We thank the Lord that among Christians today, the Lord's recovery has the greatest, deepest, and clearest utterance on the gospel of the kingdom. As long as we have the heart, we will be able to find the appropriate materials from our publications for our pursuit and edification in the home meetings.

In the suburb of Taipei, there is a Christian group that has experienced an increase of one thousand people in ten years. They have a practice similar to our home meetings. They put out messages for edification using the materials in the Lord's recovery and make them available to the believers free of charge. The first message they put out is "Joining the Church," and the second is "Reading the Bible"; both are taken word for word from Brother Nee's *Messages for Building Up New Believers*. This group has had the highest rate of increase over the past ten years, and they use material from our publications.

If we look closely, we will find that we do not use our own materials as enthusiastically as others. It seems as if we do not treasure the blessing that we have because we have been continually eating this good food for many years. Therefore, our problem is not a lack of riches; rather, our problem is that we would not avail ourselves of what we have. The truth that the Lord has given to His recovery is the most comprehensive. We do not need to think of what to say or how to say it. Even if we were to strain our mind and exhaust our effort to think of something to say, we may not say anything better than what is in our published materials. The materials in the Lord's recovery are rich and plentiful. We have not only hundreds but thousands of messages. We should learn how to use them properly and choose a message or half a message to supply the home meetings.

Thirty years ago I taught the co-workers to first digest the messages and then release them from the podium. Now I take this back and say that it is not necessary to do this anymore. All we need to do is to repeat what the book says, reading with repetition, emphasis, and prayer. Allow the saints time to digest the materials in the meeting and speak them to one another. If the co-workers in Taiwan had done this over the past twenty years, I believe that there would be four times as many saints in the Lord's recovery today. Many other Christian groups, knowing that they do not have much content and realizing their own lack, borrow the riches from the Lord's recovery. In the end, they bring in a manifold increase and cause many to be saved and edified.

Today in the church in Taipei there are almost five thousand saints, and not many of them participate in the church service. In the past thirty years the church in Taipei has not increased even by a thousand people. The other Christian group, which I mentioned earlier, was started by a couple, a husband and wife. They moved to a certain place and practiced meeting in their home using the materials of the Lord's recovery, and now they have increased to one thousand people in ten years. This proves that we are so rich in our family assets, yet our co-workers have been laboring day after day without much result. We have no excuse. We have brothers and sisters in the churches who love the Lord, not only in the big cities but in smaller towns and villages as well. Hence, compared to other Christian groups, we have an easier job. But over the years we have accomplished very little. This is worthy of our consideration.

Of course, we cannot put the blame entirely on the co-workers. The underlying reason is that our system was wrong. I regret that I did not come back to Taipei to change the system five or ten years ago. Now we must realize that our former practice is not working and is outdated. Today we must be realistic; we need to receive a practice that is according to the revelation in the Scriptures.

By observing the situation in all of Christianity, we see that the Lord's riches are truly in our midst, in His recovery. However, because we have not done things in a proper way over the past twenty years, we have come to a standstill. At the same time, others have overtaken us because their practice is more advanced and because they use our truth. In the end, they multiply and increase. However, we should still be joyful that the truth in the Lord's recovery is spreading.

Our eyes need to be enlightened. We need to discard the old ways and forget about trying to give better messages. I hope that all of us will aggressively use the truths in the Lord's recovery. If the elders can prepare messages for the saints to pursue after the Lord's table meetings, prayer meetings, and in the home meetings, the saints will be greatly nourished and edified. According to the statistics, the number of saints attending the truth classes is higher than that of the big meetings. This shows that the saints genuinely like to study the truth. For this reason, we need to learn how to make use of the rich material in the Lord's recovery in a living way, not in a formal, rigid way. We have a large amount of assets in the abundance of the truth, which is accessible and inexhaustible.

I hope that we all can change our concept to shift all of our attention and effort from the big meetings to the home meetings. We should highly regard the home meetings, setting them as our goal and stress because the practice of the home meetings is the life pulse and the life line for the increase in the church. Through the home meetings we can gain people, keep them, and at the same time carry out the functions of begetting, nourishing, and teaching. This is truly the practice for changing the system. I hope that the elders will consider this matter and pay much attention to it.

QUESTION AND ANSWER

Question: We have group meetings in our homes, but sometimes we also meet where we work in order to make it more convenient to bring people to the Lord and to edify the new ones. But some of our colleagues live in places that belong to different halls. How should we take care of the statistics and to which hall should we report the number of our small group?

Answer: It is better not to know, because once we know, there will be no increase. Revelation 3 says that the church in Laodicea thinks that she is wealthy yet does not realize that she is poor. This is to say that when we think we know, we are poor. Only when we do not know can we be wealthy. And only when we are wealthy can we multiply home after home and have home meetings from house to house. In the past we were too clear in our distinctions, and we eventually became deadened. Even though now we may seem unclear, as long as we are living, everything is fine; we should not worry too much. As long as there are the statistics in heaven, that is fine. We do not need to count the number on the earth.

LEARNING THE REAL WAY TO WORK— WORKING WITHOUT PREACHING

Home meetings have many advantages. What the big meetings can do, the home meetings can do also. For instance, in a home meeting last Saturday two new ones were baptized in the bathtub. Big meetings bind people, and preaching kills people. But the home meetings stir up the organic function of the saints and encourage them to fulfill their function. In a recent co-workers' meeting, I told the co-workers that to learn the real way to work is to learn to work without preaching. The Lord Jesus was the best example. He did not have a set style of speaking. Sometimes He spoke two or three sentences, and at other times He gave a long discourse. Moreover, He did not have a set place or a set time to speak. He could speak anywhere and at any time. This is what we co-workers should learn. We must go against the dead rules and regulations of our past.

PRACTICING ACCORDING TO THE SCRIPTURES AND ADVANCING ACCORDING TO TIME AND CIRCUMSTANCES

On the other hand, I strongly advise the elders from all the churches to receive this new leading and practice. We may have taken care of the church in our locality for thirty years, but the church has remained the same. It would be best to find someone who is younger who can be a helper. He might not be as experienced as we are, but this does not mean that his ability to do things is inferior to ours. We should give him an opportunity to learn to serve.

We have always been faithful to the teaching of the Bible

and have not been willing to take a way that is inconsistent with the Scriptures. Therefore, regarding some important matters, we must consider again and again what the Bible reveals to us. Concerning the appointment and qualification of co-workers and elders, we can view this from two angles. On the one hand, we should follow the Scriptures. On the other hand, based on our long-term history, we know that some of our co-workers have been harmed because there has been no evaluation of their service. Today in various big companies and government organizations there are examinations with grades. Even diplomatic officials must take examinations. We are human beings. Even though we have been saved, we cannot deny that our nature is still fallen. We may have much spiritual learning, but as long as we have not been raptured, our fallen nature is still in us. I absolutely believe that if we had systematically evaluated the co-workers in Taiwan over the past thirty years, the co-workers would have been more fruitful than they are today.

The same applies to the elders. I have considered this matter for many years. In the Bible we cannot find any length of time for the service of an elder. According to our understanding, it seems as if an elder should serve his whole life, like a justice on the Supreme Court. If an elder is constantly learning and making progress and is truly an elder among the saints, this is all right. But if one has been an elder for twenty or thirty years, and the church under his management is only mediocre, this proves that the time has come for him to voluntarily yield his position to someone who is younger but more qualified and experienced. If we wait for the co-workers to address the issue, it will be embarrassing and unpleasant for everyone. I hope the elders will consider their situation to discern those who have been manifested by the Holy Spirit and let them take the lead. In this way the churches can have a new beginning and a new hope.

In reality, our system must be updated. We are too old. We are still adhering to the way we learned thirty years ago. Our thinking has not kept abreast of the times, our equipment is outdated, and our plans and methods are old. Today we cannot remain old-fashioned; we need to learn aggressively. If our co-workers are not willing to learn new ways, once the system is changed or once they leave Taiwan, they will be unemployed, having nothing to do, because they will not know how to do anything. However, some co-workers may feel that the old way is still better and that it is not good to change the system and have a new beginning. I would ask them, "If your way is good, where is the increase?"

THE IMPORTANCE OF CHANGING THE SYSTEM

May the Lord forgive me and may all of you bear with me as I boast a little. Twenty-three years ago I went to the United States empty-handed. I did not have anything—no helper and no support. I labored alone and relied entirely on the Lord's provision. When I first began my work in America, there was no meeting hall. I started my work in a Chinese brother's house, which was in a neighborhood where there were predominantly black people. When I departed from Taiwan, I left the co-workers with rich assets of meeting halls in all the main cities and tens of thousands of brothers and sisters. In the past fifteen years, because of the proper leadership of the government in Taiwan, there has been a rapid economic development in Taiwan, and the offerings of the saints have been strong. Yet we have not made any progress in our work. This is all because of an improper method.

I do not mean to put the blame on anyone, but I want us all to be awakened to see that our old ways are not right, and our system is also not right. We need to have an overall review and a complete change. We must begin everything anew. We are elders of the biggest church on earth, having twenty-one halls in our hands. We must realize that the only solution to our problem is to change the system. Under the present shining, we need to ask ourselves, "Am I too old? Is my way too stale? Am I still qualified to take the lead?" We need to keep asking ourselves these questions. Today we are all living before the Lord and are responsible to Him. One day we will need to give an account to Him. We cannot wander about and live in a carefree way. Twenty years are a long time, but they have gone by fast. In the past twenty years we neither increased nor decreased in number. We should be awakened to discard the old things and adopt new things. If we are willing to forget the things which are behind and stretch forward to the things which are before, the churches under our leading will have the beautiful prospect of an increase.

CHAPTER SEVEN

THE CHANGING OF THE SYSTEM IN CONTRAST TO RELIGION

BEING DELIVERED FROM THE DEGRADATION OF CHRISTIANITY

Christianity has become degraded because it has given up four crucial matters—Christ, the Spirit, life, and the church—and has fallen into forms, methods, organizations, and systems, which result in religion. History tells us that before the Western missionaries came to China, there was not the term *chiao-hui*—"church"—which literally means a religious gathering. It was after the missionaries introduced Christianity to China that there was the need to invent the term *chiao-hui* to express a religious gathering. After two hundred years this term has been widely accepted and is now even borrowed by other religions, such as certain Buddhist sects, to describe their organizations. This shows that the term *church* has fallen into the realm of religion. It is on the level of religion. The church as we know it today has actually become a religion.

From the time of the book of Revelation, the Lord has been calling believers throughout the centuries to come out, not from the true church but from the degraded religious system. Revelation chapters 2 and 3 show that even after the church became degraded, the Lord still wanted the believers to remain in the church and be the overcomers. However, chapters 17 and 18 of this book show that the Lord calls the believers to come out, not from the church but from the religious system, the religious gathering, which is the religious organization. Up until today, however, we still have not witnessed a clear deliverance from the influence of that religious organization. This is true even in the Lord's recovery. We say that we have left religion behind, but we are still somewhat "dragging our feet in the mud." We have not completely rid ourselves of it; there is still "mud" all over us.

THE PRODUCING OF RELIGION

The Need within Man for God

The beginning of Genesis shows that when God created man, He created a spirit within him in order that man may contact Him, receive Him, contain Him, and express Him. For this reason, there is always a need within man for God. This need is innate in man; it is created by God, and it spontaneously manifests itself within man. No matter how fallen man becomes, there is still this need within him for God. This is an undeniable fact.

The Creation of Culture
Replacing Man's Need for God

Six thousand years of human history reveal that all people, whether cultured or barbaric, have a desire to worship God. The reason for this is that there is a spirit in man. This can be compared to saying that man needs to eat because he has a stomach, but whether or not he is eating the right food is a different matter. In the same way, we have within us a "spiritual stomach," which is our spirit. This spirit creates in us a need for God. Before man fell, he did not have a need for religion because at that time man could come to God, contact Him directly, and enjoy Him as his satisfaction. There was no need for regulations, forms, organizations, or institutions to help him, for the living God was leading and guiding him directly. However, man fell again and again. First, Adam fell and departed from God. Then Cain fell further and was driven from the face of God, losing God's presence forever. Because of the fall, man needed a replacement for God, and religion came into being.

Genesis 4 shows clearly that the descendants of Cain invented human culture to satisfy man's need as a replacement for God. Man had lost God and had fallen away from His face. He was estranged from God and could not meet the deepest need within his being. The only thing he could do was to invent human culture to satisfy his need. We have covered this matter clearly in the *Life-study of Genesis* (see Message 24, pp. 323-329). In order to satisfy his human needs, man invented all kinds of things in his culture. He invented husbandry, weaponry, and music. Husbandry is for food, which is for sustenance; weaponry is for protection, which is for defense; and music is for entertainment, which is for enjoyment. This is a natural consequence of man's effort to satisfy his fallen needs.

Religion Being the Crystallization of Human Culture

Man's culture was created based on his need For example, because man was not satisfied with the mule-wagon for transportation, he sought for advancement and invented the automobile. Later he became dissatisfied with the automobile and invented the airplane. Then the airplane did not satisfy him because he wanted to go to the moon; as a result, he invented the rocket. The reason that man invented music and the various musical instruments, such as the drum, the flute, and the stringed instruments, is that he needed entertainment and enjoyment for his soul. After man fell, the earth was cursed, and food production became limited. As a result, men fought with one another. So in order to satisfy his need for safety and protection, he invented weapons, such as the sword and the spear. Eventually, however, man discovered that his greatest need was in his deepest part, his spirit, and this need he could not satisfy. He discovered that he had a need to worship. As a result, he invented religion and began to turn to idol worship.

Today in the twentieth century we live in an age of unprecedented developments in science and culture. Taiwan is an example of this. Everything here is advancing and moving ahead; education is highly emphasized, and technology is advancing. Yet at the same time, idolatry is abounding everywhere. The radio, the television, and all the mass media indicate that religion is welcomed everywhere. This is especially true with Buddhism. As long as there are teachings concerning doing good with the reward of heaven and doing evil with the threat of hell, people will be gullible and swallow it. What we see in America is also difficult to believe. A nation as advanced and highly educated as the United States finds some of its own people pursuing the Eastern religions, dressing themselves in priestly gowns with pony tails and chanting to the sound of Buddhist instruments. If I was in Africa, I would not be so surprised, but I am in Los Angeles. This puzzles me. It seems as if modern man is so hungry that he will eat anything. Because of an unabating need to worship God, man turns to all kinds of "medicine" to cure his "ailments."

Religion is something that human culture developed to satisfy human longing. Sixty years ago I read a book entitled *The Two Babylons,* which speaks of the record in Genesis 11. There man built a tower at Babel which was to reach heaven. Every brick on that tower was engraved with the name of an idol. This shows that at the time of Genesis 11, the entire earth was engaged in idol worship.

This is the reason Joshua told the children of Israel in Joshua 24:2-3, "Thus says Jehovah the God of Israel, Your fathers dwelt across the River long ago, Terah the father of Abraham and the father of Nahor; and they served other gods. And I took your father Abraham from across the River and brought him throughout all the land of Canaan." While the world was worshipping idols, God called Abraham out from among the idolaters and caused him and his descendants to serve the one true and living God. In the New Testament the Lord Jesus, who is God manifest in the flesh, also called His disciples to follow Him and charged them to disciple all the nations, spreading the gospel of the kingdom to the entire earth to be a testimony to all people. Yet Christianity once again lowered such a salvation from the Lord's standard to the level of a product of human culture. It became a religion, an organization in human culture.

WHAT IS THE LORD'S RECOVERY

God's Word Being the Track

God is certainly a wise God. Had there not been the Pentateuch at the time of Moses and had the other books of the

Bible not been written, we would not have the Bible today, and the world would be in an unimaginably fallen state. We thank the Lord that no matter how much human history has been on a downward path and no matter how fallen Christianity has become, we still have the Bible. The Bible is a lamp in the darkness and a light for the world that shines in the dark age. The Bible is also like a track laid before men, leading men to the right path. Although men can choose whether or not to take the track, the track is nevertheless there.

The Work of the Lord's Recovery
versus Degraded Christianity

Degradation has no bottom to it. Not only are the world and humanity degrading day by day; even Christianity has become an ever-degrading religion. Its trend is forever downward. Nevertheless, the Lord has had His recovery throughout the ages. He has continued to raise up many groups of lovers of Jesus. In the Old Testament, Elijah was zealous for the Lord, and he was persecuted by Jezebel. He became afraid and was discouraged to the point that he ran far away and asked to be allowed to die under a broom shrub. However, an angel strengthened him, and he walked forty days to Mount Horeb, where God appeared to him. He began to accuse the Israelites by saying, "The children of Israel have forsaken Your covenant, thrown down Your altars, and slain Your prophets with the sword; and I alone am left, and they seek to take my life" (1 Kings 19:10). God answered him as if to say, "Elijah, do not accuse the Israelites before Me. You are wrong. You are not the only one left. I have reserved for Myself seven thousand who have not bowed unto Baal and have not kissed him" (cf. v. 18).

I say this to remind you that not only at the time of Elijah, but after his time and throughout church history, God has reserved for His own name "seven thousand" people, even during the darkest hour of the church's degradation. A number of people have written books on church history. The best one is by a Brethren scholar by the name of Edmund Hamer Broadbent. His book, *The Pilgrim Church,* is written with keen spiritual insight. It is a church history with the highest discernment. He traces the line from the time of the apostles to the present age, identifying those "seven thousand...all the knees that have not bowed unto Baal."

We have no intention to be proud, but we must say that since sixty years ago, when we were raised up by the Lord in China, we have had this burden and desire within us. We have told the Lord, "We would be the 'seven thousand' which You have reserved for Your own name in this age." What is the Lord's recovery? Strictly speaking, the Lord's recovery is the Lord's reserving "seven thousand" for His name. Because we have adopted this attitude and taken this ground, our actions and behavior have been a cause for some misunderstanding by others. We are misunderstood by society and by our relatives and friends. We do not follow tradition, and we do not even follow religion. Religion is going downward, while the recovery is going upward. Within three to five years after the Lord's recovery came to the United States, Christianity began to oppose us. This does not mean that the truth in the Lord's recovery is wrong. The truth in the Lord's recovery can be compared to pure gold. Pure gold does not fear the fire, and the more it is beaten, the more it shines. The real reason behind the opposition is that it is easy to flow downstream and difficult to go upstream.

I am a small Chinese man, not worthy of attention. Before I was fifty I had never traveled to the West and had never been in the United States. Yet for the sake of the defense of the truth we hold among us, I was forced to resort to the law of America; I was forced to appeal to "Caesar," the United States Constitution. More than two hundred sixty publications throughout the fifty states of the United States rose up to attack this little, insignificant Chinese man. What is the reason behind this? It is because a little Chinese man has dared to blow the trumpet in the face of the colossus of American Christianity. However, the truth is the truth. The Lord covers me with His blood. This great Christianity could do nothing to me because I was walking absolutely according to the truth and according to the law. Since the 1960s there have been rumors about me in Christianity, and anonymous letters even came to me in a plot against me, accusing me of being a Communist. Some even stirred up the Federal Bureau of Investigation to make an inquiry concerning me. I was not afraid of these things because I had done nothing against my conscience. I was not worried that I would be put to shame by the law. I cooperated with the investigations, and in the end it was proven where I stand.

THE LORD'S RECOVERY TAKING
THE DOWNWARD TREND

In general, while Christianity is on a downward trend, the Lord's recovery is on an upward trend. Today it is altogether right for us to promote the home meetings. This is the unique way that the Lord's church has taken since the first day it was on the earth. It was because of the degradation of Christianity that the church degraded into a formal and organized religion and annulled the home meetings. This is the situation we are in today. However, we need to admit honestly that even until today we have not rid ourselves completely of the traditional influence of Christianity. Please give me the liberty to say that over the last twenty years we have stopped advancing. Instead, we have been drifting downward and have fallen into a situation akin to that of an organization.

Now you can understand to a small degree why I stressed so much the changing of the system when I returned to Taiwan a year and a half ago. I wanted to overturn everything so that we could practice the small group meetings. I publicly acknowledged my mistake before everyone, because I also had fallen into the same trap. My blood was not fully purged of that religious influence. We have said that in the small group meetings we do not have any leader but that everyone is a leader. Yet after a while we came up with something called the "Training for the Core Members." You were not the only ones who were thinking in this way; I was thinking in the same way. You were not the only ones who were not fully purged from the influence; I was not purged from the influence either. To designate "core members" in a small group meeting is in effect to kill the small group meetings.

Perhaps some would not agree with me. Perhaps we think

that the small group meetings would not have survived until today had there not been some "core members." However, to my feeling, it is the presence of these "core members" that is crippling the small group meetings and limiting their development. If we are fair and compare the results, we will see that those small groups without "core members" are actually thriving. They are bustling with people, and everyone participates.

CRUCIAL POINTS RELATED TO CHANGING THE SYSTEM

Removing Human Hands, and Trusting in the Lord's Gracious Hand

In the previous chapter we pointed out that there are four hundred small groups in the church in Taipei. We have been practicing this for more than a year and a half, yet we still have not seen any subdivision of the groups. I have said from the very beginning that the best thing that can happen to a small group is for every one of its members to have regular meetings and for every home to have a group meeting. In this way, there will be no need for "core members" or so-called leaders. There will not be any hierarchy. Everyone will be able to lead the meeting. Everyone will be able to pick songs, pray, expound the truth, prophesy, and testify. Everyone will be able to speak God's word. The church in Taipei was the first place where I released such a message, but up until today, the church in Taipei has not done this. The most likely obstacle in this matter is the elders and the co-workers. To put the matter in a polite way, the elders and co-workers are too conservative and too faithful; they dare not let go. They are afraid that if they let go, disaster will follow. The truth of the matter is that they have been holding on too tightly and controlling too much. As a result, the saints are hindered from advancing and growing.

I have often prayed to the Lord concerning such a condition among us. On the one hand, I admire our faithfulness to the Lord's recovery and our fearfulness that something might come in to damage the church. If possible, we would embrace the church like a child embraces his pillow when he sleeps. This is true in particular with the older saints. Their faithfulness is not a matter of three to five years; they have been faithful for almost their entire lives, at least over twenty or thirty years. I believe that our consecration to the Lord is valuable in His sight and will be remembered by Him. Yet I hope that we will realize that sometimes we are a little too much; we have delayed the Lord's business in this way. We have gone a little overboard and have held things too tightly in our hand. This has become a limitation.

Control Limiting Growth

Let me give two examples of how control kills. During the 1940s, Honor Oak in London was a place of high spirituality. We read the books they published and received help from them for many years. In 1955 and 1957 I invited their leader to visit us, and in 1958 I accepted his invitation and visited London, where I stayed for four weeks. I saw many things during my stay there, one of which was that the leader, because of his high spiritual view, considered everyone unqualified. There were more than a hundred young people, all of whom were very capable. Not a few among them were college graduates. They were all under this leader and had been trained by him for many years. Eventually, they all wanted to go out to begin a work for the Lord, but the leader considered them unqualified and substandard. He held all of them in his hand and kept them in his own "pocket."

One day all these young ones invited me to a picnic. A few of the leading ones among them asked me a question: "Brother Lee, we have been trained and perfected here for so many years. Our goal is based on one burden, which is that we would go out to work for the Lord. But we are forbidden again and again to do this. What should we do?" Their question put me on the cross. I tried to follow the Lord's leading within and spoke something inoffensive that would not upset the situation.

My point is that we must be very clear that control and restriction only drag down the church and the saints. The more control there is, the more stunted the growth is, and the more our numbers dwindle. Before long, only a few will remain. That brother was at one time greatly used by the Lord, but before he passed away, the church and the saints were almost choked to death. In 1965, only seven years after my visit, all the young people who fellowshipped with me that day were dispersed. They drifted away as a result of that kind of control. This shows that as long as there is "birth control," there is no possibility of multiplication.

A second example is the Brethren assembly in my hometown of Chefoo. Almost the next day after I was saved, the Lord brought me to a Brethren assembly. The leader in that assembly was an old British brother by the name of Mr. Burnett. From his youth he was taught at the feet of Mr. Benjamin Newton, the famous Brethren teacher. Later he became a missionary of the China Inland Mission and went to Szechwan to preach the gospel. As time went on, he felt that the China Inland Mission was wrong because he had received light from the Brethren teaching. He quit his post and was led to Chefoo to begin a Brethren assembly there.

At that time this brother was sixty, and I was only twenty-one years old. At first, his ability to expound the Scripture attracted people to follow him, but all those gained by him were eventually killed by him in their spiritual function. The reason for this is that he exercised a tight control over them. He worked in Chefoo for a few decades without experiencing any growth or advancement, and his group remained a small assembly. I met with them for seven and a half years without seeing any growth year after year. In fact, the number dwindled year after year until eventually almost no one was left. I realized that there was a problem. The truths he expounded were high, but there was no advancement. It is a good thing that there were other denominations in the Shantung province which were preaching the gospel and contacting people. Otherwise, the gospel would have been squelched. When I saw that, I knew that there was something wrong with his way and that I could not take that way.

I mention these two examples to warn the elderly saints among us. I would like the senior co-workers among us to consider for a moment whether we have been behaving in the same way for the past twenty years. We have had a certain kind of spiritual standard. We preached spiritual messages concerning the cross and resurrection, and it is right for us to preach these things because they help us to meet God's standard. Yet these very practices deter us from letting go. We are afraid that once we let go, we will create problems, and the saints will fall into indulgence and become unspiritual, giving up the way of the cross, drifting from the path of life, and walking contrary to the leading of the church. The result of our way is that, on the one hand, our messages sound spiritual, yet on the other hand, we do not experience any growth or spread. This shows that there is a problem with our kind of spirituality.

Refusal to Let Go Resulting in Religion

On the one hand, we cannot say that during all these years our spiritual stature has remained stunted. To be honest, however, our growth has been very slow. A situation has developed among us that has limited and restricted our spiritual growth. The church is a seed of life. If we provide opportunity for it to fall into the earth, if we till the earth so that the seed can go deep into the soil, and if we allow water, air, and sunlight to work on it, it will surely grow and bear fruit. During the past ten years, our "tree" has been standing here, but year after year there is no growth. There is no branching out, no harvesting, and no multiplication. The only reason for this failure is that we have bound ourselves up as with a chain, and this binding factor is our religion. In other words, it is our method of working that has bound us up.

Allow me to tell you why I appointed fifty-two elders in one night when I returned in October two years ago. Since 1979, every time Brother Chang Wu-chen came to the United States, I asked him to appoint a few elders in the church in Taipei to help in the administration. In 1975 when I returned to Taipei, I made a change, because at that time the elders were too old, and there were signs of deterioration in the leadership of the church as a whole. There was the need to add a few brothers to the eldership, but it was impossible to raise up so many elders in a short time. I therefore asked the three Brother Changs to temporarily take the lead, with the hope that more brothers would shortly become qualified to become elders. However, by 1979 no elders had been raised up. I fellowshipped with Brother Chang Wu-chen to see if some suitable brothers could be appointed, but there was still no nomination. I had no choice but to wait longer. The next year, in 1980, we considered the matter again, and the result was the same; no one was considered qualified. We waited in this way for six years, but there were still only a few who were considered qualified to be elders.

Please give me the liberty to speak an honest word here. By October of the year before last, when I returned to Taipei, there were only three to five elders besides the few senior co-workers here. Even with these, a healthy eldership was not established. Even though there were a few elders, the work and administration of the church were still in the hands of a few co-workers, and there was no true administration by the eldership. In 1949 when I first began the work in Taipei, I spoke sternly that all the matters related to the church, whether great or small, must be brought to the elders' meeting. The elders' meeting at that time was on Saturday afternoons. Many times we would meet until eight or nine o'clock, eating a sack dinner along the way and continuing to meet after we ate. But gradually, these meetings became co-workers' meetings, and a few co-workers made all the decisions. Even when some elders were present, they were only "tag-alongs."

When I returned two years ago, I looked at the list of names of all the responsible ones in all the meeting halls and discussed them one by one with all the elders and with Brother Chang Wu-chen. Generally speaking, all the responsible brothers of all the twenty-one halls were quite good. They all loved the Lord, they were all for the Lord, and they were all consecrated to the Lord. I told the brothers, "Since they all love the Lord and are given to the Lord, and since all the meeting halls are in their hands already, they can all be elders." The brothers did not disagree. In fact, they felt quite good about this. As a result, we did away with our past cautious conservatism. On that night we appointed fifty-two elders. We thank the Lord for this big change. We overturned the control. We no longer tried to manipulate with human hands. Instead, we allowed the Lord to lead and control these saints from within.

After half a year, we appointed another twenty-eight elders. Altogether we appointed eighty elders, and later we added a few more. I did this to show that the church should not be under any individual's hand. Only the Holy Spirit has the absolute right over the church, and only the Head is qualified to exercise control over the Body.

Absolutely Delivered from Any Kind of Control

Please give me the liberty to speak. Since we have changed the system, everything that we do, all the arrangements that we make, and all the methods that we use are an experiment. We are doing everything in an exploratory way. Even until today we are still in the experimental stage. I have a concern for the eighty elders, which is the same concern that I had for the co-workers before them. I am concerned that subconsciously we are exercising control again. The thought of control is in our very blood.

Consider the situation in a family. If three children are playing together, no one needs to teach them about control. The oldest one will spontaneously boss the two smaller ones. He will spontaneously try to be the king. The thought of control is in our blood. In the past we were only "responsible brothers" in the various halls, but now we are the elders, and we may feel that we have been "promoted." We feel great, and our family feels flattered. I am fully aware of such sentiments. It is unavoidable. But if we adopt this kind of attitude, and if we say in our heart, "My, I am an elder now!" we can be sure that the brothers and sisters will be killed by our control.

My sixty years of experience as a Christian and living in the church has confirmed to me the reality of such a concern. For this reason, I charge again and again not to exercise any control. We should take our hands off, allowing the brothers and sisters to do things by themselves. With some of us, our practice in the past was to allow the saints to meet in the homes only after we granted them permission. Until the elders had an interview with a candidate, he could not be baptized, and even when he was baptized, he was baptized by the ones who were approved by the elders. Some may say, "Brother Lee, this is what you taught us to do thirty-five years ago." Since I was the one who "tied the knot," of course, I need to be the one to "untie it." That might have been the right thing to do thirty-five years ago. At that time the light we received was not strong enough, and we saw only so much. Today, however, I have awakened from my "dream." I see that something is wrong, and I am sounding the call to change the system. Whoever does not agree with me and still wants to exercise control must be responsible for the tangled "knot."

Although we cannot claim full success for the new way, we can already perceive some results. Today we can meet in the homes at any time and anywhere. There is no need to be under any control. There is no more need for a formal interview to be baptized. As long as a new one is willing, those who preach the gospel to him can baptize him. There is no need to visit the baptistery in the meeting hall very often; all the saints have bathtubs and water in their homes. They can baptize the new ones in their homes immediately. During a recent gospel meeting, about fifty to sixty saints were baptized in the bathroom of the apartments above the meeting hall. Both the arrangements of the baptism and the interviews were carried out in an organic way. The saints took care of them organically. When I saw this, I was very happy, and I was happier when I attended the small group meetings. People were ready for baptism right there on the spot, and the saints quickly filled up the bathtub. Two "small soldiers" of no special rank baptized them in the bathtub. This kind of organic practice is the best and most accurate way revealed by the Scriptures.

Not Replacing but Encouraging

In the summer of 1933 one seeker of the Lord came to me in the evening at about seven or eight o'clock. Because it was hot and my home was close to the sea, we went for a walk by the beach. After we arrived at the beach, we sat down, and he began to ask me about the truth concerning baptism. At that time I was already enlightened by the Lord concerning this truth. I gave a long discourse about the qualifications for baptism, the place for baptism, the person to administer baptism, and other matters, all of which were very scriptural. I remember how confident I was in my speaking and how I quoted all the verses. By the time I finished, it was past ten o'clock. The person said to me, "Mr. Lee, if what you said is true, you need to baptize me today." I said, "I dare not do this, because I am not an elder. I am not even a junior deacon. I cannot baptize you." He answered, "You just told me that whoever does the preaching can do the baptizing. Why are you saying that you cannot do it now? Did you not also say that as long as there is water, one can be baptized? Before us is the sea, and the water in Chefoo is calm and clean. Let me be baptized now." I was forced to go along, and on that day I baptized him.

Later, in taking care of the churches, I decided that baptism should be approved by the elders and interviews should be conducted by them. The baptizers should either be the elders or brothers serving in the capacity of the elders. I was the one who made all these arrangements. I thank and praise the Lord that during the past one and a half years, even these bonds have been broken. We can now baptize people everywhere. Whoever preaches can baptize as well. This is a wonderful thing. It proves that we have been released from the bondage of religion and are on the way toward true scriptural practices.

Yet I am concerned that the old ones among us will feel that their children and grandchildren are now turning things upside down. The Chinese are especially concerned about "family rule" and "family tradition." This is true not only with you but with me also. Some of my daughters are already grandmothers, and some of my sons are grandfathers, yet I still consider them children and do not have full confidence in them. Sometimes I rebuke myself, saying, "Foolish man, the Lord should take you away. Otherwise, you will damage your children." We know that capable parents many times do not produce useful children. A mother who is a good cook often ends up with a daughter who cannot cook. The reason for this is that the mother cannot tolerate the daughter's ineptness and tries to do everything herself. If the mother can hold herself back, even when the food is burnt or spoiled, and if she can encourage the child and not replace her, the child will eventually become a good cook.

Today we are not for the Eastern way or the Western way. We are for the scriptural way. The young people are easy to be trained and easy to be molded. We need to lead them and encourage them in wisdom. Brother Nee once said that after thirty years of age a man's character becomes set, and it becomes difficult for him to change. Hence, we must do our best to be trained in our character before the age of thirty. My point is that the elderly saints should be at ease. They should not think that once things are in the hands of the young ones, they will be ruined. Do not think that once things pass into their hands, the church will be finished. My dear, faithful, elderly brothers, be at peace. Simply encourage and do not replace. Once we do this, the young saints will receive the perfecting.

Some have asked, "If the members of a small group include saints from other halls, how should we reckon their attendance? Whom should they belong to?" Actually, numbers are not that important. The important thing is to have the real increase. As long as the small group meetings are bringing people to salvation and as long as there is the increase and the spread, why worry about the method of reckoning the attendance? If a person has many babies, he will not have enough time even to take care of their feeding. Where, then, will he find the time to do the statistics? At the present time I have twenty-two children and grandchildren. I can still count them, but I wish I could lose count of them. To lose count of them means that I am fruitful and multiplying. If a church or a meeting hall can report its number clearly, it proves that the number is small. If a church or a meeting hall has so many saints that no one can count them, this means it is growing; we worship the Lord for this.

Dear saints, we must be clear that the grace of the Lord is with His recovery. Christianity is going downward; it does not please the Lord. For the past one and a half years it seems as if I have been constantly rebuking. It may appear that I have never said anything good and have never praised anything.

I have been continually pointing out our shortcomings and mistakes. It seems as if I have been constantly shaking my head, criticizing, and picking on everyone. Actually, I would like us to know that the Lord's grace is rich. He truly loves His recovery. As long as we are willing to work for Him, He is ready to pour out His best for us. The number of regular attendants in the church in Taipei may be under ten thousand, but if we include those who do not meet regularly, we have over ten thousand saints. As long as we are willing to practice the God-ordained way, I believe that God will add to our number daily. One day the number in the church in Taipei will be more than we can count. May we all have faith to realize how abundant the Lord's blessing can be.

Controlling Factors in the Church

From now on, if anyone prophesies in the meeting improperly or poorly, we should not stop him. We should only pray to the Lord and look to Him to somehow make up the lack. We are not a worldly society, and we are not an army. We should not think that once we give up our controlling hand, everything will be out of order. In the church we have no right to control anything. There are, however, a few precious things that control us. First, we have the Lord's life. All the brothers and sisters have the Lord's life within them, and this life controls them. Second, we have the Lord's word. His word gives light, and it enlightens. Third, we have the Lord's Spirit. We believe that the Lord's Spirit is in every brother and sister. Fourth, we have the Lord Himself. We believe even more that the Lord whom we have believed into is in every brother and sister. Fifth, we have the Lord's love. We believe that the Lord's love is in every brother and sister. Even if a believer has not been meeting with us for a long time and is deeply fallen, within him he still has a love for the Lord and the church. These five things are all within the brothers and sisters. This is the reason that we should never control. We should only allow these five matters to function within the brothers and sisters. If we exercise control, these five matters will not have an opportunity to operate. We must look to the Lord. We need to pray for everyone and allow these five matters to operate and become effectual in the brothers and sisters.

We should have a testimony that we are neither a worldly society nor an army. We do not need any human control. We are the church. We have the Lord's life, the Lord's word, the Lord's Spirit, the Lord Himself, and the Lord's love. All the brothers and sisters have these five things within them. Even the weakest believer, and in particular those who are newly baptized, have these five things within them. If we exercise control, we will frustrate the Lord, but if we do not control, we will actually help the Lord. We will provide the Lord an opportunity to work within people. In any meeting we should not control, even if the saints are exercising their flesh. On the contrary, we should pray, "Lord, this is Your business. I will not control." Perhaps we may think that this is too extreme, but I am not afraid of being too extreme. I am afraid only of depriving the Lord the opportunity to work within the saints. It is possible that at first we will have some confusion, but eventually the Lord will step in to do His work because this is His recovery.

For this reason, I am bold to say that even if the brothers and sisters turn the meetings upside down, we should still thank and praise the Lord. His Spirit is among us, and His life is also among us. All we need to do is to pray. We can pray, "Lord, thank You. Your life is in us, and Your word is among us. You are the Lord! Even if the heaven falls, the earth shakes, and the waves billow, You are still on the throne on high. You alone have the authority to control everything!" Only pray this way; do not try to restrict or control. Today we should all take our hands off. Do try not to control. The co-workers in particular should not try to control the churches. Do not be concerned that the church will become deformed or distorted. Do not try to preserve anything. We must all be impressed with one thing: Do not control!

This being the case, what should the co-workers, the elders, and the full-time serving ones do? On the negative side, we should not control, but on the positive side, we should focus on stirring others up. We should stir up the saints house by house. In the last message we said something about delivering the meetings to people's homes. Now I say again that we must do the work of stirring up the saints house by house. Some saints have not been meeting for a long time. The co-workers and the elders must take the lead to stir them up in their homes. This is what we ought to do. I hope that we can understand what I am saying. Only by "burning all our bridges" can we go forward single-mindedly. Only by being "backed up against the wall" will we be forced to risk everything.

Not for Uniformity but for Vitality

We should pay attention to one thing in this new practice; that is, we should be for vitality rather than uniformity. My grandchildren are very active and growing. Whenever they come together, they create a mess, and there is no order. When they come to visit me, I tell them ahead of time that they can stay for only ten minutes. They are like a demolition crew, specialists in destruction. They feel that they must look at whatever I have on the shelves, touch them, and sometimes kick them and even throw them. They cannot resist jumping on my sofas, and they love to hop off the back of my couches. Before they come, I insist that I be warned by telephone ahead of time. My wife then hurriedly says, "The demolition crew is coming. Hurry and hide the glassware, the pots and pans, and the ornaments, or they will all be wrecked and torn apart." Although this is a bothersome affair, I am always happy at their coming, because every one of them is full of energy and vitality.

Let me ask the brothers and sisters here: Do we want our house to be orderly and clean yet empty and silent, or do we want the "demolition crew" to come? No one likes an empty house with only two elderly people living in it; this is boring. Everyone likes to have the "demolition crew." They are full of energy and noise. In the same principle, we should be afraid of the church lapsing into deadness, but we should not be afraid of the church becoming messy and noisy. I admit that I may be too much, but I fear that even my correction may not be strong enough. I would rather see the matter overly corrected than not corrected at all. I hope that none of us will exercise control. Instead, may we only encourage.

Praying for the Lord to Do the Work, Rather Than Stretching Out Our Own Hands to Do the Work

The church belongs to the Lord. It is God's house. The church is not a law court, and it is not a police station. In God's house we are not rulers lording over God's children. We are slaves serving the saints. In doing everything we must be proper and right. If a brother has committed a serious sin and has not come to a meeting for many years, we should not refer to his sin when we visit him. Some may ask, "If we do not deal with the sin, what kind of church are we?" We need to understand that our hands are not qualified to exercise control over others. Even if we try, we cannot do it. Our hands are dirty. We should never think that our hands are clean. Even if our hands are clean, we must realize that only the Lord is qualified to deal with the sinning one. If we try to deal with him, we may end up in fleshly wrath after two minutes and may fall into sin ourselves. It is difficult to find a clean person. We can only ask the Lord to do the work and allow Him to do the work. This is the best way.

From my youth, I learned to serve the Lord. When I saw some situations that I thought were wrong, I hoped that one day I could do something about them. However, after a few years, I realized that I myself was not clean. I was not pure within. For this reason, I dared not touch those matters. If a surgeon does not first sterilize himself and all his instruments, his surgery will create problems. Without surgery, a patient may at least be protected from certain kinds of germs. To have an operation in a room full of germs, with unsterilized instruments and doctors with germs on their hands, will merely aggravate the patient's condition.

Dear co-workers and elders, do not presume that it is always right to deal with the matters that stumble. It may be right to know about them, but if we are not clean persons and our "instruments" have not been sterilized, we have no way to deal with these matters. In trying to deal with defeated and backsliding saints, some co-workers and elders have stepped into a situation without adequate knowledge of the weaknesses of the saints, and the result has been a problem. It is better to stay away from such situations than to end up with a problem. As long as a person is a child of God, he has the Lord's life in him, and this life will take care of the situation. It will fight the germs, and the germs will be eliminated. However, if we try to operate in the dark, we will bring in harmful infections. Many times nothing happens when we do not touch a situation, but the minute we touch it, we spoil everything. I believe we have experienced this.

The Lord's Word Being the Main Ingredient in the Home Meetings

In short, we should not control but should stir up people in a positive way. Our most practical goal should be to stir up the saints house by house and to incite them to open up their homes. Let me give a few words of advice. First, no matter how disorganized a home meeting is and no matter how low the condition of the meeting is, we should not be discouraged. We should pray in secret and encourage in public so that the meeting can continue week after week. It does not matter how many people show up; as long as they can meet, we should encourage it. Second, the co-workers and the elders should set the direction of the meetings. Every home meeting should have the Lord's word. According to our experience, if we do not prepare some material, and if we do not have the Lord's word, everyone will be free to speak what he wants to, and the freedom will degenerate into confusion. In the church in Taipei, for example, the best way is for the business office of the church to select some nourishing, enlightening, and anointed messages and make them available for use in the home meetings. The co-workers and the elders then must encourage the saints to dig into these messages and progress through them.

The home meetings do not need to be formal. Rather, they need to be living and organic. These meetings are prone to be somewhat disorganized. They may begin at seven o'clock, but it may be half past eight before all the members arrive. After an initial period of mutual cherishing, the group can begin reading the message after half past eight. At least there should be twenty minutes when everyone is together to pursue the message together in a living way. This can be compared to eating a meal. The meal may not be a large one, but at least everyone is well fed. Do not think that this is a small matter. If every week or every other week the saints can gather together in such a home meeting, and everyone has the word planted into him, in time this will produce a certain kind of result.

The human body can incur some long-term illnesses that need long-term care. The cures for these illnesses do not come quickly. The same can be said of the weaknesses of the saints; because they cannot be cured immediately, we should go slowly. Every time we see the saints, we should dispense a little of God's word. Every opportunity we have, we should nourish and cherish a little. Then in time the saints will grow in a healthy way. We cannot be impatient. Release a word or two once a week, every week. In the beginning we may not see much result, but over a long period of time the result will become quite obvious.

After a few weeks of practice in the home meetings, I have observed that the home meetings in the church in Taipei are gradually getting on the right track. They are no longer dependent on the "core members" or on spiritual giants. Every member is functioning in an organic way. When the saints come together, they are like a heap of coal, and the minute fire is applied, the whole meeting lights up. Now I am concerned that although the fire is lit, there is not much of the Lord's word in them. The gatherings generate a congenial atmosphere, but after such a meeting, not much of the Lord's word has been imparted into the attendants. There is no pursuit of any message, and the meeting merely goes on and on with light talk. This is a serious shortage of the home meetings. We should use whatever means we have to impart the Lord's word into the saints. His word is the only vital ingredient for the home meetings.

The Home Meeting Needing
to Stir Up Man's Spirit

In short, in leading the saints to care for the home meetings, the elders must pay attention to stirring up the spirit of every person in every home. Do not expect to stir up every home the first time. Rather, work on the homes one by one. We are not afraid of being slow; we are afraid only of not moving at all. If every elder can stir up one home per week, three elders can stir up twelve homes in a month. After the saints' spirits are stirred up, we need to teach them so that they are fed by the Lord's word. Each home meeting must always render a portion of supply to the saints. This is a crucial matter. We can try to accomplish this in whatever way we please, but the spirit has to be living and fresh. If a message is too long, we can split it up into sections. Some who come early can receive the supply from the first section, and some who come late can receive the supply from the second section. Even if someone comes late and leaves early, we should still give him a portion of supply. We should accompany him to the door, read a portion to him, fellowship a little with him, and ask him to read the material when he gets home. He may not read it when he gets home, but if he does, he will receive the supply. This is a very important step.

Not Coercing but Begetting, Nourishing, Teaching, and Building

Another point we must pay attention to is that we should not coerce anyone or drag anyone to go along with us. One unfortunate effect of our changing the system is that the brothers pay too much attention to numbers. Every church and every meeting hall tries to compare its results with others. As a result, everyone is concerned about the numbers in the group meetings and how these numbers should be reckoned. I hope that we can all be delivered from the concern for numbers. The numbers merely show us whether we are advancing or falling back, and even this is not a very accurate measurement. It is wrong for us to attract people from other halls or churches for the purpose of boosting our number. We should never do this kind of thing.

A saint should go to a meeting that is close by his or her home. Do not say, "This person was baptized and revived in our area. Therefore, he or she must join the meeting in our area."

When we labor for increase and revival, we may accidentally trample on others. It is better that we be trampled on and others be revived. Is it not wonderful that we die and others live? We must be clear that we are here to spread the gospel and save the sinners. After the sinners are saved, we should nourish, care for, teach, and perfect them. This is our goal. If we are focused on this goal, we will not carefully bargain about everything but will generously give our new ones away.

Concerning the new ones, we need to prepare some material at the suitable time to lead them to know the church. We need to show them what the church is, and we need to help them to realize the importance of the church. Our old concept tells us that if a person does not come to the big meetings and does not attend the Lord's table meeting, he is not a part of the church. We must drop this concept. Those who are a part of the church are those who have the Lord's life. As long as a person possesses the Lord's life, he is a part of the church, and we must receive him.

CHANGING THE SYSTEM FIRST INVOLVING
A CHANGE OF CONCEPT

We need to change our concept entirely. We should not seek a regimented, grand, or spectacular façade. In fact, we should not pay attention to the façade at all. Rather, we should pay attention to something practical. We need to pay attention to every home meeting. We should put our hope in every saint having meetings in his home. If we do this, everyone among us, whether he is burning or cold, strong or weak, young or old, will have the opportunity to be stirred up and to develop and fulfill his organic function in the Body. The Lord's recovery will then be a nation of a fighting army, and there will be continual growth and increase. However, if we hold on to our old concepts, many saints will be quenched from functioning in an organic way through our demand for uniformity. I hope that we can thoroughly change our concept and that we can practice everything properly and absolutely according to the pattern of the new way.

CHAPTER EIGHT

CRUCIAL ASPECTS OF THE HOME MEETINGS

CRUCIAL POINTS REQUIRING OUR ATTENTION IN THE HOME MEETINGS—NUTRITION AND HYGIENE

In the previous chapter, we spoke about dividing the four hundred home meetings in the church in Taipei into a thousand smaller units. On the one hand, I am for this, but on the other hand, I am somewhat concerned about this. If we are not diligent, persistent, and proper in this practice, we will kill everything. Originally, there may be one small group meeting. However, with the division of this meeting into five smaller home meetings, everyone may become lost and the whole group may disband. For this reason I am burdened to share something further in this chapter.

It is a joy to have births. But while there are births, there is also the danger of infant mortality. In the past in China, when hygiene was not properly attended to, the infant mortality rate was high. Around 1945, the average life span of the Chinese was approximately forty years. One of the reasons the life span was so low was that the high infant mortality rate lowered the statistic. The ancient Chinese said, "Rare is the man who reaches seventy." Today, however, medical science has advanced so much that the average life span has increased to more than seventy years. The standard of living has also improved. These improvements can be attributed to the advancement in the food supply and hygiene.

My point is that we cannot congratulate ourselves merely with the fact that all the small groups have been subdivided into the homes. Of course, the number is encouraging, but we still need to pay attention to "hygiene," "medical supplies," and "good nutrition." If these things are not in place, our "infant mortality rate" will still be high. The subdivision will bring in death, not life. I hope that all the elders and co-workers will take note of this danger. If there is malnutrition and lack of hygiene, the death rate will increase. What then should we do? We must approach the problem from a few directions. On the one hand, we need to enhance our hygiene, which includes immunization. On the other hand, we need to pay attention to nutritional care. All the co-workers, elders, and full-time serving ones have a responsibility to look into these two matters. We need to bear the burden of these one thousand home meetings. For this reason, I beg the co-workers and elders to spend much time praying together and seeking the Lord together. Consider the weaknesses and the needs that exist in each home meeting.

After we subdivide the four hundred small groups into a thousand homes, there may be some sloppiness at the beginning, and we may easily become discouraged with the situation. At such times the co-workers, elders, and full-timers should bring in much encouragement. They need to keep the brothers and sisters encouraged. My youngest daughter had a premature delivery when she had her first baby. When the baby was born, he was less than six pounds. The hospital put him in an incubator. When my wife and I visited him, he looked like a pitiful little frog to us. We looked at each other and wondered, "Can he live? Will he grow up?" However, he is now nine years old. He is not only tall but also strong. He is a member of the football team in school and is even one of its best players. He was able to grow up so well because his mother took good care of him; there was adequate attention given to hygiene and nutrition. He ate well and properly, and the result was healthy and vigorous growth.

COMFORTING THE DISCOURAGED ONES AND ENCOURAGING THE WEAK ONES

The most common negative mood that saints fall into is discouragement. This is actually a characteristic of the Christian life. The Chinese are especially susceptible to discouragement. It is strange that in other things the Chinese are aggressive and striving. They can press forward in the midst of all kinds of adversity. The more they suffer, the more they stand up. During the few thousand years of their history, the Chinese were subdued by different races many times, but eventually they absorbed and neutralized their conquerors. The Chinese character is quite indomitable. However, in spiritual things they have a different characteristic. Once they encounter hardship and difficulty, they give up. This is because they think that whatever is of the Lord will be blessed by Him. They also think the Lord's blessing should come without any difficulty because the Lord is omnipotent. This kind of mentality results in much discouragement. Thus, they may think, "Since we have turned to the Lord and are living for Him, He will bless us. Since it is of the Lord that we subdivide into the home meetings, He will bless us." On the one hand, this is right, but on the other hand, we cannot be superstitious. This may be compared to planting a crop; we need to do our part to sow. This is also like gardening; we need to plant and water. If we do not sow and water in the right way, we will kill everything.

I once planted a peach tree and a plum tree behind my house, and they both grew well. I decided to trim them myself. My way was to trim them in a neat and tidy way like giving a haircut. Eventually, however, the trees did not bear any fruit. I was quite frustrated. One young American sister, who came periodically to help me, said to me, "My father used to trim trees. He told me that the young shoots should not be cut off. It is the young branches that bear the fruit. You have cut off all the young branches and have left behind only the old branches. To be sure, you will not have any fruit." I had cut off the young shoots because I considered them untidy, yet it is these untidy branches that bear fruit. Do not complain that the home meetings are going nowhere. It is possible for us to damage them through our "trimming." When this happens, it means that we are not doing things the right way.

Later I learned the lesson concerning trimming fruit trees. Last year my wife and I went to my daughter's house for a rest. For years she had sent me many sweet and juicy plums. When I arrived at her house, I went to her backyard to take a look at her plum trees. They were extremely ugly. All of them looked scruffy and untidy. My daughter said to me, "Do not despise these ugly branches. Under their boughs are many fruits." I looked carefully and discovered that indeed all the branches were bent over with fruit. I began to say to myself, "Man, do you want fruit, or do you want tidiness?"

Dear co-workers and elders, after we divide the small group meetings into the homes, we may expect all the home meetings to be tidy and neat. If they are not tidy and neat, we may want to "trim" them. But we need to remind ourselves again and again that once we trim them, they are through. We must allow these home meetings to have an opportunity to grow and develop by themselves. If they grow in the wrong way, we should still let them go. They should be free to grow in whatever way they want. As long as the branches remain, they will bear fruit. Do not try to trim them in an artificial way. Do not think that their way will never work. Do not think that since many have been dormant for a long time, something should be done to trim them a little. If we do not trim them, they may still live. Once we trim them, they may die and no longer bear fruit. Our work is not the work of trimming, but of encouragement, help, and stimulation. We need to do these things until they all grow.

THE CO-WORKERS AND ELDERS TAKING THE LEAD TO EXERCISE FAITH AND NOT BE DISCOURAGED

The church in Taipei has now been practicing the small group meetings for more than a year and a half. For a time the situation did not seem promising at all. Everywhere there were complaints that this way does not work and that the saints were dying. Some groups could not go on by themselves and decided to join with other groups. Now after a year and a half, everyone has learned some lessons. It was an impossible task for some at the beginning, but those who endured to the end saw the result. After two or three weeks, or a couple of months, the group meetings resurrected. It is an easy thing to resuscitate the small groups. If two or three people are too few for a meeting, all we need to do is to bring two or three more into the meeting, and the meeting will become strong and vibrant again. After another two or three months, we may have more than twelve people. At that time we can even subdivide the group.

I suggest that the co-workers and elders first be encouraged themselves. We must never be discouraged. Once we are encouraged, we should encourage the other saints. We should tell them that we would join their meeting and strengthen them whenever there is a need. Of course, to strengthen does not mean to replace. We must encourage the saints to take care of the meeting themselves. It does not matter whether they are skillful at taking the lead in the meeting, or whether they know how to sing. If they cannot sing the hymns, at least they can read the words. As long as we have the Lord's word and as long as we have His Spirit, there will be life, and life will enliven men. Whatever we do, it is better than not doing anything at all. If we consider a person unqualified to begin a meeting in his home, that person may never again be able to open up his home. He may remain unqualified for the next twenty years. We must always encourage the saints and support them. In the long run they will rise up. I believe that if we practice this more and more, we will find the secret; we will know how to render the proper hygiene and the proper nutrition to people. For this reason the co-workers and the elders must never be discouraged; they must have full confidence and a steady faith.

THE BENEFITS OF MEETING IN THE HOMES

A big meeting may consist of three hundred people. If fifty are missing from such a meeting, no one will notice it; the meeting will still look proper and full with the remaining two hundred fifty people. When the co-workers and elders look at such a meeting, they may be led to think that the meeting is very good. However, once we break up this big meeting into the homes, we may have only five or six people in each meeting. As we look at such a meeting, we may feel that it is a very sloppy meeting. Everyone may be a disappointment and discouragement. After joining a few of these meetings, we may even lose our heart for working as a co-worker or an elder. To us, these meetings are too poor. Indeed, when we break up the whole into pieces, the sight is not always comely. After some time, however, when we add the pieces together again to see the whole, we will find that the total number has increased.

Moreover, we believe that when someone opens up his home for meetings, his home will be blessed. The unsaved ones will be saved, the backsliding ones will be recovered, the fallen ones will be uplifted, the cold ones will begin meeting again, and the dormant ones will begin functioning. This is not all. The family life in that home will also improve. There will be light, and there will be the proper testimony. No one will dare to be loose. Of course, the fruit-bearing may not come immediately, but the situation will only go upward. It will not deteriorate, because gradually, one by one, everyone will learn to know something of life.

In short, it is always better for a home to have a meeting than to not have a meeting. Some have asked, "Do we not emphasize the matter of having a proper testimony in the Lord's recovery? What testimony is there when some people bring the meeting to the homes? These meetings are sloppy. Some even play cards and smoke right up to the time of the meeting." Of course, this kind of thing is possible, but we should never be discouraged. If we enter a home and see the people playing cards, do not stop them. Wait until they finish their game. Then take out the Bible to meet with them.

Some may criticize, saying, "What kind of church is this? They have a card game and then follow it with a meeting. You allow such people to have meetings in their homes? Even if you allow such people to have meetings in their homes, I would not dare to bring any new ones to their homes. If we bring someone to the door and they see the card game, are we not corrupting them? Have we not spoiled the testimony?" I cannot argue with that. However, we should consider the matter from a long-term perspective. We cannot look merely at the present situation. It is true that this home has a card game today, but after two weeks the card game may move to a hidden place. After another two weeks the game may disappear altogether, and after another month the host may decide to burn the game. This is the story of life. At the beginning the host may not be able to overcome the game. To be sure, he will eventually overcome it. He may even throw away the card table. If we look back at that time, we will see that had we not brought the meeting to his home, he might still be playing cards. He may not have experienced any growth in life even after five or ten years.

NOT BEING DISCOURAGED, NOT LOSING HEART, BUT BEING STRENGTHENED TO WORK FOR THE LORD

This is the kind of gospel work that we should have. The gospel is the power of God unto salvation (Rom. 1:16). Through the gospel, life and incorruption are brought to light. Some become weak after they are saved and turn back to idols. We should not be alarmed, much less give up. We must be bold and encouraged to go to them to nourish them. If we cannot pray or read the Word when we stand in front of an idol, it proves that we are not strong enough. If we are strong, we can pray, read the Word, and sing, even if we are in hell. The co-workers and elders must be that strong before they can do a persistent work. Nothing can turn us back. We should be able to work under any circumstance.

I am not joking. I have personally experienced all these things. When I was in north China, I was frequently busy with the gospel work. Now I have other burdens and do not have the time to be personally involved in the gospel, but at that time, every day I rode my bicycle to visit people from door to door. Some homes had idols in them. Some homes were possessed by demons. I was bold to preach the gospel to all of them. I went to work for the Lord. I went to preach the gospel and to announce the glad tidings. I was dispensing the Lord to them. The Lord Jesus said, "Those who are strong have no need of a physician, but those who are ill" (Matt. 9:12). We all need such a spirit to work for the Lord in a bold way.

THE PROPER WAY TO PREACH THE GOSPEL

Do not think that the big meetings are better than the small meetings. Do not say, "We have been elders for so long, and the situation has been so prosperous all this time. Now that we are broken up into small meetings, nothing seems to be working properly anymore." Some overseas brothers have taken the time to come purposely to visit and observe us.

They may say, "You tell us to come and see. What is there to see? Are there merely these home meetings? Some home meetings are conducted in the coffee shops at 9:30 P.M. after the waiters finish their day and the shop is closed. What kind of meeting is this?" Outwardly speaking, there is nothing to see, but there is a different perspective. This coffee house was once void of believers. Now everyone is a believer and is bringing others to the Lord. We need to bow down and worship the Lord for this. How wonderful it is that when the coffee shop closes, everyone gathers around the tables to study the Word, fellowship, and lead other workers to Christ! In such a meeting, there is no boss, no cook, no waiter, and no cashier. Everyone is a member of God's family. If we consider it from this angle, we will say, "What a glory this is to the Lord!" This is the kind of gospel work to which we should give ourselves.

Consider the four Gospels in the New Testament. When the Lord was on the earth, did He always do things in a "proper" way? Is it not true that often the Lord performed His work in a seemingly messy way? Outwardly speaking, there was no glamour in anything He did. If we were with the Lord, we might have said, "Lord Jesus, we heard of Your name, and we were told that You have a very successful work. This is the reason we came purposely to see You." To be sure, the Lord would answer us by saying, "What do you want to see? Do you want to see how the Pharisees oppose Me? Do you want to see how the Sadducees tempt Me? Do you want to see how Peter denies Me? Do you want to see how the disciples desert Me? What are you here to see?" If what could be seen was all there was, it would have been a very poor situation indeed. But the truth lies deeper than the surface. The Lord accomplished God's will; He finished all of God's work. In the end, in spite of the persecutions, oppositions, and denials, He gained one hundred twenty people who prayed in one accord for ten days in a little room in Jerusalem and brought in God's kingdom. This is the view we should have. I have felt during the past few years that we owe the Lord much, and we are also much indebted to the people of this land. The Lord sent us here. We have been here for more than thirty years, but even now we have not fully presented the gospel to them. This is certainly to our shame.

DEVOTING OUR FULL TIME
TO THE WORK OF THE LORD'S RECOVERY

I am an "old hand" in the matter of serving the Lord full time. I know what the young full-timers are thinking. You waver whenever you think about your future. When you were in college, you may have been called to serve the Lord full time, but at that time you may have thought that the time had not yet come. You told yourself that you should wait until you graduate from school. However, after you graduated, you still waited, and the waiting took many years. One day the Lord raised up the environment to blow away all your concerns. You could not wait any longer; in a sense, you were forced to drop everything. I have already told you that when I began to serve full time, I was prepared to go anywhere for the gospel. If I thirsted, I was ready to drink the water from the mountain. If I hungered, I was ready to eat the roots of the trees. However, when I actually quit my job to serve full time, I did not need to live that kind of life at all. We do not need to worry that much. The Lord is everything to us.

Today on this earth, no profession will abandon a person to starve to death. The only way that a person will starve is if he does not work at all. As long as we are willing to do something, we will surely not starve to death. The full-timers should not be afraid that there will be the need to starve. Our profession is the highest profession. Our Lord is the One who holds the keys of death and of Hades (Rev. 1:18). Death will not find us. We should not think that serving the Lord is a way of poverty. I can say strongly that while any profession can lead to poverty, serving the Lord will never lead to poverty. Serving the Lord is a golden profession. If we have the burden to serve the Lord, no one can frustrate us. It is something that is full of glory. Who among the full-time workers here has suffered hunger? Who is suffering from poverty? And who does not have the sense of glory in him? Therefore, we must not worry about our living.

Of course, since the Lord cares for our needs, we must be

faithful to Him. We cannot become careless merely because we have a golden profession. We need to labor diligently. We should not waste our time with mere mental knowledge. Rather, we should give ourselves to the Lord in a selfless way. This is the reason that I exhort us all to have small groups and to subdivide the small groups into the homes. In this way everyone will have something to do, and everyone can function. At present, the church in Taipei has a thousand homes. We all need to rise up to labor together. If every one of us would work on one home a week, in a month we will have worked on all one thousand homes. If we do this, all the home meetings will surely be made alive by our work.

DROPPING OUR OLD CONCEPTS AND CARING ONLY FOR FRUIT AND NOT FOR APPEARANCES

I hope that we can all drop our old concepts. Do not care for uniformity. Do not care for appearances. Rather, care for the fruit. What we want is an orchard, not a garden. A garden is for show, but an orchard is for fruit. Once our concepts are changed, we will act differently when we go to a home meeting. When a meeting is dying, we will not give it up. Rather, we will immediately administer some "booster shots"; we will do some "CPR" by stirring up, encouraging, and consoling the saints. We will do this until the meeting is revived again. We must not be discouraged by anything, and the host of the home where the meeting is held must not be discouraged by anything. We should pray together, read the Word together, and visit and shepherd together. At least, we need to shepherd and encourage each other. We must learn to do this.

HAVING AN AGGRESSIVE, BOLD, AND DARING SPIRIT

I hope that we will have the boldness and the confidence to open our mouth to speak for the Lord. We must not be afraid, and we must not be shy. Such are not the attitudes of one who is serving the Lord. What I mean is that when we go to a home meeting, we should fire up the meeting. We must not be afraid if the meeting does not have fire. We must not worry when instead it pours cold water on our head. We must have a strong determination that anytime we go to a meeting, we must light a fire in that meeting. If we are shy and hesitating, we will only quench the fire, even quenching it quicker than any other person will. We will not be able to fire up anyone. We are all young people. If we want to work, we must work with enthusiasm and impact. We need to be like Elijah, who called fire down from heaven even when the ground was covered with water (1 Kings 18:33-38). We all need this kind of attitude, this kind of spirit.

Twenty-three years ago I went alone to America as a sixty-year-old Chinese. I did not have any theological qualifications, and I never studied in America. That was the first time I worked in America. I had to learn their language in order to preach to the Americans. At that time I encountered cold water everywhere. All around me was chilling ice. Yet I did not care for any of these frustrations. I had the confidence within that as long as I was selling treasure, someone would buy it. In the end, the water was dried up by the fire; everywhere I saw churches being raised up.

When the Chinese went to Brazil thirty years ago, the easiest way for them to make money was to carry a knapsack on their back and sell their wares from their sack. The Chinese who had just migrated to Brazil had very little else they could do because they could not understand Portuguese. At that time a favorite item for the Brazilians was embroidery work. This was the only kind of business the Chinese knew to do. They would wrap all kinds of Chinese goods inside a sheet and carry it on their backs, going from house to house to make sales. The Brazilians are very hospitable people. Whenever they saw someone coming to their door with a knapsack, they would open the door and invite the person to come in for tea. The Chinese may not have known the language, but they surely could communicate with their hands. After unwrapping their sack and settling on the price, they would make their sale. Sometimes they were able to sell their goods in this way by the hundreds. In time, they could communicate in the native language and were able to make even more sales.

Today in working for the Lord, we should be like those who carried their goods on their back. It does not matter if we cannot communicate very well. As long as we can open up our "sack" and show people our "goods," that is sufficient. It does not matter if we are not able to make ourselves clear; we should simply repeat the same words a few more times. We have the goods. If we have this spirit and this attitude, surely we will be able to sell our goods. If we go to the home meetings with the same spirit, I guarantee that every home will be fired up. Even if it was dead before, we can do what Elisha did; he laid mouth to mouth, eye to eye, and palm to palm, stretching himself over the one who was dead and dispensed life to him (2 Kings 4:32-37). At most, we need to do this for two or three weeks; then the people will come alive. We must believe that the eternal and incorruptible life is within all the brothers and sisters. As long as we work aggressively enough, they will come alive. I believe that we can all testify to this.

Many times some co-workers asked me, "Brother Lee, what is the secret of your work?" I can say that the secret of my work is that I do not know what difficulty is. I know only to give myself to work. I do not care for the result; I care only to labor diligently. We can say that my secret is simply to work. I do not care about the circumstances; I care only to work. The result of this work during the past sixty years can be seen. As long as we work, there will be the result.

Thirty-seven years ago, the situation in mainland China changed suddenly. At that time all the co-workers gathered together in Shanghai to prepare for the change. Brother Nee said specifically in that co-workers' meeting that I should leave the country. Eventually, I was the only one who left; all the rest stayed behind for the Lord's testimony. At that time, Shanghai was the largest city in all of Southeast Asia. The church in Shanghai was the leading church among more than four hundred churches in the Lord's recovery. Every week we published one periodical. All of this work was under my care. We even spent one hundred five thousand dollars (U.S.) to buy a piece of land and were prepared to build a three-thousand-seat meeting hall that would also accommodate two thousand people outside. Then suddenly I was sent to the small island of Taiwan.

When I first arrived in Taiwan, I did not know where I should meet. The brothers in Taipei invited me to speak on the Lord's Day. When I went to the meeting place, I found out that it was a run-down house that occupied only a few square feet. As I entered the door, I had to take off my shoes. I was from north China; according to our custom it is impolite to take off one's shoes. I had never taken off my shoes in public, but on that day I had to speak without my shoes on. I was afraid that I would not be able to deliver my message and that my spirit would be gone, but I went against my will and spoke. There were only a few dozen people sitting around in a scattered way. I groaned within. When I returned to my dwelling, which was a small place with only two rooms, I fell on my bed and stared at the ceiling. I asked myself, "What am I doing here in Taiwan?" As I looked at the pebbled streets outside the window and listened to the sound of the wooden clogs clattering on the road, I wondered what kind of work I could do there. I did not understand the native Taiwanese dialect, and everything around me was disappointing and discouraging.

However, since I was already in Taiwan, I reasoned, "What can I say?" The Chinese have a saying that when the goods arrive at the doorstep, the deal is done. Since I had already moved my "goods" to Taiwan, I had to "sell" them. If I did not sell my goods, they would spoil. After two months a thought came to me, and I believe that it was of the Lord. I asked myself, "Why don't you take a trip along the railway route?" At that time there were a few hundred brothers and sisters in Taiwan who had just moved from mainland China. They were scattered in the few major cities along the railway route. So I took the train and visited Shin-ju, Taichung, Zhia-yi, Tainan, and Kaohsiung along the way. That visit gave me a burden. I felt that much could be done. When I returned, I fellowshipped with the brothers, and we decided to begin the work there.

I believe the senior co-workers among us remember that at the beginning of our work in Taiwan the first meeting hall in Taipei was only one-half the size of what it is today. The land was donated by two overseas Chinese brothers, and we erected a temporary canopy with wooden beams for our meetings. Once we began our work, God's blessing was there. We decided to preach the gospel, but the meeting place was not large enough. The land across the street from the hall was an unassigned plot, and nothing was on it yet. We decided to contract some people to enclose it with bamboo fences, bricks, and wooden props. It provided a temporary overflow space for meeting. That space later became the "Workers' Home." This was how we began our work in Taiwan.

We should not allow any circumstance to quench our burden for the Lord's work. We work even if the worst hardship befalls us. We work even if harsh poverty meets us. As long as we are clear that we are serving the Lord, we should charge forward without any fear. Do not think that if we are rejected, we will have no more places to go. Do not say that it is impossible to have a home meeting that has only one believer because the rest of the household worships idols. This is to pour cold water on ourselves. This is to quench the fire. If we do that, it is no wonder that we cannot bring life into the situation. No matter how difficult the situation is, as long as we have the Lord's presence, we can go against all odds. One characteristic of a Christian is that he can go against the tide and move forward by beholding the Lord's face. When the missionaries came to China, they also faced trying situations. Everywhere they went, they faced opposition and cold water. Rocks were thrown at them, and some were even martyred. Yet they were not discouraged. They pressed on and did not turn back for a moment. Eventually, they opened the door of the gospel in that old, conservative land.

Today to spread the Lord's gospel in Taiwan and to evangelize the whole island, we need the spirit and perseverance of the missionaries who went before us. If we sit here hoping that evangelization will come, that is a dream. If we wait until all things are ready, and if we think that we can preach the gospel from an easy chair, we will never see anything of the gospel. When the Lord charged the disciples to preach the gospel, He told them not to bring any shoes, staff, or money. This means they needed to have the attitude that if there was no food, they would simply press on in hunger. If there were no shoes, they would simply move on bare feet. If we have such a spirit, the gospel will surely prevail.

Dr. Mateer, the chairman of the translation team that put out the Chinese Union Version, was one of the seven renowned scholars in the East Pacific region. When he came to China, he lived in a carpenter's home in Penglai in Shangtung province in north China. The father of one of our senior co-workers was a student of his in oceanography. When Dr. Mateer first came to China, he and his companions could not find a place to live. No one was willing to rent, much less sell, a room to him. In the end, some among them had to live on the streets, and some were forced to take shelter in idol temples. This was how they persevered in the gospel. I say this to show that we are not qualified to do the Lord's work if our intention is to wait for all things to be ready before we preach the gospel. If we want to be in the Lord's work, we must learn to strive even when there is nothing for us to work with.

In short, we should not be deterred by anything. Rather, we should charge forward with no thought of turning back. We must not allow anything to cripple our aspiration to build up the home meetings. We must have the will to "do or die." I hope that the co-workers, the elders, and all the full-timers will pick up this burden and spirit. The home meetings are not a product of our imagination but they come from the Lord's revelation. As long as we are willing to work, something will be worked out in a proper way.

LABORING FAITHFULLY AND
DISPENSING FOOD AT THE PROPER TIME

Concerning the home meetings, we must pay attention to three things. First, all the elders, co-workers, and full-timers should learn to minister God's word to the home meetings at every opportune time. However, do not try to preach; that will only lead to failure. Do not try to be big. If there are only three people in a home meeting, do not be disappointed. Even if there are only two people—or even one person—we should still not be discouraged. Always minister a little of God's word and render others some timely help. This is what the

Lord meant when He spoke of dispensing food at the proper time (Matt. 24:45).

Second, we need to prepare ourselves ahead of time for the home meetings. Do not prepare a long message. Rather, look to the Lord and seek Him. We should be prepared to speak only the few words that we have enjoyed that day. Some people will not be saved even if we deliver two or three long messages to them. Other people are saved when we speak to them only for five minutes. Do not go into a long discourse in the home meetings. Rather speak with wisdom by addressing the peoples' need. We can cover some of the *New Believers' Lessons* if we have a newly saved person, but with the unbelievers we should speak something about the gospel.

Third, even after we have prepared something, we should not take up all the time. Rather, allow the brothers and sisters to speak. We should supplement their speaking only when they run out of things to say. This will give them the opportunity to learn.

BELIEVING IN THE LORD'S TIMING

We must believe that every home meeting will survive. In order for that to happen, we must endeavor with our all, but for what should we endeavor? We should endeavor to give "injections," to fight the adverse environment, and to supply nutrition, which is the Lord's word, in order for the saints to grow. We must believe that not only every word in the Bible is God's word but that all the truths we have released according to the Bible are also the Lord's present speaking. As long as it is the Lord's word, His Spirit will bear witness to it with His work. The Lord's Spirit delights in working upon and strengthening His own word. The minute we speak the Lord's word, His Spirit will follow such a word with His work, and there will surely be the result.

I believe the words that I have spoken are from the Lord. I believe the Spirit will also follow such words and work within us in a silent way. This work is of life, and this life is something that human language cannot describe. It is something that human feeling cannot fathom. When a seed falls into the ground, after a period of time it brings forth flowers, yet we cannot explain how the seed has grown and blossomed. The same can be said about our home meetings. We should speak something in every meeting. Even if there is only one person, we should still speak something. We may think that we are speaking in vain, but we do not realize that we are actually sowing. We have not spoken in vain. In the long run we will see the result, and the result will be rewarding. When we speak to one person, we may not realize that in five years our word will produce results in that person. He may perfect another one, who may turn out to be a great vessel of the Lord. We can never anticipate such things. Yet such things do happen all the time.

LEARNING TO SPEAK BY SEIZING THE OPPORTUNITY

For this reason, we cannot look merely at the present condition. We need to believe that our work is a work of life; it has eternal value. What we speak is the truth of the Bible, and life will follow this truth and work on man. We must learn to speak in an organic way. We should not preach in a dead way. Suppose we need to visit a sick and elderly sister or a busy and heavy-laden brother. If we ramble on mechanically about "the organic functioning of the believers" the minute we meet him, we may not be able to impart anything to him. Such speaking is neither organic nor effective. But if we take care of people's situation by seizing the opportunity, we will meet the needs of all kinds of people.

For example, we can say to a sister who is lying on a sick bed, "Sister, 1 Peter 2:24 says that the Lord Jesus bore up our sins in His body on the tree, and by His bruise we are healed. Simply call on His name and He will deliver you from your sickness." We may not have the absolute assurance that she will be healed, but we should believe that she will be comforted by the Lord's word. After this we can lead her to pray, "Lord, I commit my sickness to You. You know my pains. Have mercy on me." If we seize the opportunity in this way, there will be a perfecting work in her. We can then turn around and speak a little to her family. Do not give a message on the "organic functioning of the believers." Instead, seize the opportunity to say a suitable word. We all must learn this.

Concerning the truth, we must be absolute. We cannot discount anything with regard to God's truth, and we cannot discredit God's word, but in our practice we need to be flexible and skillful. Take baptism as an example. Strictly speaking, as soon as a man is saved, he should be baptized. However, we cannot say under what condition a man is qualified to be baptized, nor can we say with surety what way we should baptize people. To do this will not help a person to be saved. When John the Baptist baptized men, he did not baptize in a certain prescribed way. He lived in the wilderness. When men went to him to be baptized, they did not need to change their clothes. They did not need to be in a prearranged place. As long as there was water, he baptized them. Regarding the truth we must be absolute, but in practice, we must learn to work as the opportunity arises.

A PRACTICE FOR THE INCREASE AND SPREAD OF THE CHURCH LIFE

Once the small groups are divided into the homes, the opportunity for everyone to speak greatly increases. No longer is it like the big meetings, where one's mouth is sealed the minute he walks into the meeting. Such big meetings are actually "mouth-sealing" meetings. Once the saints arrive at the big meeting, their mouths are sealed. The elders in particular have taken the lead to shut up their mouths and have allowed the co-workers to set up their little "platforms" and erect their "stages" to deliver their wonderful, savory, and well-rehearsed messages. In the long run, however, such meetings deprive the saints of their organic ability to function. This is a great loss to the Lord's recovery! Let me say a frank word: We have been doing this in Taiwan for more than twenty years. Every meeting was impressive, but what is the result? Where is the increase today? How many saints are functioning?

We are not here to do the work of gardening; we are here to raise orchards. We are not for appearance; we are for fruit, for the increase, and for the spread. In order to achieve this goal, we need to do the following two things: First, we should not lose heart, not be discouraged, and not give up. Rather, we should be strong, be persistent, and have a will that does not settle for anything less than the determined goal. Second, we should learn to dispense food at the proper time, apply the Lord's word suitably at the right time, and make the home meeting a meeting where everyone speaks.

CHAPTER NINE

DEFINITE STEPS FOR
THE PRACTICE OF THE NEW WAY

MAKING THE CHURCH LIFE
A PART OF OUR DAILY LIFE

In the past our church life has been too dead, and not many people have functioned. Even when some did function, they functioned in a formal, religious, and organizational way. The church life has not been a part of our daily life. For example, in the past when a person wanted to be baptized, we arranged for a baptismal meeting, set up a formal façade, prepared the baptistery, and baptized the person in a formal way. All of our meetings were conducted in a proper order. There were definite ones assigned to call a hymn, sing, pray, or preach. Everything was in order, yet when such meetings were dismissed and the saints returned to their daily life, there was no change in their behavior. There seemed to be no connection between the church life and their daily life. However, everything is changed now. If there are two hundred people meeting in a hall, all two hundred people need to function. One can be baptized anywhere and at any time. The church life has become a common "everyday affair" and is easily within everyone's reach. Such a practice vitalizes the church life and increases its impact.

Recently Sister Lee said to me, "After dinner tonight I will go and watch my old classmate be baptized. She was saved, and tonight she will be baptized at hall six." I asked, "Is there a baptismal meeting?" She answered, "No." This is very different from what we used to have. However, this is still not sufficient. We need to be more spontaneous and normal so that our church life is a part of our daily life. I hope that every day the saints will see people baptized into the Lord in their own bathtubs. This will bring a great revival into the church.

THE PRACTICAL STEPS
TO CARRY OUT THE HOME MEETINGS

We have spoken about the burden for the home meetings. Now we will go one step further to consider the practical steps to carry out the home meetings. First, I would recommend that the elders, the co-workers, and the full-timers conduct a survey in their area this week. They must gather up all the records on file for the saints and take a "census" of the saints. Every year the number in the church fluctuates. Some saints have moved away, and others have moved in. Some dropped out of the church life because of their circumstances or their physical weaknesses. Some have not been able to stay abreast with the church life because of their work or schedule. Many have lost contact with the brothers and sisters. We must consider these situations one by one.

These saints have all been baptized into Christ, and they once met with us in the Lord's recovery. It is easier and more profitable to contact these than to contact new ones. Although they may have drawn back or become cold because of their weaknesses or other reasons, they are nevertheless the Lord's children. As far as responsibility goes, we have no excuse; we must take care of them. In the past it was our lack of concern or shortage of care that brought them to their poor condition. This is a shortage on our part. Now the Lord is leading us to recover the organic function of all the members. This is the business not only of the elders, the co-workers, and the full-timers but also of every child of God. The new way that the Lord is leading us to take today is a way in which everyone functions organically, every member operates effectively, and every home serves fervently. If we do this, we will nourish and care for more people, and the church will increase and spread.

After such a "census," the elders should announce in the meetings that they intend to create a file of all the saints who reside in their area, whether or not they have been meeting regularly with us. Even those believers who no longer live like believers, but live like heathens, should have their names in this file. If we do this, a hall with two hundred members may suddenly find itself with more than five or six hundred names. After this, the elders, co-workers, and full-timers should take the lead to divide up the regular attendants into groups to make a "grand sweep." This may be compared to conducting a spring cleaning, where lost stationery and other items are found one by one. Then the saints must visit the homes one by one to find and recover the lost saints who were saved many years ago.

After such an initial visitation, the elders should assign the saints to care for and revisit the lost ones based on the strength and capacity of the saints and the practical needs. The elders should call a meeting, gather the brothers and sisters together, and present the real situation to them. They should be charged to pick up the burden to seek the lost sheep. If all the brothers and sisters do this, even though we may not witness a complete success, the results will be decisive. If there are too many names and the assignments cannot be completed in one meeting, they can be distributed gradually at other opportune times.

We may take hall sixteen as an example. At present, there are about two hundred saints meeting in fifty homes. If there are two hundred fifty dormant ones, every home will need to take care of only five names. Such a burden will not be too heavy on any one home. If every home is faithful to rise up, in a short time more than half of these dormant ones will be recovered. If the one thousand homes in the church in Taipei will all do this, recovering one person per week, one thousand people will be recovered every week. I believe if we work faithfully and diligently in this way, in three months we will recover at least a third of these dormant ones. This is not a small matter. Hence, this is the first thing that we need to practice.

I hope that the elders will practice this immediately. Gather the records of the saints together, classify them, and convey the burden of the care for these dormant ones to the brothers and sisters through local conferences. The elders should consider each home as a unit and in the meetings should solemnly charge the head of each household to take care of these names. They should charge the head of each household to pick up the burden to lead the entire family to pray for these names. To be sure, as long as that home will pray for these people, every spirit in that home will be revived and rekindled. I believe the Lord's grace will accompany this work, and the Spirit of the Lord will join us in our labor. If we do this, in three months we may recover three thousand people.

From now on, we cannot take care of our work in a general way. We must work according to a schedule with a proper budget. Our goal is that in three months we will recover one-third of the dormant ones. If we do this three times, we will need only nine months to recover most of the saints. Where there is a will, there is a way. It all depends on whether we are willing to do this. To be sure, if we do not clean up our house, the house will be a mess. If no one "sweeps," surely we will find trash everywhere. However, if I sweep a little, you sweep a little, and every person and every household takes care of its sweeping, the cumulative result will be a clean neighborhood.

In everything, the most difficult step is the first one. If we are to do this, the responsible brothers must take the lead. This is our responsibility. We must go back to our halls to stir up the spirits of the saints. Do not speak in a general way; that will not work. Instead, we need to plan out a definite course of action and work out a schedule. For example, we can set a goal of recovering one-third of the dormant ones in the first three months, the next third in the second three months, and finally the last third in the last three months. The elders and the co-workers must be definite and "scientific" in the way they work. We must pass out the records to the saints, take the lead in the practice, and supervise the work every step of the way.

We must not merely give orders; that will not work. Learn to fellowship with the brothers and sisters and offer some practical suggestions and proposals. These dormant saints were baptized by us. They are our responsibility, but for many years we have neglected them. This was our lack. Now the

Lord has given us a new leading and a new practice to make up our lack. We should all rise up to respond to this. Of course, this does not mean that we should ignore the big meetings. We should still take care of the Lord's Day morning meetings. For the sake of those who need such a meeting, we should not dismantle this structure. However, we should pay attention to the small groups. The small groups are our life pulse. We must give our all and be desperate for the small groups. Although it is not easy to overturn tradition, we should look to the Lord's blessing, and we should pray that the home meetings will bring in a success in the near future.

The principle of the New Testament is the principle of incarnation. In the New Testament, God cannot do anything without the cooperation of the "flesh." I have never heard of anyone being saved through an angel alone; the preaching of the gospel must come through human beings. In Acts 10 the angel could only tell Cornelius to invite Peter to preach. If I were Cornelius, I would have said to the angel, "Since you are here already, why not preach the gospel to me directly? Are you not more qualified than Peter? Why don't you preach to me?" The interesting thing is that the gospel must be preached through human beings. It must be preached in the principle of incarnation.

What I fear the most is our "spiritual" teachings. I cannot tolerate such "spiritual" teachings. These teachings say that we should not do anything in an artificial way. We should not promote anything, but we should look to the leading of the Holy Spirit and the prompting of the Lord. I would ask the ones who have taught such teachings, "Where is the result of your looking and waiting?" Thirty years have passed. Where is the result? If we are to meet the practical needs, we cannot settle for mere theories. If we continue to wait, Taiwan will not be evangelized in another thirty years. The dormant ones will remain dormant.

We need to wake up. The older elders and co-workers among us have been "waiting" and "seeking" for the Lord's leading for more than thirty years. Some of our sons have become elders during this time, but what has become of the church? I hope that we will all wake up and realize that this is a dead-end street. We should not be stuck in a blind alley. We should not wait to die. Even if we were to wait until the Lord comes back, our "waiting" and "seeking" would result in a dead end. We must take another way. We are frustrating the Lord's leading. The timing is not in the Lord's hand but in our hand. Any time we rise up to work, the Lord's leading is there. What is the Lord's timing? It is whatever time we stand up to do something for the Lord.

My fellowship today is not meant to be a yoke. Everyone can practice this. It is not a burdensome yoke for each family to take five names and joyfully visit them as believers in the Lord. It is a light burden. In practice, when the saints go out to visit, we can tell them that they do not need to make all five visits in one evening. They can visit these families one at a time. Neither is it necessary to knock on their doors; they can first call them on the telephone. As long as we persist stead-fastly, we will surely see the result. This is the principle of spiritual blessing. All living things grow in small increments, yet eventually such growth fills the earth. Now the Lord has shown us a clear picture. We need to overturn our old practices and habits. This is not merely a "diversification" movement, but a turn to make everyone grow and function. I hope that we will take this advice and carry it out in a practical way.

THE ONLY WAY
BEING TO LABOR DILIGENTLY

Although such a practice is not a burden, it requires much labor. In farming, for example, one must work with his two hands. Removing stones, digging, plowing, tunneling, and irri-gation require one to work with his two hands. Every day the farmer needs to do some work. When I was young, the older generation told me, "The size of the harvest depends not only on the land but also on the hand." Even when we were snowbound in winter and no one could work in the fields, we were not idle at home. The entire family worked in preparation for the spring. The Chinese divide the year into twenty-four "seasons" with certain tasks for each season. This reflects the cumulative experience of their labor throughout the centuries.

Today we are in the scientific age. Everything is done by machines, yet labor is still necessary. Science and machinery can reduce only the work but not the labor. If the owner of a business does not labor day and night, he cannot compete with others and cannot make money. If we are managers but work only as much as our employees do—eight hours a day for five and a half days a week—our business will soon shut down. There is only one way to succeed—laboring and endeavoring with all of our time.

We must not think that the Jews are much more capable than others. Their success lies not in their capability but in their endeavoring spirit. In New York there are more than three million Jews. They have become what they are through their hard labor. While others work eight hours a day, some of them work more than ten hours a day. A Jewish friend of mine told me these things. Now some of the Chinese are taking this same way in the United States; they give themselves to work, and they are making progress quickly. Some Chinese were not this way when they were in their home country, but once they migrated to the United States, they realized that the circumstances did not allow them to relax anymore. When they relax, others move ahead of them. Today many Chinese students are ranked at the top not only at the college level but also at the high school level. They are forced into such achievements by their circumstances.

Many times I have considered before the Lord how to present this matter to the brothers and sisters. I have considered how to convince all the saints to labor diligently and practically. To be sure, if we take this way, the churches in Taiwan will have a breakthrough. I cannot pray, "Lord, grant all the saints sufferings and persecutions so that they will be forced to strive and labor." I can only exhort and bother everyone patiently. We must take the actual steps one by one. Do not try to take any shortcuts. Do not try to be quick, and do not expect too much. Never think that as long as the elders come together to fast and pray for a week, the church will have a great revival. This will not work. Do not take this way. Of course, we need to pray, and I hope that the elders would spend more time praying. But I also would like to see us spending

the time every day to work while we pray. Do not merely tell
the brothers and sisters to work; we have to work ourselves,
and we should bring others into the work and labor with them
side by side.

LABORING WITH GOD
TO WORK ON THE HOME MEETINGS

I hope that the co-workers will labor in the same way. I
have been a co-worker for many years. I know what you are
thinking. Every worker desires to have power and a gift. He
likes to see dozens, even hundreds, listening to his preaching.
However, today we must go to every home. We need to visit
the weak, strengthen the sick, and recover the dormant ones.
Is this beneath you? This is not beneath us. This is what the
co-workers should be doing in the first place. There are all
manner of burdens upon me that prevent me from doing this,
but if I were not so burdened, I would happily engage in this
work and contact the saints one by one. I hope that from
today onward, the co-workers would not crave the big meetings but would love the home meetings. Do not despise the
home meetings. Their results last forever, and they increase
and multiply. Perhaps we serve one home today. When the
relatives of this home are touched, we may end up with a fivefold multiplication. This is the genuine way for the church to
increase and spread.

In the past we spoke, shouted, and labored from the
podium for many years. What was the result? Every so-called
Christian worker has the secret desire of becoming a spiritual
giant. Even if a co-worker among us cannot be a Peter, one
who now is dead and gone, he at least wants to be a Billy
Graham or a Witness Lee. This is a terrible thought. The
young brothers and sisters among us should not have this
concept. This will kill our spiritual life. We should not have
this kind of concept. I have said before that when I first began
to serve the Lord, I did not dream of any great success. I was
ready to take my Bible to all the villages and hamlets to
preach the gospel, drinking from the mountain streams and
filling my hunger with roots and the bark of trees. I hope that
we will have a right motive, a clean heart, and a proper spirit.

Even if we have a doctorate degree, we should still serve the Lord in this way.

THE PATTERN OF THE MISSIONARIES

Since my youth I have admired the missionaries very much. In my hometown the missionaries were all highly educated scholars. They came from England and the United States. Many of them were more than sixty years of age, yet they still had a spirit of sacrifice, a willingness to suffer, and a heart to give up everything. I was very touched by them. Even though every one of them was a scholar in his own field, they were all willing to go to a backward country like China to preach the gospel and contact people in the rural countryside. One of the most elderly among them was Mr. Go. He was ninety years of age, but he nonetheless went to the streets to contact people. He also gave away a great deal of money to the poor and used this as a means to contact people. His work was very effective. When the Boxer Rebellion broke out in 1900, the unbelievers called the missionaries the "First Devils" and the Chinese Christians the "Second Devils." At the height of the rebellion, the unbelievers had a slogan: "Among the Second Devils spare Chao Tu-nan; among the First Devils spare Mr. Go." Why did they say this? These two were especially kind to people. I saw all these things with my own eyes, and I have to admit that they produced a deep impression on me.

LEARNING BASIC LESSONS
THROUGH THE HOME MEETINGS

I hope that the young full-timers would have the understanding that it is a joy to consecrate ourselves to the Lord. Yet we must not think that we have consecrated ourselves to be a spiritual giant with a great name and a large following. The Lord may be gracious to us, and He may make us such a person one day. But surely that is not the way for us to take today. If we want to serve the Lord and work for Him, we should begin from the homes. We should go to people's homes and meet with them in their homes. Since the church is led by the Lord to practice the home meetings, we need to consider the homes as the goal of our work. We must work on the homes. We must not wait for the elders to make the arrangements, nor should we wait for the senior co-workers to take the initiative. Simply pray, "Lord, I have to work on the home meetings. I must work on the home meetings." We must not choose only the good homes to work on. The good homes do not need us; to work on them is merely to add more icing on the cake. We need to work on the homes that are not so good, on those who are weak, backslidden, lacking in nourishment, dormant, and even at the brink of denying the Lord's name. We must squeeze our way into these homes. We may not succeed in getting into every one of these homes, but I believe that at the very least we can succeed in getting into one home.

If we work on the home meetings conscientiously, we will learn many lessons. The period in which I learned the most lessons in preaching the gospel and contacting people was during the years around 1940. I spent more time in those years than in other years preaching the gospel. From 1938 to 1943 I preached the gospel very often. In my hometown of Chefoo, on my bicycle I visited both the saints and the unbelievers every day. During these visits, I met people who were possessed by demons, people who were sick, and people who were in all manner of strange conditions, and I dealt with them one by one. From these experiences, I learned many lessons. There is nothing wrong with being trained and receiving spiritual education. But we still should enter into the practice, and we must learn how to deal with people one by one.

A FEW POINTS
CONCERNING OUR PRACTICE

If the elders, co-workers, and full-timers in the Lord's recovery will pick up this burden, and if all the churches and all the halls will practice this, that is, to sort out the records and charge the brothers and sisters to take action together, the impact will be tremendous. If we do this, I believe that in three months one-third of the dormant saints will be recovered. If the saints pick up the burden to recover the dormant ones, they themselves will be firmly established and rooted. There will no longer be the need to worry about the saints. We must be clear and firm about this point. We need to labor and strive diligently, and we must be thorough in our endeavor.

Do not despise this kind of practice. Do not think that lofty spiritual theories and deep spiritual principles can be easily applied in practice. Do not think that all we need to do is to go to the homes and stir up people, and that there is not much to this work. If we have these kinds of thoughts, we are very wrong. Do not think that it is a simple thing to stir people up. With some people, we simply cannot do anything with them, yet when another person comes along, he is stirred up. There are secrets, keys, and skills to this. The key is the truth. We must study the truth very much. If we are rich in the truth, our labor will not be in vain, and the chance of failure will be minimized. When others hear our speaking, they will know that we have a high standard of spiritual education. We cannot fake this. Some jobs cannot be done by people with only a junior high education; they require someone with a higher education. In order to carry out our present practice, we need the equipping of the truth.

Before I dropped my job to serve the Lord full time, I was working in a foreign firm. Sometimes the young courier working there could not deliver packages to the customs office or the post office, and he would come back and report this to me. I would rebuke the courier for his inefficiency. Then, since I was the only senior staff member in the office who could speak Chinese, I had to take the courier with me and make the trip again. When I got to the post office, I had to say only a few words and the matter was done. The courier was furious, yet he could not lose his temper in front of the postal clerk. The same was true at the customs office—what the courier could not accomplish, I was able to complete with only a few words. Why was there a difference? The young courier did not have enough constitution. When others asked him a question, he could not give an answer that was to the point. When he asked others a question, he also could not make his point. However, when I answered people, everything I said was to the point, and things were handled efficiently and properly according to the correct procedure. This was the reason that I could accomplish the task and he could not. I can say the same thing concerning our home meetings. We must be properly equipped. The more we are equipped, the richer the meetings will be.

There are two sides to the present leading in the churches. On the one side, we need to take care of the big meetings. This will take care of those who come only for messages. On the other side, we need to send the meetings to people's homes. We must care for and nourish the dormant ones and the newly saved ones. On the one hand, we need to apply diligence toward people; on the other hand, we need to have the church meetings. With our present church life, we have both sides. We have the big meetings on the Lord's Day, the bread-breaking meetings, and the prayer meetings. We also have the small group meetings and the home meetings. All these will take care of the needs of the saints as well as bring in the increase and spread of the church.

To have the home meetings is not simply to break up the big meetings into the homes. We have spent much time to study this topic because the home meetings are the life pulse of the church life. They are the key to the increase and spread of the church. When we promote this matter, I hope we will take it seriously. We must pick up the burden from the Lord and work on it in a practical way. On the one hand, we must pass out the records to the saints and charge them to work on the names. On the other hand, we must encourage them to pray much and to persevere in the patience and love of Christ. As long as we do not lose heart, become discouraged, or beaten down, and as long as we continue to seek out and visit these ones, we will see an abundant harvest.

I also hope that the co-workers, elders, and full-time serving ones will take the initiative to labor and work with the brothers and sisters and not allow them to do whatever they want. We cannot merely conduct a survey and then invite those who are "willing" to open their homes to come to meet, but we need to take the initiative to gather the saints and bring the meeting to their homes. Otherwise, some time later the effect will be weakened, and fewer saints will be willing to cooperate. This is an exhausting and laborious job which requires the co-workers and elders to pay undivided attention to promote this.

CONCERNING THE CARE
OF THE FULL-TIME SERVING ONES

A year and a half ago, we spoke about the matter of producing full-time serving ones. At that time, based on our experience and through our observation and study of the ways in which Christians have served throughout the centuries, we were convinced that we could not take the way of organization. Instead, we had to follow the Lord's leading. In Taiwan we have a particular situation with its particular needs and particular means of supply. We felt that we could produce almost a hundred full-timers a year. It is right, of course, not to trust in any organization. But it is not proper to be floundering around without any definite leading. For this reason I suggested that we should produce one full-timer out of every twenty saints. His or her needs would be taken care of and covered by the other nineteen saints. This is a basic principle. In practice, if a church or a hall produces a full-timer, that church or hall should take care of that full-timer. All the elders and co-workers should be clear about this.

However, until now this arrangement has not been implemented in a practical way. Some full-time sisters have given birth to a baby. Other full-time saints are sick. How should we take care of these special cases? These are details, but I would like to cover them in a clear way. In principle, when a full-timer is produced by a church or a hall, that church or that hall has the responsibility to take care of him in a good way. This means that the elders should contact those who have a desire to serve full-time. We should try to find out if such ones should actually serve full-time and, if so, for how long and how they should be cared for. With those who are already serving full-time, the elders should look into their living. Some may serve for only one or two years, after which they will take up a job again. Furthermore, some may be supported by their family or their own savings and do not need any support from the church. With others, the church must take care not only of the serving ones but of their families as well. We need to fellowship these matters with the full-timers in a thorough way. We should know their real situation and find out their real need. Then we must take care of them according to their condition and their present circumstances.

It is easy for us to take the way of organization. But if we do not take the organizational way and instead take the way of following the Lord absolutely, we must be watchful moment by moment, and we need to exercise diligent care and oversight. Actually, we do not have a choice; we can take the Lord's way only. This is the genuine way of those who love the Lord and who have consecrated themselves to Him. Nevertheless, the elders have the responsibility to fully know the condition of the full-timers. In this way we can supply them according to their need. In practice, the elders should not be too legal or set. We should have much fellowship and should try to understand the real situation. We should render the proper supply with full consideration of the overall economic situation of the community. In this way there will neither be an overabundance nor a lack in their care.

The elders must put their heart and mind to this matter. We should care for the full-timers like caring for our own children. We should be flexible and address the needs as they arise. This will cover all the needs in a good way. All parents know that even though all their children are their own offspring, they cannot treat them all in the same way. There are differences in condition, need, character, and disposition, and each must be treated properly according to his or her situation.

The full-timers themselves need to have a clean living. They should not be lavish but should take care of their conscience before the Lord, not being greedy or covetous, and not exhibiting their secret needs before men with the hope of getting more help. This is wrong. They must do their best to have a clean living before the Lord and to maintain a proper conscience. If they receive more from the Lord, they should learn to give away some of what they have. The Lord Jesus taught us that it is more blessed to give than to receive (Acts 20:35). We do not like to have outward regulations, control, and restrictions. Rather, we want to give everyone the opportunity to learn to live before the Lord and to fear Him.

Some have asked me, "If this is the case, will not some

take advantage and receive more?" My answer has been, "We must trust in the Lord." Such selfishness can happen in the world, but it cannot happen in the church, because we all take care of our conscience to have a clean living before the Lord. Everything is in the Lord's hand; the Lord will uphold His own testimony. To be sure, if we take care of others, the Lord will take care of us. If a co-worker or full-timer is faithful to the Lord, he will truly find excess in his hands; then he must learn to give it away—the more the better. We must exercise not to waste anything, spend little on ourselves, and save as much as we can so that we can care for others.

There are two sides to this matter. On the one hand, the brothers and sisters along with the whole church should care for the full-time serving ones before the Lord faithfully in love. On the other hand, the full-time serving ones should take care to maintain a clean living and an unfeigned conscience. If by the Lord's grace we do our best to give to others, the Lord will richly bless us and place us in abundance. If we practice this, the Lord will have a way among us. Those who receive much will not be in excess, and those who receive little will have no lack.

CHAPTER TEN

BRINGING THE CHURCH TO THE HOMES
AND BRINGING THE SAINTS INTO THE TRUTH

In this chapter we will speak about the principles of the home meetings, which are everyone speaking, no one assuming the headship, and every home having a meeting. In order to have everyone speaking, we need to begin with the training meetings of the co-workers and elders. This training of the co-workers and elders has continued for five or six weeks, yet the more we have met, the more silent many of us have become, and I have become the de facto "head." It would be contrary to spiritual principle to ask all the saints to speak when we ourselves remain silent in the co-workers' and elders' meetings. If the co-workers and elders say nothing in these meetings, yet speak much when they return to their own localities, their speaking is a kind of performance. This is hypocrisy.

In translating the book of Matthew, we found out from the original language that the word *hypocrisy* actually means "the putting on of a mask." This indicates a performance. In Greek this word means not merely a false show or pretense but the putting on of a mask or make-up; hence, it is a performance. For example, a young man can put on a mask of an old man and thus present himself as an old man. I hope that the co-workers and elders are not performing or putting on masks. Instead, everyone should be speaking. Instead of making me the "head," all of us should forget about being the "head."

When a person opens his mouth, he is immediately exposed. Matthew 26:73 tells us that after Peter denied the Lord three times, someone identified him, saying, "You also are one of them, for your speech also makes it clear that you are." The best way to hide oneself and remain anonymous is to remain silent. But remaining silent is actually the putting on of a mask. Once we open our mouth, our real self is exposed. This should in fact be the way we are in the home meetings. We should be open to one another. There should not be any masks. We should come simply as we are. Once we come as we are, we are no longer pretentious, and it becomes easy to mutually support one another in spirit, to supply one another, and to be built up together. We must drop our masks and speak the truth in love. This is one secret to the home meetings.

At present, we are in "the season of speaking"; everyone should speak. If we do not speak, it is like a rainy season with no rain. I beg the elders and co-workers to open their mouths to speak because I want to know how we are all doing in the above three matters.

THE NEW WAY BEING THE LORD'S LEADING IN HIS RECOVERY TODAY

I hope we will understand that the new way is the Lord's leading among all the churches in His recovery today. We should not consider this matter to be merely my burden or concern. All of us need to change our concept and accept this burden as our burden. It will be difficult to carry out the new way if we do not have the same burden and feeling.

In order to have a feeling for this matter, we must first have a clear picture. Christianity has made all the life matters unclear and muddled, including the operation of the Spirit and the function of the Lord's word. Christianity has taken on many kinds of ways. For example, organization is one of their ways. Control is a way; outward arrangement is a way; fund-raising is another way. The effectiveness of Christianity today depends fully on these four ways: organization, control, arrangement, and fund-raising. If these four things are taken away from Christianity, nothing will be left.

We should examine the present condition of the Lord's recovery in the light of these four things. If we take away organization, control, arrangement, and fund-raising, will the church still exist? Before the Lord we have received a concern and burden to rid ourselves of these four things in His recovery. We want only the Lord's life, His Spirit, and His word. We do not want any organization, control, arrangement, or fund-raising.

In mainland China the Communists took these four things away from Christianity. They thought that by doing so, Christianity would be through. It is true that Christianity as a religion was through, but Christ is not through. The Lord's life, His Spirit, and His word are not through. The taking away of the above four matters actually provided an opportunity for greater growth. This surprised the Communists, so they began to organize their own kind of "Christianity." Actually, they are atheists; they do not believe in Christ. Their purpose in organizing was to control, restrict, and thus curb Christianity. The enemy knows that if he fails to destroy the Lord's work through persecution, he can still resort to control through organization. Among the so-called Christian countries, the result of the development of such organization in Christianity has been the evolution of the clergy-laity system.

I would like to point out that we are not blind. The Lord has shown us clearly that while He was on earth, there was no organization, control, arrangement, or fund-raising. When He had needs, some of the women gave their money to minister to those needs and those of His disciples (Luke 8:2-3). In Acts the apostles did not resort to any kind of organization, control, arrangement, or fund-raising. However, I am afraid that the brothers and sisters are still under the influence of old concepts. They may have heard the truth, but the old concepts still remain with them. I hope that all the co-workers, elders, and full-time serving ones would rid themselves completely of these old concepts and fully pick up the new way that the Lord has led us to take in His recovery.

In the Bible we do not find such things as organization, control, arrangement, and fund-raising. The Bible reveals to us that God gave man life and breath, and He wants man to receive Him as life by taking the tree of life. Although man fell, Christ came to accomplish redemption. Furthermore, He became the Spirit to reach man and to speak to man. Life, the Spirit, and the word—these are the three precious things that God has given to man. From the beginning of the Old Testament, we find these three things, but Judaism came in and gradually developed a kind of organization. God sent the prophets to the Jews to speak to them, and the Spirit followed the prophets. Once the prophets spoke through the inspiration of the Spirit, life followed and worked on man. The picture is even clearer in the New Testament. The Lord Jesus came as life (John 11:25), and He came to speak God's word. Moreover, He gives to us the Spirit without measure (3:34). We need to preserve and maintain these three precious things— life, the Spirit, and the word. We must reject anything apart from these three things.

Some may ask, "Do we still need the meeting halls?" Strictly speaking, we can do without the meeting halls. The meeting halls are dispensable. We can meet even if we do not have the meeting halls. When the Lord Jesus was on the earth, He did not have any meeting hall, yet He met with the disciples all the same. A genuine church will increase continuously even when it does not have a meeting hall.

The four Gospels tell us that when the Lord Jesus was on the earth, He used the Jewish synagogues. He was not there to participate in the so-called "services"; He went to call men out from the fold. He led people out of the Sabbath tradition on the Sabbath day. Christianity, however, has created another, new Sabbath; it has invented its modern "synagogue." We also see this with the disciples of John the Baptist. John came out of Judaism and rejected the legal Jewish formalities, but his disciples created a new religion based on his work. This is regrettable. The Lord Jesus said, "John came neither eating nor drinking" (Matt. 11:18). John the Baptist did not eat or drink because he was for life, and he had the Spirit with him. However, his disciples preached abstinence as a religion. When they saw that the Lord dined and drank with sinners, they interrogated Him, saying, "Why do we and the Pharisees fast much, but Your disciples do not fast?" (9:14).

Today we need to change our concept. For two thousand years God has been doing the work of recovery, the goal of which is to reject everything that is not of life, the Spirit, and the word. Eventually, however, man again has come up with an organization and a way of control. When John Wesley was raised up, he was full of the Spirit and life. But later, when the person was gone, the Spirit, the life, and the word left also, and all that remained was the Methodist Church. One hundred seventy years ago, the Brethren were raised up by the Lord in England. They rejected everything and upheld only the Lord's word. Brother Nee said that the light that came through their exposition of the Word poured out like a cascading waterfall, but among them today life is gone, the Spirit is gone, and the word is gone. The things that remain are the organizations, such as the "Closed Brethren" and the "Open Brethren." We are fearful that we could end up the same way. We should learn the lessons from those who have gone before us.

This is the reason that I am fully determined to risk everything to knock down the old ways practiced by Christianity today and to "sink them under the sea." I hope that the co-workers and elders could see this and respond to this burden. We should change our concept. We are not here for the big meetings, because the big meetings can take care of only some of the people. We must see that it is not enough to depend on the big meetings alone. This is not the way. There is no prospect and no future in this. The Lord Jesus did not go to the synagogue to build up the synagogue. He knew that there was no prospect and no future in such work. He went to the synagogue to gain a group of people. The apostle Paul did the same thing. He was clear that he was sent by God not to build up the synagogue but to bring people out of it. Dear brothers, if we see this, we need to preach this faithfully with all boldness.

In the book *Church Affairs* Brother Nee stressed that our Sunday morning message meeting is absolutely a practice of Catholicism and Protestantism. For us to continue in this way is to walk "in the statutes of the nations" (2 Kings 17:8). He proposed that we overturn this tradition of having a Sunday morning message meeting and change it instead to a gospel meeting. Although he spoke about this, the churches did not respond, and no church took the lead to do anything. If I were to ask today whether or not we want to maintain the Lord's Day morning meeting as we have in the past, we may all say yes. However, if we do this, it will be difficult to promote the practice of the new way.

I do not mean that we should drop the big meetings or that we should disband them. It is good to utilize them, but it is not good to consciously build them up. This is similar to what the Lord Jesus and the apostles did. They utilized the synagogues, but they did not build up the synagogues. Brothers, we should all be clear about this, and we should pick up this burden to return to our localities to speak and promote this. The first task of a revolution is the work of propaganda. In the same way, in practicing the new way, we must first have the promotion. Recently I heard at least three brothers who stood up and said, "We need to propagate Brother Lee's burden. We need to work out Brother Lee's burden." I beg you not to say this again. We must say, "We need to carry out the Lord's burden. We need to propagate the things that God has entrusted to us." I hope that we all will have this concern and burden and that we will settle for nothing less than the complete overturn of all the old things.

Of course, we must still take care of the big Lord's Day morning meeting because there are still some people who prefer the big meetings. If we do not take care of the big meetings, these people will be lost. However, we must be clear that there is no future or prospect in building up the big meetings. We thank the Lord that recently all the big meetings have been changed to small meetings; each meeting has been split into different places. According to our old concept we wanted to see as many people as possible coming to the big meetings in order to gain new ones. But now in terms of practicing the new way, we would like to see fewer people in such meetings. If a day comes when only five people are left in the big meetings, we should jump for joy. Of course, if there is not an increase in the other meetings, we would mourn in sorrow. What I mean is this: If a day comes when we have five to six hundred people learning the truth in classes of forty or fifty each, but there are only five people left in the so-called big meetings, we should consider this a cause for celebration.

Today we still need to keep the door open to the big meetings. One day when no one "comes to the shop" any longer, we can "close the shop." If, however, the big meetings become bigger and bigger in number, we should find the reason that they are increasing. Let me repeat: The practice of the new way takes care of all aspects of the church life. This is similar to what the Lord Jesus and the apostles did while on the earth. When Paul was in Philippi, he went to a place of prayer by the river (Acts 16:13). This was the place where the Jews and devout Gentiles would go for prayer. Paul did not go there to build up something. He was merely using that place to achieve his purpose. Today we need to do the same. We must use the big meetings, but we are not here to build up the big meetings. Sometimes when the saints have friends and relatives whom they want to bring into the church life, they prefer to bring them to the big meetings. The big meetings are still a place for gaining people. We still need to take care of these meetings, but our emphasis is the home meetings, and we must build up the home meetings.

THE FOUNDATION OF THE CHURCH
BEING THE HOME MEETINGS

A nation is not built upon a school or a club; its foundation is the homes. Without the homes a nation cannot exist. In the same way, if the church is to prosper today, the homes need to rise up. If the homes in the church are strong, the church will have a good prospect and a bright future. This is the new way revealed to us in the Bible. Today in mainland China, Satan hates the churches that meet in the homes. These churches comprise more than fifty million believers. The authorities condemn the "shouters," who are predominantly those who meet in the homes. Some saints have written telling us how strong and revived these home meetings in mainland China are. They have no apparent leaders. Whoever tries to be the leader is asking for trouble because the authorities focus their attention on the leaders. However, when everyone is a leader, the authorities can do nothing.

This is one reason that we are practicing to have no "heads" among us. Rather, everyone should be a speaker. Whoever assumes the headship is asking for trouble. We must learn from the brothers and sisters in mainland China. They have no pastors or preachers. Everyone preaches, and the more they preach, the stronger they become. One preaches to ten, and ten preach to a hundred. In this way the gospel becomes more and more powerful. No one could have believed that within a period of a dozen or so years more than fifty million Christians could be raised up in mainland China. It is possible that in a few years the number could double to one hundred million. One county alone has more than one million Christians. The leading ones have all been imprisoned, and no one wants to be the "head." Yet the saints are still very active and powerful in preaching the gospel. Some of the imprisoned ones have been sentenced to terms of fifteen years, yet they still have small group meetings in their prison cells with some of the guards trying to join them in secret. This is even more than what Paul did. Paul brought the Philippian jailer to salvation, but he did not have meetings in his prison cell. This shows that the practice of everyone speaking is truly the way the Lord ordains and blesses.

We need to see that the real prospect and future of the church lies in the homes. In order to evangelize Taiwan, the first thing we must do is build up the home meetings. Once the home meetings are built up, Taiwan will be gospelized within one or two years. However, if we still depend on our old ways, old organization, and old arrangements, and if we only depend on our past training, I am afraid that Taiwan will not be gospelized in fifty years. I hope that the co-workers and elders would change their view. We need to see this clearly. Once we see it, we will have the burden, and when we speak, our spirit will be released.

The most pressing need now is for all of us to promote this and to persuade others to do this in the various meeting halls. We need to take the lead. The saints will follow us. It will not work if we try to push others to do this but are unwilling to do it ourselves. But if we do it and urge the brothers and sisters to do the same, the result will be a success. I am concerned that the co-workers and elders may feel that they are merely following and obeying the training, merely doing what they have been told. If this is the concept that we have of the practice of the new way, we have failed. We must have the inward light. Our concepts must change. Our eyes must be opened. Only then will we have the boldness to push the saints aggressively. I am not asking that we busy ourselves with the arrangements of the home meetings. I am asking that we stir up the burden and stir up the saints until the saints fight to go to the home meetings. When a person is sick, he has no appetite for food. We cannot force food down his throat. The best way is to stir up his appetite. Once he becomes hungry, he will want food. I hope that the co-workers and elders can make every saint in the churches or the halls a "glutton" for souls; everyone will be starving to save some souls. If we can do this, the home meetings will be successful, and the evangelization of Taiwan will be accomplished.

If we do not change our concept, and if we think that the new way is merely a change of method, from managing big meetings to managing small meetings, from managing small meetings to managing home meetings, and if we think that this can be accomplished easily by mere arrangements, we will find ourselves facing nothing but failure. It would be better if we did not make any arrangements. The minute we make arrangements, everything dies. If we make arrangements for one home, we kill that home. If we make arrangements for a second home, we stifle that home. Then if we make arrangements for a third home, we bury that home. The homes are like plants. If we do not move them, they live, but once we move them, they die. Now we ourselves must first rise up, taking action in an aggressive way. Then we will see others taking action who follow after us. When that happens, the new way will sprout.

A tree is known by its fruit, and parents are known by their children. If we are active in the new way, and if we are hungry for the home meetings, the ones who are saved through us will also be active and hungry. But if we are indifferent and unconcerned about the new way, the ones who are saved through us will also be loose and unconcerned. If we take this attitude, Taiwan will not be gospelized in one hundred years. In a positive sense, all the co-workers and elders from now on must be "hungry wolves," actively gaining people and caring for them.

HAVING MUCH AND ADEQUATE PRAYER

The co-workers and elders must also strengthen their prayer. We need to consider this matter as a burden and pray for it. In order to be a hungry one, one must first be a fasting one. The co-workers, elders, and full-timers need to fast and pray often. It is not too much to fast and pray weekly. We must pray by fasting, saying, "Lord, You must turn the church around absolutely from the old way of Christianity. You must turn us to the home meetings. Burn in every home! Stir up every home!" To merely act a little after I speak is not the way. We need to pick up the burden in a genuine way and pray with this burden pressing heavily upon our shoulders.

Fasting is the result of heaviness of burden and pressure in the spirit. When one becomes so pressed that he is unable to eat, he is fasting. Once we pray according to the burden within, the Lord's Spirit will come upon us. When the Lord's Spirit comes upon us, something will happen. This is different from a mere change of method. Although we speak of changing the system, we are merely borrowing this expression for convenience. In reality, if we have only an outward way without a burden that burns within us, and if we do not fast or pray, this "change of the system" will be an empty shell. It will never bring forth any results.

I have no way to describe the heaviness of my burden. I hope we all will see this and pick up this burden. The need in the Lord's recovery is great, and there is no way for us to meet the need. I have mentioned before that throughout my life of serving the Lord over the past fifty or sixty years in both the East and the West, I have never seen a place like Taiwan today where needs abound. The way the high-rise apartment buildings are constructed today is simply a preparation for the gospel. Within one building there are sixty to seventy homes, and they all share a common entrance. It is easy for everyone to know everyone else. Are we not touched by the situation? Our need today is people. At present, there are approximately ten thousand saints in the church in Taipei.

Among them only four thousand are active members. If we do not work on the homes, and if we do not stir up every home, how can we answer to the Lord, and how can we answer to all the saints?

PRACTICING THE HOME MEETINGS
AND TRAINING THE SAINTS

I have heard that many denominations are now turning their attention to these urban communities and have gained many people from them. However, they are still carrying on their practice in the old way. I hope that when we go to these communities, we will be different. We should practice "universal conscription"; everyone should be a soldier, and every home should rise up. If we stir up the homes with the homes, and if we perfect the homes with the homes, soon twenty homes will be stirred up in a community. Perhaps in two years many home meetings will be established in that community. This requires our labor. To depend solely on the one or two hundred co-workers and elders that we have here can be compared to attempting to quench one's thirst with only a drop of water. What we need to do is stir up the homes. Of course, we cannot wait until all the homes are stirred up before we begin our work. On the one hand, we need to make personal visits to the communities, and on the other hand, we need to train the saints through the practice of the home meetings. If we cannot break through in the matter of the home meetings, we will not be able to have an army. Every home that is stirred up becomes a part of the army.

During the Second World War, after the bombing of Pearl Harbor, the United States could not enlist the adequate number of fighting men by the standard way. The government opened up the opportunity for anyone interested to join the army. As a result, the number of volunteers more than met the demand. The American government also diverted its resources and turned many factories into arsenals. In this way all the needs were met. Today in Taiwan we need to evangelize the entire island. The Lord has provided us with an open door. If we have three to five thousand people responding to this need, we will gospelize Taiwan in at least two years.

I have heard reports of the visitation work in the communities. These reports are very encouraging. We are well received and many people are open to us. Although we do not have the adequate manpower, we should still endeavor to do this work. In particular, the full-time trainees should go out at least twice a week. I have made the decision that when we go out again, we will match two young full-timers with one older saint. I believe that there will be more open doors because of this, and people will take our gospel even more seriously. The training center in Taipei needs to plan, and the co-workers and elders must take the lead to encourage the working saints and the elderly saints to dedicate some time to go with the full-time trainees to visit the communities and to bring the meetings to people's homes.

BRINGING THE MEETINGS TO THE HOMES

To bring the meetings to the homes is the very heart of the God-ordained way. It will be a great failure in the Lord's recovery if we cannot bring the meetings to the homes. For the past twenty years in the Lord's recovery, we have been bringing people to the meeting halls. The more we work in this way, the fewer people we have, and the worse the condition of the homes becomes. More and more our meetings have become a kind of Sunday morning service. In Christianity many people "go to church" to listen to the singing of hymns and to attend the "service," but their homes are deplorable; their tables may still be scattered with mah-jongg game pieces. In the morning the family attends the service, but in the afternoon the mah-jongg game goes on in the homes. In order to overturn this degraded situation, we must bring the meetings to the homes. I hope that every home will be mobilized, that everyone will become a soldier, and that together we will become an army of the Lord.

At present in Taipei there are about sixty new urban communities. Let us suppose that we can set up a center for meeting in every community, and every center takes care of fifty people. Immediately we will have three thousand people. If each center takes care of one hundred people, we will have six thousand people. This is not a small matter. This is the reason that we must endeavor to work on the communities.

BEING LIVING IN TEACHING *TRUTH LESSONS*

Recently I took some time to observe the teaching of the truth classes in hall one in Taipei. On the one hand, the brothers took my word and stayed away from free expounding, keeping themselves instead to teaching the text. On the other hand, as the brothers have followed my words, they have become somewhat "robotic"; they no longer act according to the leading of the Spirit. If asked why they are doing what they are doing, they may say, "Brother Lee told us so." I would like to point out the shortages here according to my observation.

First, your spirit is not strong enough. When you are teaching, you are not exercising your spirit. There are two ways to teach. One way is the institutional teaching, the teaching in the schools. In this case the teacher reads or teaches, and the students are occasionally asked to read. This kind of teaching does not require the exercise of the spirit. The other kind of teaching is the teaching in the church. This requires the spirit. If we do not exercise our spirit, we will turn *Truth Lessons* into a school textbook. If neither the teacher nor the students exercise their spirit while reading *Truth Lessons,* the result will be a killing meeting where people come merely to warm the pews and sleep. Throughout all these years, we have been taught that our meeting is a matter of the exercise of the spirit. Any time we meet, we must stir up our spirit and exercise our spirit. This is not a matter of being loud or soft. It is a matter of exercising the spirit. When we exercise our spirit, we can read in a living way. If we do not exercise our spirit, we will read in a mechanical way. I have pointed out that there are many ways to read *Truth Lessons.* We can read them with life, with repetition, with emphasis, with prayer, with explanation, and with singing. However, no matter how we read them, the key is to exercise the spirit.

In our reading we should not be legal but flexible. While we read, we can ask questions to emphasize the main points. As I have said before, in order for a chicken to live, it needs feathers, skin, and bones. The feathers are worthless, but without the feathers the chicken cannot exist. In the same way today, while we are serving others, we must remove the "feathers" and the "skin" from the "meat." Once in a while we may also serve the "bones," but the main thing we serve others is the "meat." When we ask questions, we should not concentrate on the "feathers" or "skin." Rather, we should give others the "meat." We need to know what the meat and the feathers are. If our questions are on the main points, we can ask ten questions, and the time will still be well spent.

We may take the outline of the Old Testament as an example. I have no intention to teach the brothers and sisters history. Yet most of the thirty-nine books of the Old Testament are a record of history. Without history, the Old Testament would be like a chicken without bones, feathers, and skin. However, if someone merely focuses on the history when reading the Old Testament, he will be lost, unable to understand what he is reading. For this reason, in writing *Truth Lessons,* I gave a general sketch of the history of the Old Testament. The main points, however, are the spiritual matters related to life. If we have the discernment, we will spontaneously pick up the meat, that is, the spiritual points and the points related to life. We will not read the lessons in a dead or legal way.

We should not merely run through a lesson in a nondescript way. To do so is to take the way of classroom teaching. Such reading does not differentiate the meat from the bones and feathers. In reading, we must separate the bones, feathers, and skin from the meat. When we come to the important points, we need to read with emphasis. If we do this, the meeting will be living, and the message will be nourishing. In editing the materials, I have purposely left out many bones, skin, and feathers and have kept the meat. For example, with the twelve books of the Minor Prophets, the main points are the meaning of the names of the prophets and their prophecies, especially their prophecies concerning Christ. The main purpose of the material is to show everyone that all the prophets in the Old Testament spoke of Christ. Although I included the background, history, and dates related to these prophets and their spiritual significances in the lessons, the goal of the lessons is to show the reader a picture of the entire "chicken." When we teach, we need to bring out these main points. The thing that bothers me the most is that none of us have presented these main points in a clear way. This is a great loss. It defeats the whole purpose of teaching *Truth Lessons*.

At the end of each lesson there is a summary and some questions. This is the most crucial portion of the lesson and contains the real significance of the entire lesson. All the teachers should first study the summary and ponder the questions. Then they will know the main points. In teaching, we should impart the main points into others. We should speak, ask questions, and answer with our spirit, and we should read these portions with repetition and emphasis. If we do this, in one hour we will give the attendants an impression of the main points concerning Christ.

THE RESPONSIBILITY OF THE ELDERS

First Timothy 3:2 says that one of the qualifications of an elder is to be apt to teach. I hope that every elder would participate in the teaching of the truth lessons on the Lord's Day morning. The elders should not excuse themselves from this responsibility simply because others can teach better than they can. They must be teachers. First Peter 5:3 indicates that the elders must take the lead in everything, becoming patterns of the flock. If the elders do not take the lead in teaching but assign this responsibility to others, they are acting contrary to God's word. Even if others can do a better job of teaching, they should still take the lead in teaching. By doing this, the elders will be forced to learn the truth and speak the truth. In principle, the elders should know more of the truth than the other saints.

Today in practicing the new way, we need every saint to speak. If the elders only encourage others to speak, yet they themselves do not speak, they are left without any excuse. No elder in the Lord's recovery should be an "honorary" elder. Every elder should be a practical and useful elder. The first responsibility of an elder is to teach. This is the greatest need of a church. If we read the Bible carefully, we will find that there is not much mention of the affairs that the elders should handle. This proves that the scriptural requirement concerning the elders lies in teaching, supplying life, shepherding and care, becoming patterns of the flock, and not so much in the arrangement of affairs or the management and organization of the church. Strictly speaking, once the church life is built up in the saints' homes, there will not be much need for the arrangement of affairs and organization. At that time the elders should take the lead even more in learning the truth, learning to speak, and teaching the truth.

This is the grace that the Lord has reserved for the elders. You need to be a few steps ahead of the saints. You should know the truth a little more than the saints so that you can fulfill your responsibility in the church. The foremost requirement of the elders is to be apt to teach. Never surrender such responsibility of teaching to other brothers and act merely as an overseer. Even if others are more gifted, the elders should still take the lead in this matter. By taking the initiative and participating, they induce others to follow. By this practice a good foundation will be established.

The Chinese have a saying, "Champions are found among the students, not among the teachers." Sixty years ago there was a famous opera singer in Chinese drama; everyone knew him, but no one knew who his teacher was. I am not a "champion," but I truly hope that everyone taught by me would become a "champion." If you learn and put into practice what I have taught you, I believe you will do a better and more excellent job of teaching than I can. If you do this, the teaching of the truth lessons will be living, with much spirit, having a good grasp of the main points, and with much supply of life.

In Chinese cooking, one famous dish is plain steamed fish. The whole fish is steamed, and the original taste of the fish, including the head, the fins, the tail, and even the bones, is retained in the cooking. The fish is very tasty and fresh. Because Westerners do not like the bones in fish, they usually cut the fish into fillets and throw away the head, the fins, the tail, and the bones. However, the taste is sometimes lost in this way. Today we are not here to serve merely the "fish fillet"; we must learn to cook our "plain steamed fish." If we teach the truth lessons in this way, we will make them tasty and appealing.

A FINAL WORD

The burden in this message is first to bring the church to the homes, and second to bring the saints into the truth. If we can achieve these two points, the new way will succeed, the gospelization of Taiwan will be realized, and there will be a bright future in the Lord's recovery. Therefore, we need to give our all to do these two things. We must build up the home meetings, and we must teach the truth. I hope that we will pray much before the Lord for these two matters.

CHAPTER ELEVEN

HOW TO USE THE SPIRITUAL PUBLICATIONS AND HOW TO TEACH *TRUTH LESSONS*

THE PRACTICE AND PROGRESS OF THE NEW WAY

In this chapter we will continue to fellowship about the practice of the home meetings and the teaching of *Truth Lessons*. As a result of the last few meetings, we have seen some results. The brothers are very faithful in putting into practice what they have heard. In their practice they have found some secrets and have made some improvements. I believe that we will make much advancement in the coming days.

I received a very encouraging report. After we divided the small groups into the home meetings, in three weeks our attendance increased by fifty percent, from three thousand to four thousand five hundred. Those attending the truth classes have increased by twenty percent to the current number of three thousand five hundred. This proves that the new way is the right way.

THE NEED TO CARRY OUT THE SMALL GROUP MEETINGS AND THE HOME MEETINGS SIMULTANEOUSLY

We need both the small group meetings and the home meetings. We should not stop the small group meetings because we now have the home meetings. We cannot have home meetings without having small group meetings, that is, meetings that combine two or three families together. On the one hand, we need to encourage the brothers and sisters to open up their homes for meetings. On the other hand, we need to encourage them to have spontaneous small group meetings in their neighborhood with a few other families. They do not need to meet every week; they can meet once every two weeks for fellowship, encouragement, nourishment, mutual help, and inciting. The home meetings and the small group meetings must go together, like the two feet of the human body. The foundation, however, rests mainly in the homes.

We look to the Lord to bring the church on in its practice. As soon as a person is saved, the first thing we should do is open up his home and have meetings in his home. On the one hand, we bring people to salvation through the home meetings. On the other hand, such saved ones, being saved in their homes, will spontaneously have a good impression of and a strong inclination for the home meetings. This is one advantage of saving people in the homes. It is different from the way that we brought people to salvation through the big meetings. Those who were saved in the big meetings did not have a good impression of or a strong inclination for the home meetings. As long as a person is open, even if he is not yet saved, we can bring a meeting to his home.

BRINGING THE MEETINGS TO THE HOMES

The result of bringing meetings to people's homes is considerable. I have story after story to confirm this. Some dormant ones were revived through the saints bringing the meetings to their homes. Many relatives have refused the gospel for many years, but as soon as the meetings go to their homes, they believe, receive the Lord, and are baptized. This is a wonderful thing. It proves that the Lord's leading and what we have seen are right. As soon as we contact someone, we should bring the meetings to his home. The minute he is saved, he should immediately open up his home. He can do this because he was brought to the Lord through the way of bringing a meeting to his home. In the Lord's recovery, this practice should be the fundamental factor in building up the church.

Mormonism is a great heresy in the United States. It tells people that the Lord Jesus was born of a marriage between Mary and Adam. This is a blasphemy. Although Mormonism accepts the Bible, it has its own Book of Mormon in addition to the Bible. Today in America, Mormanism enjoys a strong increase. Its influence worldwide is also quite phenomenal.

Recently in Taiwan, I studied this matter. I was very surprised by the results of my investigation. The Mormon publications clearly state that its "church" is built up by the efforts of its members in opening up their homes. Its practice is the same as what the Lord has impressed us with and commissioned us to carry out. To be sure, we did not pick up anything from them, nor did they learn their practice from us. From the very beginning, they have been teaching their members to build up their homes. In 1973 alone, they increased by one million members. The Mormons now have a presence in Taiwan. Although they have not been in Taiwan for a long time, they are very aggressive. When some of our brothers and sisters visit the homes of new ones, they meet Mormons in the new ones' homes. We need to pray. I feel that Satan is working here, because he knows that the Lord is carrying out the new way in Taiwan during these few years, and he is trying his best to frustrate the Lord's move with his counterfeit move.

USING THE LORD'S WORD TO TEACH ONE ANOTHER IN THE HOME MEETINGS

The Lord has shown us that every saint should meet in the homes. We are now practicing this. At this point in time, we need to pay attention to the use of the Lord's word in a proper way in the home meetings to nourish and lead everyone. We should not ask the saints merely to open their homes, sing a few songs, pray and fellowship a little, have a snack, and then send everyone home. We should help them to realize that all the attendants should learn to teach one another in a mutual way.

In a home meeting, the son in the family can call a hymn, the daughter can lead the prayer, and the mother can begin the fellowship. Everyone can be the "head." In the home meetings we should teach one another in a mutual way. First, we should teach the children, the family members. Next, they in turn should teach others. Of course, we must remember that we should not teach with our own teaching. Rather, we should teach with the Lord's word. A person will receive help in the home meetings only through the Lord's word. The Lord's word is spirit and life. For this reason, every time we have a home meeting, we should render the saints some words of the truth.

CAREFULLY SELECTING THE READING MATERIAL

Such a practice involves an effort on the part of the co-workers and the elders. We must carefully select the proper material for the home meetings. We need to spend an adequate amount of time to pray thoroughly, to observe the condition of the brothers and sisters, and to understand the need of all the homes and the groups. We need to know their conditions, and then we should search out the suitable material from our publications. A mother, in preparing a meal for the family, should consider the condition of all the members of the family. Sometimes one member of the family is sick, and she needs to prepare special food for that one. Sometimes the season changes, and she needs to shop for the proper kind of food. All this takes research as well as common knowledge.

We cannot be nonchalant in the kind of material we use for the home meetings. It is not that as soon as we have a new book, we automatically pass it on to the homes and the groups for their study. This can be compared to a mother going to the market and buying a cartload of watermelons simply because the melons are fresh and inexpensive. If she does that, some who have ulcers will end up in a worse predicament. We may say, "This is too difficult. Who can do this?" Even if this is difficult, we still must do it. If the co-workers and the elders do not do it, it will be harder for the other brothers and sisters to do it. If we make the effort to learn, sooner or later we will pick up the way. The most important thing is to take this matter seriously. We must meet the need of men in a solid way.

Recently, when some co-workers came to the United States to attend the conferences and trainings, I rebuked them, saying, "Look! Everything in Taiwan has advanced. We are the only ones who have not advanced. We are still holding the same standard and doing the same thing as thirty years ago." Now all the co-workers have improved, but we still have not reached the proper standard. We must raise the standard still higher. Although I am a little older than you are and have more experience in the work, I am still learning. I hope that we will all learn. While we work, we should learn at the same time.

Matthew 24:45 says that the faithful and prudent slave distributes food to God's children at the proper time. The meaning of distributing food to God's children at the proper time is profound. It does not mean merely to distribute food according to the seasons but to distribute different kinds of food according to the varying needs. This is something that requires time and research. Suppose we meet a new one, and without any regard for his condition we begin to share with him about the seventy weeks in Daniel. It is true that we are speaking God's word, but that kind of "distributing of food" does not nourish him. Instead, it kills him. God's word is life, but if we do not use it in a proper way, it becomes a killing factor to others. It can spoil a person's appetite; the taste to come to the meeting will be spoiled because what he has heard has not benefited him.

I may have exaggerated a little, but I want us to see the absolute necessity of preparing the right kind of reading material for different meetings. This is in the principle of distributing food according to the proper time. The advancement of the various kinds of meetings hinges on this very matter. Whether or not a meeting brings profit to a person, attracts him, or stirs up the desire within him to join depends fully on this matter.

In 1937 Brother Nee had a co-workers' meeting in Hankow to release the messages on *The Normal Christian Church Life*. I arrived early in Hankow. One day I went to an Episcopalian Church to study its service. I observed the prayers and the sermons. Everything was printed on a sheet of paper. When it was time to pray, the pastor simply turned to the page and read. When the time for the sermon came, he simply read from the pamphlet. That was truly a kind of public reading. It was definitely not in the way of following the Spirit. We cannot follow this way in teaching *Truth Lessons*. On the one hand, we are reading some messages in the meeting, but on the other hand, we do not read them in a formal way like the example of the pastor, assigning one portion for one week, certain material for certain occasions, and praying certain prayers on certain days. We prepare reading material for the meetings because we realize that in the various meetings we cannot expect everyone to be able to deliver a message. In the past the Lord has given us so many riches; our storehouse is full of all kinds of food. As long as we use it in a wise way, we will have more than we need to meet the needs of the saints.

All of us know that during the past years, it was no small achievement for us to have twenty-one meeting halls, each maintaining a message meeting week after week. Now there is no need for us to strain our mind to find the material for a message. We have food in store already. In applying it, however, we should be living and flexible. If we are living and flexible, our delivery will be full of the Spirit. For this reason, we should select the material carefully. This is a matter of life and death. If the material is well selected, others will live. If it is selected poorly, others will die. We can send people home with their hands full or with their hands empty. It all depends on the material we pick. This is a very crucial matter.

I hope we will not listen to the outsiders who slander us. They say, "Brother Lee has changed. He does not want others to speak. He only wants people to read his books. In the past he urged people to read the Life-studies. Now he is going one step further; he is asking people to take his messages as reading material in the church meetings. He is doing this to shut everyone's mouth. No one can speak anymore; everyone has to read his messages." I have read some writings that accuse us of discouraging people from reading the Bible and of restricting people to Witness Lee's publications. These are evil words; as Paul says, "We are slanderously charged and as some affirm that we say…" (Rom. 3:8).

HOW TO USE THE READING MATERIAL

One point needs special attention: In selecting the reading material, we should precede each portion with a few crucial verses. Every time we meet together, we should first have the attendants pray-read the verses. This will plant the Lord's word into man's heart. His word is living, operative, and full of power. We hope that those who come to the meeting will receive nourishment and truth and will testify that we are here for the spreading of the gospel and the presenting of the truth.

Do not underestimate the practice of pray-reading in the meetings. There are three to four meetings a week, and fifty-two weeks in a year. In time, the deposit will add up. As the saints pray-read the Lord's words into them, these words become a deposit in them and serve as their timely supply. We need to pay much attention to this. Never neglect this practice by saying that there is not enough time for pray-reading. No matter how long the meeting is, there should always be three to five minutes for pray-reading a few verses. Even if there is not enough time, we should still take care of this, because this is an indispensable element of the meeting.

In reading the publications, do not be dull or monotonous. A few ways of reading should be avoided. First, we should not have everyone read together except when we come across the crucial sentences. If the whole congregation reads through half a message or an entire message together, that will kill the meeting. Next, we should not have one person read through an entire paragraph. According to my experience, observation, and personal investigation, the best way to read in the small group meetings and the home meetings is for each one to read one sentence. This kind of reading may be difficult at the beginning, but in time it will become easy. I hope all the halls, small groups, and home meetings will promote this kind of reading. I would like to see this practice developed until it becomes our "family tradition."

The churches in the Lord's recovery meet three to four times a week. In one year we meet more than two hundred times. For this reason, it is crucial that we learn to read the messages in a proper way. This can be compared to a ball game; with practice and training, there will be the improvement in skill. If the playing is capricious and there is no restriction and limitation, one can play for years and still not know how to play the game. Today the co-workers, elders, and full-timers must pick up the responsibility. We must take the lead to do it and to learn how to do it. I am asking that we take the lead; I am not asking that we replace others. I am asking that we do it *with* others, not *instead of* others. While we are doing it, we should point out the secret, the key, so that everyone can learn something. The co-workers, elders, and full-timers cannot be silent in the meetings. We cannot close our eyes and simply meditate. The meetings are the times when we "play ball on the court." We need to take the lead to play ball. If the brothers and sisters are playing very well, we can step back. But if they are not playing in the right way, we need to step forward and render the timely corrections. Do not barge in or take over. Rather, teach others until they can play. If we spend time and effort to do this, the church will be built up by our work.

In teaching, we should help the saints to focus on the main points. Take John 3:16 as an example. It says that God so loved the world that He gave His only begotten Son. We need to learn to bring out the word *gave;* that is a main point. Lead the saints to emphasize the word *gave.* Repeat that word. Learn to point out the main points. We do not need to spend much time to explain them. The saints will realize by our hints what the main points are. We must see that our exposition does not carry much weight. The most effective way is to bring out the Lord's word and have everyone pray-read it, directing everyone to the main points. In this way, we will provide everyone with the opportunity to function. No one will stand idle. In order to achieve this, we need to continually lead the brothers and sisters to practice this in the meetings. I believe that in fewer than six months the church in Taipei will produce a model for others to follow.

HOW TO USE *TRUTH LESSONS*

In the past I pointed out that in teaching *Truth Lessons* we should not expound but should only read. The brothers are all very faithful. They took my fellowship. However, there are different ways to read. If we appoint one person to read one paragraph and the next one to read another, we "hang ourselves by a noose" with such a reading. What I mean is that if that person happens to read well, everyone will enjoy his reading, but if that person is a poor reader, the whole meeting will be awkwardly held in suspense. If that person does not exercise his spirit in reading, he will even kill the entire meeting. In teaching *Truth Lessons,* we cannot ask one person to read an entire paragraph.

Directing Everyone to the Main Points in the Reading

I agree that at some crucial juncture we should ask everyone to read together. But the teachers need to control the speed of the reading. We must also direct everyone to the main points. When we come to the main points, we should read with emphasis. While it is true that the teachers should not engage in long expositions, they ought to direct everyone to the main points. From my observation, I have noticed that some teachers fail to direct people to the main points at the crucial junctures. Some are worse; they allow the readers to mumble inaudibly over these crucial points and do not do anything to correct them. The main points are thus completely skipped. Sometimes the main points are contained in only one sentence. The reader may read the entire paragraph but miss that one sentence. Some teachers allow such negligence to occur. This kind of teaching is very poor. It amounts to no teaching at all. If the teachers cannot direct others to the main points and if they allow them to be glossed over, why do we need these teachers at all? The job of the teachers is to direct everyone to the main points.

Take as an example lesson 14 of *Truth Lessons,* Level One, Volume 2. Almost all the teachers have committed the same mistake. The main point in this lesson is that the prophecies and types reveal Christ. There are many prophets in the Old Testament, and whether they speak in types or in prophecies, their focus is Christ. In Luke 24:44 the Lord Jesus told the disciples, "All the things written in the Law of Moses and the Prophets and Psalms concerning Me must be fulfilled." In John 5:39 He said, "You search the Scriptures...and it is these that testify concerning Me." This shows that the entire Old Testament is a testimony, typifying and prophesying Christ. Both the major prophets and the minor prophets have Christ as the focus and the highlight of their prophecies. Unfortunately, most of our teachers do not direct everyone to this point.

Asking Questions

When we teach *Truth Lessons,* asking questions is an expounding, so we need to highlight the main points. When we ask questions, we should not ask about trivial matters. For example, we can ask, "Which prophet had the most detailed prophecies concerning Christ?" When people look at lesson 14 of *Truth Lessons,* they will find that Micah's prophecies concerning Christ occupy only a few lines. He prophesied concerning the birthplace of Christ, when He was to become a man in time, and the goings forth of His Godhead from eternity. But David's prophecies concerning Christ occupy one and a half pages. He spoke about the Lord Jesus from eternity past, passing through His creation, incarnation, human living, death, resurrection, ascension, enthronement, coming back, and receiving the kingdom, all the way to eternity future—His years being without end. If we read the Bible carefully, we will find that even though the Gospels are rich in content, some matters related to Christ are not spoken of as clearly as in David's prophecy. For example, the matter of Christ's being a Priest forever according to the order of Melchisedec is not mentioned in the four Gospels.

When we focus on the prophets, we should ask the saints, "How did this prophet prophesy concerning Christ?" The main point of this lesson is that in the Old Testament there is a group of prophets who prophesied concerning Christ. The Lord Jesus clearly said that both the Law of Moses and the Prophets testify concerning Him. This indicates that the prophets in the Old Testament are for testifying Christ. Hence, when we compiled *Truth Lessons,* we put a special emphasis on this point in presenting the prophets of the Old Testament.

Focusing on Main Points, Not on Dates

Some saints are attracted by dates, and they pay much attention to memorizing them. This amounts to what Paul called "unending genealogies" (1 Tim. 1:4). All the Jews were trapped by this, and Paul said that we should not engage ourselves in this. Of course, history has its place, but history merely tells us that something has happened. There is no need to argue about the dates. From my research and study of the Bible, I have found out that there are at least four or five different schools of identifying dates in the Old Testament history. They all differ by a few years. It is not only impossible to accurately identify dates from a few thousand years ago, it is also sometimes difficult to ascertain dates from only a hundred years ago. The dates are not the main points. The main point is Christ.

I say all this to impress us that we are not here to teach history, geography, or language. We are here to minister Christ. We are here to point out the things concerning Christ in the Bible. For example, in talking about the eight persons in the book of Genesis, we need to point out what we see in Adam, Abel, Enoch, Noah, Abraham, Isaac, Jacob, and Joseph. If we can point out the focus of God's work in these eight persons, we will unveil the meaning of the entire book of Genesis. Throughout the ages many scholars have not seen this. They think that the Bible is a book of history, geography, or science; they have not pointed out the spiritual light hidden within these pages. This, however, is the main emphasis of *Truth Lessons*. We must spend time to enter into all these points.

At present, many places throughout the world are using *Truth Lessons*. In the United States, Europe, Australasia, and Africa, many places are welcoming this publication. They welcome it because it ministers Christ. It points out the things related to the Spirit and life. In teaching these lessons, we must minister Christ. We must point out the things related to the Spirit and life. Everything else is background material. The accessories that come with a diamond ring, such as the frame and the box, are important, but the focus is the diamond itself—its color, the number of carats it has, its shape, and its weight. In teaching *Truth Lessons,* we need to point out the focus and teach by bringing out the emphasis.

CONCLUSION

The key to the success of the new way is the spiritual material we use in the home meetings and the way we teach *Truth Lessons*. If we neglect these two points, we will not reap much result. The focus of *Truth Lessons* is Christ, the Spirit, and life. It is not history, geography, or linguistics. If we exercise these keys in a proper way, I believe we will reap a tenfold harvest. I hope that we will pray much for this.

CHAPTER TWELVE

THE PROPER PRACTICE
IN THE LORD'S RECOVERY

Scripture Reading: Rom. 16:5, 10-15, 23

THE HISTORY OF THE PRACTICE OF THE NEW WAY

One and a half years ago the Lord granted us a new direction in His leading as a means to turn ourselves fully away from the way of traditional Christianity. This is a fact that we all acknowledge. Christianity has made the Lord's church altogether an organization. An organization derives its existence from big meetings with one man speaking and everyone else listening. Such big meetings kill the spiritual life of the believers as well as the function of the members of the Body of Christ. We have seen this clearly from the beginning of the Lord's recovery. Regrettably, in our practice we have been groping for the past fifty to sixty years. As early as 1934, Brother Nee pointed out that the kind of Sunday morning "worship service" where one person speaks and everyone else listens should be dropped. To him that was "the custom of the nations." After fifty to sixty years of searching and groping, we still did not find the way to have the proper practice.

After many frustrations, losses, and setbacks, the Lord has finally brought us to our present way of practice. Thank the Lord. Concerning this way, I still need to fellowship a few points. First, this does not mean that after we have the small group meetings and the home meetings, we can forget about the big meetings. I have said from the very beginning that these two kinds of meetings are like the two wings of an airplane; we cannot have one without the other. The two must go hand in hand. I believe when we put these words into practice, we will see that while we still have the big meetings, our way of carrying them out is entirely different from the way of the denominations.

During the past fifty or sixty years, we have been experimenting with the proper way, but we were not that accurate in our search. As a result, more or less we were still under the old habit of meeting. Now that we are suddenly changing everything to a new way, many of the brothers and sisters may feel uncomfortable about the change. They may not be accustomed to the new practice. Some have said that this new practice is something borrowed from the West and that it will not work in the Far East. Other co-workers have said that the new practice is suitable only for Taipei; it will not work in other places. No matter what is said, I believe one day we will see that this way works even in the farthest corner of the earth, unless, of course, one chooses not to take this way; in such a case, it will certainly not work. It is altogether not too much for me to say this.

THE LIFE PULSE IN THE PRACTICE OF THE NEW WAY—THE HOME

The crucial thing concerning the new way is to have the Lord's salvation realized in a practical way by every saint. We know that the only way anything can be sustained in human society is for it to be carried out in the homes. The home is the place where everything related to human existence is sustained. If we have only individuals in a society without the existence of the homes, nothing related to our human living will last; society will be short of the vessel needed to hold it together. The home is the basic unit of society; it is the foundation of a nation. According to God's Word, the church of God is first the house, household, or home of God (1 Tim. 3:15). After that it is the kingdom of God (Rom. 14:17). It is difficult for God's kingdom to exist without the existence of the homes. Without the home as a basis, it is difficult for individuals to exist, and it is difficult for a nation or kingdom to be established.

Christianity has fallen prey to the wiles of Satan; it has completely overlooked the homes. In Christianity only the big meetings are cared for without any thought of the home meetings. A person in Christianity finds no vessel to hold his experience together. There is no vessel to uphold the testimony and no vessel to keep and maintain the truth. Consider Romans 16. Without a doubt, during the time of the apostles, the church was built up in the believers' homes. We know that the book of Romans is a book dealing specifically with the spiritual life in Christ and the spiritual living in the church. At the end of this book, one entire chapter is devoted to Paul's greeting of the saints. From his greetings, we can see that quite a number of homes were opened to the church. This shows that the church life at the time of the apostles had a very strong home atmosphere. Under Satan's influence, Christianity has completely annihilated this spiritual atmosphere of the homes.

This is the reason that we must endeavor with all the energy, strength, and time that the Lord has given us to recover the proper atmosphere of the homes. The first thing we must do is to make every saint's home a place for meeting. At the present moment, many saints are burdened to open up their homes. This is a great step forward, yet we cannot be satisfied with this initial step. We must not only open up the homes of those who are burdened, but we must also bring the meetings to the homes of those who are not burdened. We hope that every home can be opened to become a place for meeting. Each opened home means one more place for meeting. The smallest places of meeting in a church are the homes of every brother and sister in that church.

LEARNING TO MEET IN THE HOMES

We all need to learn how to have meetings with people in their homes. The co-workers need to learn, the elders need to learn, and the full-timers need to learn. In particular, the sisters need to learn. We should learn to go to people's homes to have meetings with them. We do not need to wait until they have the burden and the desire. As long as one is a believer and as long as he or she has a home, we need to work on the home. If they do not know how to have a meeting, we should lead them and teach them to do it. If for any reason they have difficulty starting a meeting, we should help them. We should continue persistently time after time until they are able to sustain a meeting in their home. After that we can hand the meeting over to them. Such meetings are not primarily for the relatives and neighbors but for the members of the family, especially for the husbands and wives. Perhaps the couple has not been meeting for a long time. As long as we bring the meeting to their home, they will be touched by the Lord to start meeting again. This is one lesson that all the co-workers, elders, and full-timers must learn.

I would also speak a word of advice to the co-workers and elders. In the past we were accustomed to taking care of the big meetings. Now we have a new way. We are asking everyone to work on the small meetings. In other words, we need to work on every saint's home. Not only must we recover the dormant ones, but we must also recover their homes. Although many brothers and sisters are not co-workers, elders, or full-timers, they do have a heart for the Lord. There are about three thousand such saints in Taipei. If they all form units of three, we will have one thousand units which can carry out meetings in others' homes. Every Saturday we will have one thousand teams of saints looking for people to work on, whether they are dormant ones, weak ones, or indifferent ones. We can even send a meeting to the home of a gospel friend. We will not graduate by doing this only once. Such a practice must be sustained in a steadfast way. In the process of doing this, we must learn to take care of other things, such as the arrangement of chairs, the provision of food, and the preparation of the refreshments. We also must learn to choose the hymns and exercise to follow the leading of the Spirit. If we do this, I believe the result will be more than we can think or imagine.

Helping Every Attendant to Function

Another secret to the success of the small group meeting or home meeting is the singing. This is especially crucial among the older ones, those who are more than forty years of age. We have many good hymns among us. Many times we do not need to sing the entire hymn; we can sing only one stanza.

When we go to a home meeting, our singing with a released spirit will stir up the meeting. The most crucial thing is to help every attendant of the meeting to function. We can take the lead to pray and afterward ask the brothers and sisters to pray one by one. If some express reluctance, we can help them along. We can also encourage them to give a testimony of their salvation and to tell the story of their experience of the Lord's grace. This will rekindle the love for the Lord within them and fire them up. It will also stir up the heart of the listeners.

Learning to Use Proper Material

Every time we have a home meeting, we must provide the proper material for the supply of life. We must all learn to use such material. Do not be legal or inflexible in using the material. At times we may come to deep and lofty points. Depending on the actual need, we may want to skip over some of these points or cover them in a brief way. Any Scripture reference listed at the beginning of a lesson or chapter should be pray-read. Ultimately, we still need the supply of the Lord's word for spiritual nourishment. If we do this, the meetings will become living.

Preparing before Going to the Home Meetings

Before we go to a home meeting, we need to pray before the Lord, confess to Him, and ask for His cleansing. We need to wash our hands every day. We cannot say that since we washed our hands yesterday, we do not need to wash them again today. Nor can we say that since we washed them this morning, we can skip it for now. Every time we contact the Lord, and every time we touch anything concerning the Lord, we need to confess our sins and ask Him for His cleansing. We do this not as a formality. We confess our filth, weakness, lack, corruption, and evil from the bottom of our heart. Whether they are conscious sins or unconscious sins, we must ask the Lord to forgive and cleanse them one by one.

The result of such prayer, confession, and supplication for cleansing is the moving and outpouring of the Holy Spirit. We have to believe that the Spirit of the Lord today is the ultimate consummation of the Triune God. He is all-inclusive. He lives within us and is also upon us. After we confess our sins and ask for forgiveness, He will cleanse us with His precious blood (1 John 1:7, 9). After such confession, we must exercise our faith to claim His Spirit. We must believe that He is within us and is also upon us. We also must believe that every time we are with the brothers and sisters, His presence is with us. In Matthew 28:20 the Lord says, "I am with you all the days until the consummation of the age." This Lord who is with us is the Spirit. If He is not the Spirit, how can He be with us? The Lord who is with us in the meetings is the Spirit.

Once the Lord cleanses us, we must stand on this fact. Based on this faith, we should exercise our spirit in the meetings. Whether it is singing, praying, speaking, or fellowshipping, the minute we open our mouth, we need to learn to exercise our spirit. Our meeting is not a common thing. It is a holy matter. Whenever we meet, we touch God. For this reason, we must exercise our spirit. John 4:24 says, "God is Spirit, and those who worship Him must worship in spirit and truthfulness." According to my observation, when the brothers and sisters come together, most of the time they do not exercise their spirit; they do not worship in spirit and truthfulness. This is our greatest lack.

Chinese philosophy extols "inward substance" over "outward show" so that even if a person is filled with "inward substance," he should behave outwardly as if nothing has happened. To the Chinese, this is virtue and valor. But such "valor" should not be found in our meetings. In the meetings we need to have inward substance, and we need to have outward expression. Fifty years ago the most famous preacher in China was John Sung, who did not graduate from any theological school. He received a doctoral degree in chemistry in the United States. When he returned to China, he was called by the Lord to preach the gospel. Around February or March of 1933, he came to Chefoo. I went purposely to listen to him. He was like a madman. He would come in either from the front door or from the back door. Sometimes while everyone was waiting for him, he would suddenly appear and would sing in a loud voice, saying, "Down with sin, down with sin; out with Satan, out with Satan!" At that time, even Christian congregations of a thousand people would be completely silent for the entire meeting. But the minute John Sung sang in this way, every dormant spirit was awakened. When we go to a meeting, we should do the same; we should stir up other people's spirit.

We must realize that with whatever part of our being we speak, we will touch that same part in others. If we speak in a joyful way, others will rejoice. If we speak in anger, others will be led to anger. If we speak with our emotion, we will touch others' emotion. If we speak with the will, we will touch others' will. Of course, if we speak with our spirit, we will touch others' spirit. This is an invariable rule. When we go to the meeting, we are there only for one thing—to do God's business. We are there to stir up people's spirit. If we do not exercise our spirit, others' spirit will never be stirred up. If their spirit is not stirred up, they will not touch God, and they will not receive any supply. God is Spirit, and those who worship Him must worship in spirit. When we go to the meeting, we need to exercise our spirit. We must always exercise our spirit.

Some saints are always strong. They are always ready to speak and can exercise their spirit without any encouragement from us. But the majority of the saints need encouragement before they will exercise their spirit. When we go to a meeting, that is, when we deliver a meeting to a person's home, the minute we come and the minute we open our mouth, we need to exercise our spirit. Once we exercise our spirit, the meeting will be full of the Spirit. Once we speak with the spirit, others' spirit will be opened, and they will touch God.

LEARNING TO TEACH *TRUTH LESSONS*

Every Lord's Day I go to a different hall to observe the teaching of *Truth Lessons*. I feel that all the brothers are making progress everywhere. However, it seems that we are still not thoroughly clear about how to teach the main points of the lessons, and we do not know the secret of teaching. In the past I implored that we not expound but only teach the lessons.

Now I am still holding on to this principle. The reason is that the content of *Truth Lessons* is already a complete message which includes everything that should be included. It does not require us to expound any further. As long as we are able to point out and impress people with the main points, this is the best way to teach *Truth Lessons*.

Exercising the Spirit

The first and foremost requirement in teaching *Truth Lessons* is the exercise of the spirit. We need to exercise our spirit in every word that we speak. The minute we open our mouth, if we exercise our spirit, we will spontaneously stir up others' spirit. On the contrary, if we speak in a low tone without any vigor, people will be killed by our speaking. For example, in a classroom full of naughty students, if the teacher speaks without any vigor, the students will be even naughtier and will not listen to the teacher. Even though we are not teachers, we still need the same kind of attitude and manner. Once we stand on the podium, we should not speak casually or in our regular tone. Rather, we need to speak in a dignified way. Once we open our mouth, our spirit should be released. We must learn this. If we do this, our teaching of *Truth Lessons* will be entirely different. Once we open our mouth, our spirit will come out, and what we are going to say will also be spirit. The attendants will also exercise their spirit when they speak and read the messages. Hence, the exercise of the spirit is the first item that we must work on.

Applying Some Techniques

I said earlier that according to my observation and experience, the best way to read *Truth Lessons* is that everyone reads instead of a few reading or only the teacher reading. But all should not read together; rather, they should read a sentence each, one after another. Consider a basketball game. It is not one person who holds the ball all the time or five persons simultaneously playing the ball; they pass the ball to one another and take turns playing it. Based on what I saw, almost all the churches commit the mistake of not reading in the right way. I hope that we will receive this fellowship.

The advantage of teaching in this way is that in reading the lesson, everyone will spontaneously exercise to speak and we will not be the only one speaking. Everyone will read consecutively, like five players passing a basketball from one to the other. This is to be flexible. The most important thing in our home meetings and small group meetings is for everyone to speak, as if they are passing a basketball. The best opportunity to train the saints to speak is when we teach them *Truth Lessons*. We need to explain to them or even give them a demonstration of how to read the lesson.

Second, in reading the lesson, we need to teach them how to pay attention to the main points. When we come to an important point, we can ask someone to read it again, or even three or four times. If the one who reads is experienced, he may be able to stress the point a little. In this way, not only will he gain the benefit, but everyone will be benefited. The newly saved ones and gospel friends in particular will be very impressed. The teacher and the student can profit from each other. The teacher speaks; the students speak; everyone speaks. Spontaneously, we will all grow. This is not easy, but it is not too difficult. I hope we can all practice this. Do not practice this in a rigid or monotonous way; instead, do it in a living way.

Third, after each section has been read, the teacher should highlight the subject and the main point. This will give the saints a deeper impression and enable them to learn the truth and receive the supply.

If the teachers can speak with an exercised spirit, lead the saints to practice repeated reading, emphasized reading, reading that brings out the main points, and give a conclusion after each section, the saints will be able to taste the sweetness and riches of the messages. After each lesson, the saints will not only receive the knowledge of the truth but also the life supply released from the main points that were highlighted. This is a very profitable practice.

There are also a few points to which we should pay attention. When we ask questions and highlight the main points, we should not pay too much attention to trivial things, such as history, geography, or the names of persons; rather, we should pay attention to the types, prophecies, and fulfillments. Once I heard a teacher ask questions, not related to the prophecies of Christ but to the names and numbers of prophets. Some people may ask, "Since we do not need to pay attention to all these things, why did you include them in the lessons?" I have already pointed out that for a chicken to grow properly, it needs to have bones, feathers, and skin. But when this chicken is presented for man's enjoyment, the more meat there is, the better. When we compiled *Truth Lessons,* we included some of the "bones," "feathers," and "skin," but this does not mean that we want them to be taught.

I have read the Bible for sixty years. From the very beginning, I started to memorize the names of persons and places, but until today I am not able to remember all of them. If the trainees were to tell me that they have memorized only the names of the twelve minor prophets, I would not be happy. However, if they have not memorized all the points concerning Christ's prophecies, I would say that they should be dismissed and should leave the training. I am afraid, however, that many of them have memorized the names of persons but not the prophecies of Christ. This indicates that our teaching of *Truth Lessons* has reversed the order of importance—we are presenting only a pile of bones for people to gnaw on, but we cannot present the meat for people to eat. This is a big failure.

Last Lord's Day I joined a corporate Lord's table meeting in a certain hall. The saints were tested on the main points of the lessons and accordingly given rewards. I agreed with their practice. They did not test on trivial matters but on the outlines—in Adam, we see God's redemption; in Abel, we see God's way of redemption; in Enosh, we see man's need for God and man's calling upon Him to enjoy God's riches; in Enoch, we see one who was redeemed and who walked with God on the pathway of redemption. We do not need to ask questions such as how long Enoch lived or how long he walked with God. The trivial matters are not important. The most important thing is the spiritual significance.

All of the co-workers and elders should be teachers of *Truth Lessons,* and especially the younger ones should bear this burden. The older ones are already sixty or seventy years of age; the younger ones should pick up this burden. In the Lord's recovery our teaching of the truth should not be the same as the way people teach theology. For example, they teach the historical event of Abraham's being born in Ur of the Chaldees. Instead, we should teach the spiritual matters and things, such as the spiritual significance of Ur of the Chaldees being a land of idol worship. We must remember this kind of spiritual significance. The failure of theological teaching is that even though people have received theological education, their comprehension of the spiritual matters is still incomplete. What they learned are things such as history, geography, archaeology, and culture. What we teach must be matters of spiritual significance.

THE BENEFITS OF BUILDING UP
THE CHURCH IN THE HOMES

We need to realize that the way the Lord is taking is to build up His church in the believers' homes. Once the church is built up in the homes, the homes will be transformed. The husbands and the wives might have been arguing couples, but once they have meetings in their homes, they will stop their arguing. The children will also be preserved from drifting with the current of the age. As a result, the family will become proper and normal. If possible, we should compile some material to teach the brothers and sisters how they should build up their own homes. For example, we should have something to teach them how to behave as parents, children, husbands, and wives. This is scriptural. A book as spiritual as Ephesians contains teachings on being proper husbands, wives, children, parents, slaves, and masters. In the past we were somewhat negligent in this matter. All the brothers and sisters devoted their attention to the big meetings and neglected the building up of the homes. In the coming days we hope that we can compile some messages on the building up of the homes so that every saint's home would be a proper home. Once that happens, we can invite our relatives to the home meetings, and they will see the situation in our homes and will be touched to receive the Lord's salvation.

Once we build up the church in the believers' homes, we will be able to spread the gospel through the homes. All the churches that do a good job with the homes will not need to have big gospel meetings; the gospel will spread spontaneously. The home is the place that touches man's heart. It pierces and digs deep into man's very soul, even his very spirit. This does not mean that we cannot have big gospel meetings, but we need such meetings only a few times a year. The main emphasis with such meetings is in reaping, not sowing. The crucial thing is to build up the church in the homes and to spread the gospel through the homes. At the same time, we need to encourage the brothers and sisters to group two or three families together into small groups. In the small groups they should fellowship together and render spiritual help, nourishment, and care to one another. Then in the larger church meetings there should be the teaching of *Truth Lessons*. Such teaching is mainly for everyone to learn the truth. If we build up the church in such a well-coordinated way, the Lord will greatly bless us.

THE BENEFITS OF *TRUTH LESSONS*

What surprises me the most is that many dormant believers, including those in the United States, like *Truth Lessons*. Some dormant saints in the church in Anaheim recovered their meeting in order to learn *Truth Lessons*. Right before this meeting, a few elders from Kaohsiung told me that before they started the truth classes, the number of people fluctuated very much. But since they began the truth classes, more people are meeting steadily. This indicates that man has the heart to know the truth and that *Truth Lessons* is truly being used by God.

First Timothy 2:4 says that God "desires all men to be saved and to come to the full knowledge of the truth." Therefore, we cannot tolerate to see a group of saved ones merely loving the Lord fervently but not knowing the truth. We must teach with *Truth Lessons*. After God's children are saved, if they pursue the truth, the church of the Lord will have a base and foundation and be built up in truth.

After we have led the saints in this way, they will have the understanding to enter into the spiritual significance of the Bible and comprehend the revelation in the Scriptures. We have all had this kind of experience. When we were newly saved, we did not understand the Bible. After we were taught for one or two years and learned some truths, we started to understand a little. Now the leading of the new way is to have home meetings, small group meetings, and truth classes. These three matters are like a threefold cord and are very powerful. Through these three things we bring people to salvation, enable them to know and pursue life, and help them to enter into and be equipped with the truth so that they may have the way to life and the light of the truth.

A FIVE-YEAR PLAN
FOR THE GOSPELIZATION OF TAIWAN

Since October of 1984 we expected to begin a five-year plan for the gospelization of Taiwan. Now one and a half years have passed. This period of time can be regarded as a time of preparation. It may take us another year and a half to prepare. First, we need to work out the home meetings, the small group meetings, and the truth classes. After we have established the homes, we will take the homes as the starting point to cooperate with the campus work in order to raise up full-timers. In the preparation period of three years, I hope that we will produce at least one thousand full-timers. In the fourth year, they will be formed into an army with ten people in a team. These one hundred teams will set out together. Each team will work first in a town and then in the villages. They will stay in a town for at least three weeks or a month. They will establish the church by preaching the gospel through door-knocking, establishing home meetings, and bringing ten to twenty people to salvation. Then two full-timers will stay behind to continue to nourish, shepherd, and lead the new ones. The other eight will come back, re-group with new full-timers, and set out for another town. In this way, in fewer than four months we will gospelize all 318 towns throughout the island. Later a team of six to eight people will re-group to work in the villages. Then in a few years, Taiwan will not only be gospelized but also "churchized." There will be a church in every town and village as a shining testimony of the Lord. This plan is the Lord's leading. We should not think that this is too difficult.

In order to carry out this momentous task, the preparation work is more than crucial. We should consider the kind of transportation the teams will need—gospel vans, motorcycles, bicycles, or taking buses. Before the full-timers set out for the towns, we must first rent houses for them. The location of the houses must be appropriate. Moreover, the expenditure, realized in furnishing houses and providing the living expenses of the full-timers, will be very great and thus will require all the churches to prepare in one accord.

Before setting out in the fourth year, the full-time trainees who have graduated in the first three years should already be coordinating with the local saints to propagate in the communities of some major cities, such as Taipei, Taichung, and Kaohsiung. At the present time they go door-knocking every Wednesday and Friday morning and visit people house to house in the apartment buildings. The result has been quite good. I believe that three years from now, when they propagate in towns and villages, they will already have some experience to establish a certain model in the communities. By this way, we "hit two birds with one stone."

This five-year plan for the gospelization of Taiwan can be an easy task, but it all depends on the foundation we lay these first three years. This foundation is the small group meetings, the home meetings, and the teaching of *Truth Lessons*. This is the reason that I want us all to aggressively learn, because what we are learning and working out is not only a foundation but a model. I believe that if the full-timers seriously learn for half a year, when they go out, they will know how to set up and lead the home meetings. In this way, once the move of the gospelization of Taiwan commences in the fourth year, we will march with strong morale to spread the gospel and the churches all over Taiwan. We must be faithful to the Lord. Those who should give their time must give their time. The young people especially need to give their time to God to receive His glorious commission. After the gospel and the churches have spread all over Taiwan, they may be led by the Lord to continue to serve full time or to find a job. But they need to be faithful to this "military" service in these five years until every town, village, and hamlet in Taiwan is gospelized. On the other hand, those who give financially must also be faithful to God. The monthly support for more than one thousand full-timers is considerable. This is in addition to the need for the churches and the spreading of the gospel. This requires all the saints to give joyfully and willingly in one accord. If we are faithful in these two matters, the Lord will definitely accomplish what we ask and think.

FELLOWSHIP REGARDING
THE BUILDING OF THE BIG MEETING HALL

Requiring Strong Faith and Adequate Prayer

The purpose of building a big meeting hall in Lin-ko is not merely for our need locally but for the international gatherings in the Lord's recovery. This requires much prayer. Regarding the international conferences, saints from different countries came to visit Taiwan in this past year because they wanted to find out about the new way. There were hundreds from the United States who wanted to come, but I asked them not to come at the present time because our practice has not been fully developed. Last week several saints from Germany visited, and there will be a few more coming this week. A continuous stream of saints is coming from places like Japan and Brazil. Some American saints even have signed up to participate in the construction work of the big meeting hall when it begins. They all are professionals in building. Hence, when we speak of the international need, we should never think that this is an exaggeration. We are simply stating the facts. I hope that we will all have strong faith before the Lord to pray for this matter desperately.

Cooperating with the Lord's Move
to Gospelize the Whole Earth

Moreover, after the construction of the big meeting hall, we will expand the size of the training. At that time more will come to the training. We also thank the Lord that the international position of Taiwan has been raised up. The changes in the international situation are more favorable toward Taiwan. These changes are sovereign of the Lord. If Taiwan now becomes the gospel center, Taiwan will be gospelized, and the gospelization will spread from Taiwan to the whole earth in cooperation with the Lord's move.

This term of the full-time training is approaching the end. In the coming term we will have classes for different languages, teaching the trainees a third foreign language other than English, such as Spanish and Japanese. Now the need for Spanish is very great. Consider Central and South America for instance. Even if we were to send three hundred co-workers there right now, it would not be sufficient to meet the need. There are many needs all over the earth. After the gospelization of Taiwan, some may be sent to Japan, Europe, or Africa. Hence, I encourage the young people to advance in their studies. They not only need to know the truth and life, but they also need to learn more languages, including Greek.

Many Christians confess, and even those in Christianity in America cannot deny, that the Lord has entrusted us with His truth in this age. This is an irrefutable fact. We must bear the responsibility to spread the Lord's truth from Taiwan to every part of the world and raise up the Lord's testimony in every place. Therefore, the construction of the big meeting hall in Lin-ko is crucial. Taiwan is the best location. I hope the co-workers, elders, and full-timers will have adequate prayer and will also explain this matter clearly to the saints in the different halls and churches so that they also will pray much. I hope that all the churches in Taiwan will call on the Lord desperately for the sake of His interest on the earth to touch the government officials and grant the authorities the wisdom to see that this building will be beneficial to our nation, our people, our society, our economy, Taiwan's foreign relations, and even our people's foreign relationships, so that they will gladly and promptly grant us the permission to fulfill this matter.

CHAPTER THIRTEEN

THE PRACTICE OF THE NEW WAY
BEING A SPIRITUAL WARFARE

While resting these few days, I have felt that we have neglected the spiritual warfare, caring only for the work, because we have been busy with our work and busy following the new move under the Lord's leading. In particular, we have been negligent in prayer. Hence, I sense the attack of the enemy. He has even stirred up some who oppose the new way to pray against this way. For this reason, I feel in my spirit that we should all be watchful. When we are busy with the Lord's work, we must realize that we are engaged in a spiritual warfare.

The foremost need on the battlefield is to be watchful and alert, in order to know what the enemy is doing and what he intends to do. The enemy always does things in a subtle and hidden way. I do not have anything particular to fellowship at this point, but I do want to unload a heavy burden. I hope the co-workers, elders, and full-timers will receive a burden from the Lord to spend much time before Him to pray corporately. Perhaps we need to devote this whole meeting to prayer. We will see how the Lord leads us.

NEEDING ADEQUATE AND THOROUGH PRAYER
TO WITHSTAND THE STRATEGY OF THE ENEMY

Over the past two months I have been leading the meetings for the co-workers and elders. Every time we met, we were short of prayer. We had neither the spirit of prayer nor the adequate amount of prayer. Therefore, I am concerned that when the co-workers and elders meet together, there is a lack of prayers and, even more, a lack of weighty prayers. For this reason, recently when I was resting, I often felt a heavy weight on my heart. Deep within my spirit I sensed that this was an attack of the authority of darkness from behind. We have neglected this matter. I believe there may be some who are praying counter prayers. Hence, we must ask the Lord to resist prayers that are directed particularly against the work we are carrying out, against the church, and against my leading. The prayers we utter before the Lord must stand against these counter prayers. May the Lord cover us and not allow the enemy to have any ground to do damage.

A FEW MATTERS REQUIRING OUR PRAYER

We need prayers to fight the spiritual warfare. But we also need to pray for the various aspects of the work and the different needs in the Lord's new move in this new age that have arisen because of our change in the system. First, we must pray for the approval of the construction of the meeting hall in Lin-ko. We have submitted the application, and it was received. Now is the time for the brothers and sisters to receive a burden to pray for this matter. This is a crucial juncture that determines whether we will succeed. If our application is not approved, we cannot build the meeting hall, and this will delay the Lord's timing. I hope that all the churches, not simply the church in Taipei, will receive the burden to pray in one accord for this matter.

Second, we need to pray for the different kinds of meetings in our practice, such as the home meeting, the small group meeting, and the meeting for teaching *Truth Lessons*. We also need to pray for our general meetings such as the big Lord's Day morning meeting, the Lord's table meeting, and the prayer meeting. I hope that the elders will bear this burden and press toward the goal of the new way together with the co-workers and full-timers. I hope that the Lord will establish all the meetings in a strong way through us and through His grace so that He may gain what He is after.

Third, this term of the full-time training will end on June 20, and the next term will begin in August. In these days we must pray for the number of the full-time trainees. I hope that by the beginning of 1988 we will have at least one thousand full-timers who have passed through the training and are ready to be sent to different towns for the propagation. Moreover, in this coming term of the training we will teach different languages, including Greek, English, Spanish, Japanese, and Chinese. All of these items require much prayer.

PRAYER BEING THE SECRET
TO ACCOMPLISH GOD'S WORK

We need to remember that in God's work, there is no such thing as sheer luck, no such thing as gaining without effort. Moreover, there is no guarantee that if we labor and endeavor, we will succeed. We must realize that we are engaged in spiritual warfare. We must fight and be watchful in everything we do and in every step we take. I hope that we would take this word. We have been called by the Lord in His grace to gather here and receive a burden. We must know that we need to struggle, fight, and take possession of every inch through prayer. The last line of *Hymns,* #892 says, "We should, we must, we can, we will, / Fulfill God's purpose faithfully." This should be our attitude. We should not listen to the lies from the authorities of darkness; instead, we should offer prayers to God in steadfast faith.

Whenever we pray together, I hope that everyone will pray, not praying simultaneously but one after another. Our prayers should not be too loud or lengthy. They should be short and living, adding to the one before, so that all the prayers can be joined together as one strong, powerful prayer. We should pray as if we are playing basketball, knowing how to pass and how to catch the ball. I hope that our prayers will meet God's standard and requirement and be according to His desire.

I also beseech that we pray for the publication of our books. The compiling of the recent messages, especially *Truth Lessons,* is a very heavy burden. After finishing the Gospel of Mark, I resumed the compiling of *Truth Lessons.* I was exhausted. Last Wednesday afternoon while I was working on *Truth Lessons,* I suddenly felt very tired and had to stop before completing a lesson. I had used up all my energy and could not go on any longer. I had to stop to rest. This is because even though I know my own physical condition, I also realized that it was more than merely a condition in the natural realm. A spiritual battle was also being waged. The enemy was attacking and disturbing. On the one hand, in the natural realm, our strength and energy are limited, and we should not overuse our body. This is a fact. But on the other hand, in the spiritual realm, when this kind of thing happens, we should not rule out the attack of the enemy. Therefore, I hope that we will receive a burden to pray for this matter. May the Lord bless the books we put out so that they can be effective and greatly used by the Lord to reach His goal.

I repeat, regardless of the time and place, we must be led by the Lord to cry out to Him and to call on Him to touch His throne—not merely the throne of grace but the throne of authority. I hope that each of us would pray from our spirit, and no one would be silent and not receive this burden.

PRAYER

Lord, release our spirit, give us the burden, and enable us to receive the burden and to stretch out our hands in faith to touch Your throne of authority. Lord, we believe that Your church needs the land in Lin-ko. We thank You for blessing Taiwan because of Your recovery. We still ask You to pour out Your blessing in so many ways. Bless this country, bless the government, and bless the officials. Give them the wisdom to make the right decisions. Cause them to have a deep realization that this decision is a blessed decision. Lord, we are not asking this for ourselves or merely for the church, we are asking this for You and Your interest. We are here to command You to fulfill this matter.

Lord, we also receive the burden to pray for the different church meetings. Since You are the One gathering us together, cause us to sense Your presence in all of our gatherings. Now we petition You in one accord and touch Your throne of holiness. We ask You to hear our prayers. Pour out Your grace and blessing in every meeting.

Lord, we hide ourselves, Your work, Your recovery, Your church, and all the steps of the practice of Your new way in You and under the covering of Your precious blood. We ask

You to draw the boundary around us with Your precious blood and not allow the authorities of darkness to overstep. Lord, cover us in many ways. We are touching Your throne of authority and opposing all counter prayers. If there are some who oppose us before You, they are not opposing us, they are opposing Your new way and Your work. Lord, we ask You to act against all counter prayers, resisting the enemy and fighting for us. Since we are here fighting the battle, we ask You to grant us the inner peace so that we may enjoy Your fighting and rest in Your fighting. May Your testimony, the testimony You have shown us, the testimony of the end time, be a living testimony, an anti-testimony, a testimony against Christianity, against its poison, against its traditions, against its oldness, and against its old ways. May Your testimony be a genuine living testimony.

Lord, we also ask You to enable all the co-workers, elders, and full-timers to receive the burden to pray unceasingly and labor faithfully before You. Lord, we will never enjoy rest before You have obtained Your rest. We want to see You resting in all the saints' homes. We want to establish all the saints' homes and make them Your resting place. Lord, perfect thousands of homes to be Your living testimony for the release and shining forth of Your truth. Build us up and equip us with the truth. Make us good soldiers to spread the gospel, the truth, and even the churches all over Taiwan. Lord, hear our prayer.

Lord, remember that we belong to You and have been set apart for You. Remember that we are here in Your name. Our prayers are also in Your name. Lord, we believe that for Your sake and for the sake of Your interest on the earth, You will answer our prayers. Amen.

A FEW ANNOUNCEMENTS

We thank the Lord for giving us the time and the utterance to pray. We must believe that He has heard our prayers in His name. We need to continue to pray that the Lord will execute what He has heard and fulfill our desires before Him.

Regarding the teaching of *Truth Lessons,* I hope all the elders will carry this out in a serious way. We should try our best to put into practice every point we have fellowshipped in the previous two chapters regarding the teaching of *Truth Lessons*. I would emphasize again that every elder should take the lead to teach the truth by teaching a truth class in the meeting hall where he meets. If we do know how to teach, we surely should teach, but even if we do not know how to teach, we still must teach, because elders should be apt to teach (1 Tim. 3:2). Some of us may not know how to teach at the present time, but as long as there is the heart to learn, eventually we will be able to teach. If we teach according to what I spoke in the previous chapters, we will see the result.

There will be forty days from the end of this term of the full-time training until the beginning of the next term. This time is also the summer vacation. There will be many activities for college students. I hope that we could have a definite plan and arrangement for the gospel work on the campuses. If possible, we should arrange for some of them to attend the summer training on *The Conclusion of the New Testament*. This period of time can serve as a bridge to the full-time training to increase the number of those who have the heart to go. I hope that we will pray for this matter and for the full-time training and its leading. These are crucial matters.

Another matter we need to pray for is the move of propagation in the communities. Before we begin the propagation in the towns and villages in 1988, we will focus on laying a good foundation in the communities of the big cities. This is a great matter. We all need to receive the burden to pray for the propagation.

CHAPTER FOURTEEN

THE BUILDING UP OF THE CHURCH BEING A SERVICE OF WARFARE

Scripture Reading: Num. 4:3; 26:2; Neh. 4:15-23; 1 Tim. 1:18; 6:12; 2 Tim. 4:7; Eph. 6:13-14a

During the past one and a half years we have been speaking concerning the building up of the small groups, the home meetings, the teaching of *Truth Lessons,* and the preaching of the gospel. In short, we have spoken about begetting, nourishing, and teaching. I am concerned that we have become indifferent to these matters because of the frequency of our speaking on them. We also may now consider our work to be very common and ordinary. Therefore, I received a burden from the Lord to remind all of us that our work is a spiritual warfare.

THE CENTRAL LINE OF GOD'S ECONOMY

In the Old Testament, as far as God's economy is concerned, God's work was to build up the temple and the city. The entire Old Testament has the temple and the city as its center. God's work in the Old Testament age was carried out through different offices or ministries. There was the ministry of the priests, the ministry of the kings, and the ministry of the prophets. Although these three offices or ministries were different, their goal and center were the same—to build up God's temple and His kingdom, in other words, to build up God's house and His city. At the same time, the Old Testament clearly shows that the work of God's enemy was also focused on this line. He tried to frustrate, damage, and destroy God's building. This line can be clearly seen in the Old Testament.

The first time the church, which is the house of God, is

THE VISION AND DEFINITE STEPS

spoken of in the New Testament is in Matthew 16:18. The
Lord Jesus said, "Upon this rock I will build My church, and
the gates of Hades shall not prevail against it." This clearly
shows that as soon as the church is mentioned, the gates of
Hades, that is, the power of darkness, is also mentioned. This
shows that in the New Testament, the work in God's economy
to build up the church is a warfare.

THE NEED FOR SPIRITUAL WARFARE
FOR THE DIVINE BUILDING

The problem with Christianity is that it is merely a religion.
The people in Christianity see almost nothing concerning
God's building. Therefore, they know nearly nothing about
spiritual warfare. Thus, they cannot discern the enemy's tactics. They know that there is a devil, but at the most they only
know that the devil tempts men to do evil things and causes
them to turn away from God, to stumble, to sin, and to bring
shame to God's name. They never touch the crucial facts, nor
do they realize that Satan, the devil, with all his wiles and
tactics, his temptations and corruptions, has only one goal in
mind—to fight against God's building in order to frustrate,
withstand, damage, and destroy it.

Today in the Lord's recovery, we should clearly see that
we are not merely doing a work of recovery—recovering the
truth, the gospel, the experience of Christ as life, and building
up the church. We must see that all of this recovery work
is related to God's building. God's building is at the center of
His economy. His goal is to gain a house and a city, which are
the church and the kingdom. Such a building work is altogether related to the enemy's final destiny. This, of course,
stirs up his attack.

Before I saw the light concerning the Lord's recovery,
I heard many sermons, but I never heard any messages on
spiritual warfare. John Bunyan was one of the most famous
spiritual preachers among the Baptists in England in the
seventeenth century. He wrote *The Pilgrim's Progress* and
The Holy War. Sixty years ago, when I was still a young man, I
read *The Holy War.* It speaks of man's warfare with Satan.
The purpose of the book is to teach people how to oppose Satan

when he attacks and how by faith they can withstand his temptations. However, this book does not speak of God's economy and His building. It says nothing of opposing and countering the power of darkness in the midst of building up God's kingdom.

One day, God led me to see the light concerning His recovery. At that time, I was reading some English books as well as some books that had been translated by Brother Nee. Through these books I came to realize that, throughout the centuries, those who love the Lord with a pure heart and who know something about God's eternal purpose in their spirit experience a kind of spiritual warfare. They realize from the depth of their being that every step of God's recovery involves His enemy, and every step requires warfare. Yet very few have seen that there is the need of spiritual warfare in order to realize the divine building. Today we need to see that there is the need to engage ourselves in spiritual warfare for the building up of God's kingdom.

During the past few days, because of a slight illness, I was forced to set aside my work temporarily and rest. During this time I reconsidered many things, especially the things we have seen and experienced in the past. I felt that I should pick up the burden to remind us of this matter. Perhaps we do not feel any attack and do not sense any warfare. However, we should realize that even this feeling is a result of Satan's intrusion. He has injected lethargy into us so that we will become numb to all feelings.

Nehemiah 4:23 says, "Neither I nor my brothers nor my servants nor the men of the guard who followed me, none of us took off our clothes; each had his weapon at his right hand." I used to think that since the Bible is the canon of our faith, it should speak about divine and lofty matters. Why would the Bible record such a small thing as "each had his weapon at his right hand"? This word sounds too simple and shallow; it does not sound like the Scriptures. Yet we need to see that even this short word conveys much light of the truth. This short word shows the need for warfare! Nehemiah 4:23b in the American Standard Version says, "Every one went with his weapon to the water." Even when they were going for water, the builders did not leave their weapons behind. This shows that there is warfare even in the smallest matters of our daily life.

THE TYPOLOGY OF GOD'S BUILDING
IN THE OLD TESTAMENT
AND ITS RELATIONSHIP TO THE WARFARE

The building in the Old Testament was the tabernacle and the temple as the house of God. After the Israelites left Egypt and arrived at Mount Sinai, Moses saw the vision of the building of God's tabernacle. Following this, the people began their journey in the wilderness with Canaan as their goal. They did not travel to Canaan without a testimony and a goal. These two or three million people did not wander in the wilderness aimlessly, arriving in Canaan by chance. Rather, their journey in the wilderness was orderly and disciplined, and it was always centered around God's tabernacle. From the book of Numbers we can see that when they set up their camp, the first thing they did was set up the tabernacle. After the tabernacle was established as the center, all the tribes settled around it according to a prescribed order. When they set out on their journey, they put the tabernacle on their shoulders and followed the ark.

The first four chapters of Numbers show that when God ordered the children of Israel to be numbered, He considered every numbered person as a soldier. Those who were numbered were conscripts in the army. The first group to be numbered were those twenty years of age and upward. They were all drafted into the service. The Levites, however, were not numbered. Since they were required to draw near to the tabernacle to serve the priests and to minister to the tabernacle, they needed to possess a higher level of life and more maturity in life. Therefore, only those who were between thirty and fifty years old were numbered and drafted into the service of the tabernacle.

Numbers 4:3 says, "From thirty years old and upward even to fifty years old, all who enter into the service to perform the skilled work in the Tent of Meeting." The word *service* here should be translated as "warfare." Verse 2 of chapter 26 says,

"Take the sum of the whole assembly of the children of Israel, from twenty years old and upward, by their fathers' households, all who are able to go forth for military service in Israel." The phrase *go forth for military service* is based on the same Hebrew word for *service* in 4:3. It refers to those who are able to serve in the army.

The first four chapters of Numbers show these matters, because in God's eyes, in order to maintain His central testimony, all the arrangements and services around the tabernacle are related to warfare. To be a priest is to be in the army. To be a Levite is to be in the army. Even to be an ordinary citizen is to be in the army. Hence, the move of the entire people of Israel in the wilderness was a military move. It was not the wandering of a nomadic tribe. These were not nomadic people. They were an organized and disciplined army. This is the reason that they were called "the armies of Jehovah" in the Old Testament. On the way to the good land, they first defeated the Amalekites in a fierce battle. After leaving Mount Sinai, the people then fought battle after battle. While they were traveling, they were also fighting. This went on until they passed the Jordan River, completed the first war at Jericho, and marched into Canaan.

From that time on, the Israelites never ceased to fight. Their history is a history of warfare. The book of Joshua records all the wars that went on in the conquest of Canaan. The book of Judges is also about warfare. Without warfare, how could they possess the promised land of God? Without the good land, how could God's temple be built, His city established, and His kingdom set up on earth? This is the reason that the children of Israel waged war unceasingly from the time of Joshua. This went on until the time of David. David was a warrior. He was a warrior-king. He fought battles in the north and in the south, subduing all the enemies within the land and establishing peace. He left behind a land of peace for his son Solomon. At the same time, he prepared materials for the building of the temple, materials that he captured through his many battles. Hence, David's warfare not only secured a foundation for the temple; it also secured all kinds of materials for its building as well. He left all these to his son

Solomon. As soon as Solomon ascended to the throne, he ruled in peace. At that time the nation was rich, and the people lived in abundance. He ordered the work of building the temple to begin immediately, and in due time the temple was finished.

However, Satan was not willing to be idle and allow the temple to be built. He stirred up the Egyptians to attack Jerusalem; the Assyrians and eventually the Babylonians were stirred up to destroy Jerusalem. These people captured and destroyed Jerusalem, destroyed the temple, and took the holy people away as captives. At that time, God's house was gone, His kingdom was gone, and His people were taken into captivity for seventy years.

At the completion of the seventy years of captivity, God brought His people back once again. He brought them back for the purpose of rebuilding the temple and the city. During the first building of the temple, there did not seem to be much warfare, but during the rebuilding of the temple, Nehemiah 4:15-23 shows that the entire process was a warfare. Verse 16 says, "From that day half of my servants labored in the work, and half of them held the spears and the shields and the bows and the armor; and the rulers were behind all the house of Judah." Half of the Israelites were working, and half of them were fighting. In addition verse 17 says, "Those who built the wall and those who carried burdens took the loads with one hand doing the work and with the other holding a weapon." Verse 21 says, "So we labored in the work; and half of them held spears from the start of dawn until the stars came out." The second half of verse 23 says, "Every one went with his weapon to the water" (ASV). Without warfare and without a spirit of fighting, there is no building. This matter is clearly revealed in the Old Testament.

WARFARE FOR GOD'S BUILDING
IN THE NEW TESTAMENT

The recovery of the building in the Old Testament was fully accomplished by and through warfare. In the New Testament the Lord Jesus said that the gates of Hades, which belong to Satan, would never prevail against the built-up church (Matt. 16:18). The apostle Paul speaks specifically about the church in the book of Ephesians. He speaks about the church as the Body of Christ, the fullness of Christ, the counterpart of Christ, the new man, God's house, and God's kingdom. Lastly, he speaks about the church as the warrior, fighting on behalf of God's economy. Paul himself was a warrior. Before his martyrdom, he declared, "I have fought the good fight" (2 Tim. 4:7). This is the proper position and responsibility of the church.

Satan always comes behind God to damage His church. He causes the church to become fallen and degraded. Even when the apostle Paul was on earth, the church had become desolate. Paul saw the churches that he had built up with his own hands being damaged by Satan and brought into desolation. When he wrote the books of Philippians, Colossians, and 1 and 2 Timothy, he was very clear about the situation. He even said, "All who are in Asia turned away from me" (2 Tim. 1:15). The church became so desolate that it had even deserted Paul. Yet Paul was not discouraged. He exhorted Timothy to "war the good warfare" (1 Tim. 1:18), which was to fight against the different teachings of the dissenting ones and to accomplish God's economy according to his ministry concerning the gospel of grace and eternal life (v. 4), so that God, who is worthy of all praises, might be glorified (vv. 11-17).

At that time the greatest problem was the different teachings of the dissenting ones. This problem brought in great damage to the church. Paul told Timothy to remain in Ephesus to "charge certain ones not to teach different things...rather than God's economy" (vv. 3-4). For Timothy to do this was for him to war the good warfare. To war the good warfare is not to swing with our fists or kick with our feet. It is, on the negative side, to defeat and destroy the winds of different teachings, and on the positive side, to carry out God's economy. Paul clearly points out that it is insufficient merely to not teach different things; we must also speak God's economy. Today we are faced with the same warfare. Hence, to war the good warfare, to withstand the downward drift of the church, and to carry out God's economy is to preach the gospel of grace and eternal life according to the apostles' ministry.

In 6:12 Paul says, "Fight the good fight of the faith; lay hold on the eternal life, to which you were called." To fight the good fight is to lay hold on the eternal life. This life is the divine life, God's uncreated life, and the eternal life. The words *eternal life* are related more to the divine nature than to time. In our Christian life, and especially in our Christian work, we need to lay hold on God's eternal life and not trust in our human life in order to fight the good fight of the faith. Hence, the two books of Timothy and the book of Titus repeatedly emphasize the eternal life (1 Tim. 1:16; 6:19; 2 Tim. 1:1, 10; Titus 1:2; 3:7). This life is a necessary and basic prerequisite in order to accomplish God's economy concerning the church as depicted in 1 Timothy, to withstand the declining trend of the church as depicted in 2 Timothy, and to maintain good order in the church as depicted in Titus.

OUR WARFARE TODAY

Our work today is to build up the home meetings, teach the truth, and spread the gospel. In other words, it is to beget, nourish, and teach. These are things that are absolutely contrary to what Christianity is doing. It is a move against the tide. We are conscious that we are fighting a battle. We need to struggle to swim upstream. We must fight against the current. Consequently, we encounter difficulty at every stage. We all know that it is easy to flow downstream. There is no need to exert any strength; we can easily glide along, but to swim upstream requires a continual struggle. To press forward requires fighting.

Concerning these three matters, the burden within me is too heavy for words. I am already an old man, yet I still need to bear such a heavy burden. The only way I can explain it is that this is something that the Lord wants. Today the church has been corrupted by Christianity to such an extent that it has fully become a religion and an organization. In such an organization, two things are produced—a clergy-laity system and hierarchy. Through the practice of the clergy-laity system, hierarchy is built up. The Catholic Church takes the pope as its head, and the different Protestant groups take their founders as their heads. Under the pope and these founders, there is a distinct class of people who are different from others. People are separated into different categories and classes.

This completely obliterates the life relationship among God's children and annuls their organic function.

Through Brother Nee we saw the light sixty years ago that the most important matter in the Lord's recovery is that we be free from any organized religion. During the past sixty years we have paid much attention to this matter. Still, we admit that we have never rid ourselves fully of its influence even though we emphasize this so much. This is a battle. We have never been completely freed from the bondage of this organized religion because of the entanglement of the power of darkness and our sluggish disposition. Those without the spiritual insight do not see anything concerning the power of darkness. Everyone today says that religion is a good thing. Furthermore, Satan has even mixed some wicked things with our knowledge of the Bible through his cunning tactics.

The whole of Christianity is an organization of religion. It can be compared to the big tree described by the Lord Jesus in Matthew 13. It has taken root, settled on the earth, and become a huge organization. All Christians have been organized together and absorbed into it. The Lord has raised us up to stand against this great organization. We have been fighting this battle for more than sixty years, but to a certain extent, even our own brothers and sisters are not clear. Even our co-workers have become confused, considering that we are the same as Christianity. We consider ourselves the same as Christianity. Look at our situation today. How are we different from Christianity? Where are the distinctions? Some brothers and sisters even say, "Are not some Christians more zealous than we are? They are also preaching the gospel." As time goes by, black and white seem to be the same, fresh water and salt water become indistinguishable, and the pure and the polluted are mixed together. The reason such a situation has developed is that we have not fully rid ourselves of the clergy-laity system. The presence of the concept of a hierarchy results in this kind of an organization.

I hope that we will understand the fellowship in this message in a proper way. I hope that by the grace of the Lord we will take this clear word. We need to admit that two years ago in 1984 the clergy-laity system was very strong among us, even here in Taiwan. We did not have the form, but we had the fact. In order to deal with this matter, we saw from the Lord that we needed to deal with this from its roots. We must remove this practice from among us completely; otherwise, we will have no way to go on. This was why I have spoken so strongly against the big meetings and emphasized the small group meetings. I made it clear from the beginning that eventually the small group meetings should be brought into the homes. Once the meetings move to the homes and the church life is established in the homes, the clergy-laity system will have no more ground. Once the clergy-laity system loses its ground, the system of hierarchy will be uprooted and removed.

I am not speaking empty teachings. I am speaking facts based on our history. Hence, what we now need the most is for the elders, the co-workers, and the full-timers to become absolutely clear that it is not a small thing for us to set up home meetings. We are transplanting our "produce" from the realm of religion to the homes of the saints. Once they are transplanted to the homes, there will be no further opportunity for the clergy-laity system to surface. If every home has a meeting, every person is speaking, and no one wants to be the head, how can the clergy-laity system remain? However, if we cannot achieve these three ends, the clergy-laity system will remain, and the religious organization will continue.

THE BASIC STRATEGY OF THE NEW SYSTEM BEING THE REMOVAL OF THE CLERGY-LAITY SYSTEM

We must be clear that the changing of the system, the spreading, and the increase are not the basic issue. A local church may have three thousand people, thirty thousand, or even three million people; however, what is the foundation upon which the churches in the Lord's recovery are based? Are they based on big meetings, which have the clergy-laity system as their foundation and factor? Or are they based on the home meetings, in which everyone functions? The big meetings can never be free from the clergy-laity system. Once there is a big meeting, its very foundation supports the clergy-laity system. However, if the basic ingredient of the church is the home meeting, and if the element, essence, and inward reality of the church are in the homes, how can the clergy-laity system possibly exist? The clergy-laity system is the very root of the big meetings, and the big meetings are the "tree" for the clergy-laity system. The home meetings, however, remove the clergy-laity system as the root. This is the best way to eradicate the tree.

Let me repeat. I have no intention of offending anyone. Please do not take offense with me. I feel that our co-workers have been working for many years but have only produced big meetings. I believe that the co-workers do not have the intention or motive to build up a clergy-laity system, but we may not realize that our practice can be unrelated to our intentions or motivations. It is related to the principle under which we operate. If we operate under a certain principle, we will produce certain kinds of results. For example, we may have no intention of planting garlic, but once we plant a garlic seed, what will we reap other than garlic? We may say that we are not planting garlic, but we are deceived; what we are planting is garlic. Moreover, when we do things a certain way, what results is an organization. The result will manifest itself spontaneously, development by development.

I hope that your eyes will be enlightened in the same way that the Lord has enlightened my eyes by His mercy. We should not have any more regard for the big meetings. We should not think about them any longer. In the past the big meetings may have helped us and edified us, but we should not long for them any more. Some people are saved and are even edified, built up, and helped in the Catholic Church; others experience the same thing in the denominations. However, we should not hold on to such experiences. Many of us, including myself, were in such places. Later by the Lord's mercy we all left them, but regrettably, we now find ourselves building up what we left behind. For this reason, we need to be delivered from our own work. We should not hold on to anything. The Lord has shown us a clear vision. We need to build up the church in the saints' homes. We must all take this view and have this concept.

This is not an easy task for us. This is a big problem for us. We should check: After practicing the small groups and the home meetings for a year and a half, what kind of meeting do we appreciate? Do we still appreciate the big meetings, the kind of meetings where one man speaks and all listen? The meeting for the teaching of the truth is not a big meeting. In each class there are only about fifty people. The conferences are also not the big meetings, because these conference meetings are called for a special purpose. The joint Lord's table meetings are also not the big meetings; they are initiated when there are special needs. Such meetings are actually quite sweet. The big meetings that we are talking about here are the regular church meetings where one speaks and everyone listens. In these meetings the saints cannot function. But even today we still appreciate this kind of meeting.

FIGHTING EVERY STEP OF THE WAY

My point is that in order to arrive at the matter we spoke of earlier, that is, in order to arrive at the goal of the home meetings and teaching of truth lessons, we should be on the alert constantly and fight every step of the way. While some may say, "Brother Lee, we do not see any brother opposing you," we must be careful. The attack of the enemy is subtle. Today we are promoting the home meetings. Although the brothers and sisters do not oppose our promotion of the home meetings, neither do they respond enthusiastically. What is the source of this lukewarmness? Who put this in us? It is put in us by Satan. While Nehemiah was building the wall, others apparently were not opposing him, yet they were actually pouring cold water on his work (Neh. 4:1-3). When they heard that the wall was finished, they sent men to meet with Nehemiah. Outwardly, it was to help him, but actually it was to kill him (6:1-10). In order to arrive at our goal, every step of the way we need to fight.

In some halls or churches, as soon as the co-workers or elders speak of the home meetings, everyone responds favorably. Some even open up their homes immediately. This means that Satan's attacks are weak and ineffective in these places. In some other places, however, when the brothers say, "This is the Lord's up-to-date leading," nothing happens. Even after a month no one is meeting in the homes. This means that the legions of Satan's army are actively at work in these places. What should we do when faced with such a situation? Some who have not had any experience in spiritual warfare say, "We have done our best to encourage the saints, but no one is willing to open his home. This way must not work." This is the deadly attack of Satan; he turns us into a weapon in his hand and uses our mouth to launch his attacks. Consequently, we become discouraged and disappointed. Sometimes we hear reports that the home meetings are few in number and poor in attendance, and we think that everything is hopeless. What is this? This is altogether the work of agents from Satan.

If we are clear about these things, we will realize that for the past few months, Satan has been sending many little soldiers and messengers to us. Even though no leading one has ever said, "We do not agree with Brother Lee's proposal. We are absolutely against it," the enemy knows which tactics to use. He knows that he cannot fight the battle in this way, because it would only bring failure. Instead, he engages in a hidden war. Sometimes he avoids a "hot" war, and sometimes he even avoids a "cold" war; he simply brings in a war of confusion. He encourages inactivity, a sort of lethargy, making everyone feel that the small groups are difficult to carry out and that there is no need for action. All of these thoughts are from Satan.

I hope that we will all rise up and ignore these voices, fighting in one accord through prayer for the brothers and sisters. Do not interrogate them, saying, "Why are you not opening up your home?" Instead, pray for them in one accord. In all the halls and churches, the co-workers, elders, and full-timers must come together often. We should pray and even fast before the Lord together with the more seeking ones. We must counter the enemy step by step and push him back inch by inch. No opportunity must be given to him.

Satan knows that with the strong foundation in the Lord's recovery and the cumulative riches that we have inherited throughout the years, he can never succeed with a frontal attack. This is the reason he is adopting cold-war tactics. He does not send a direct blast of wind or engage in direct confrontation. Rather, he blows a little draft here and there, causing some to say, "Thank the Lord, our home is open, but regrettably no one comes." This kind of remark gives others a sour impression and discourages them from opening up their homes. On the surface, such remarks appear quite innocuous. Actually, they dampen the spirit. A car tire is usually not punctured by an iron rod but by a small nail. Once the tire is punctured, the air leaks out slowly, and soon the car comes to a standstill. Frequently this is Satan's strategy. He sends a small messenger to wear us out and cool us down.

For the past one and a half years, I was not personally involved in the church's practice, but I was observing from the side. The Lord covers me for what I am saying. I feel that even the elders do not have the awareness that we have fallen victim to Satan's tactics. We have not prayed in watchfulness. After my trip here last October, I returned to the United States to take care of many matters that were facing me there. In the midst of my busy schedule I wrote a serious letter to the elders here, reminding them in a sober way to pray and fast. However, when I returned, I found out that in the elders' meeting only the young brothers pray. Not many older brothers pray. This proves that there is not an atmosphere of prayer or a spirit of prayer among us. I am not discouraged by this. If I become discouraged, I have also fallen victim to Satan's tactic. However, the fact that the elders do not have a watchful and prayerful spirit means that they have come under the spell of the messengers from Satan.

The practice of the new way should be a great move of God. The church is on the verge of this new practice. When we come together, we should have much prayer; we should fight to pray. It is not right if I am the only one speaking every time we come together. In every gathering, everyone should pray and praise. Then the Lord will grant us some suitable words. Sometimes there is even no need for any words. This is the move of the Spirit. Currently, we do not sense much of the move of the Spirit, because we have not rendered Him adequate cooperation. He does not want to stand still; He wants to move, but He cannot move. We have stopped Him because we have not prayed.

Of course, I sympathize very much with the elders. Only

five or six of the elders are serving full time; the rest have jobs. Today in Taiwan the economy is very fast paced. Those who are working must struggle, or they will not be able to earn a living. I fully understand this, and I am full of sympathy. Still, our eyes must be opened. We need to see that no matter how busy we are, we must set aside some time to pray. Especially when the elders gather together, this time must be treasured and used for prayer. We should not merely pray eight or ten minutes and then move on to discuss business affairs. This will never work. When the elders come together, there should only be prayer. We should pray and pray until the Holy Spirit moves. The discussion of business affairs is secondary. In fact, every such matter, no matter how crucial it is, is secondary. The primary need is prayer. If the spirit is dormant and a spirit of prayer are lacking, the Holy Spirit will remain still. This is the most subtle contingency that the enemy has in his camp against the Lord's move. For this reason, we must all be watchful in our prayer.

A PERSONAL TESTIMONY

At the present time in Taiwan, my goal, on the one hand, is to study how to advance in the new move with the co-workers and elders. On the other hand, I have a great burden to work on the Recovery Version of the New Testament in Chinese. It has been difficult to have a proper version of the Bible for our meetings. The existing translations require much editing work. Since the publication of the Recovery Version in English, the Chinese saints, especially those overseas, have unanimously demanded a Recovery Version in Chinese. The saints in Taiwan are also very eager to have such a version. A few years ago I was hoping that some Chinese-speaking saints would pick up the burden to take care of this responsibility. I was even ready to spend the money to hire someone to take care of this work. However, after considering this for a few years and looking around, I realized that it was impossible to hire anyone to do this job. Such a one would need much spiritual education and should know theology as well as spiritual terminology and expressions, such as *the Triune God, the person of Christ, God's dispensing, God's economy, the essential Spirit, the economical*

Spirit, and others. At the same time, it was impossible to recruit some useful ones from the Lord's recovery and put them to use immediately. Even if we selected a few young ones and started training them, they would still need to pass through a period of training and perfecting. Consequently, I became clear that I had to sacrifice the work in the West and devote a year's time in Taiwan for this task. Based on our experience in the last few decades, I know I must enter into this work thoroughly in order to establish a good foundation.

For me to engage in this work is also a kind of warfare. It has been two months since I started this work. I have used every ounce of my energy on this. I can say that I have exhausted the strength in my spirit, soul, and body. Every day I work eight to ten hours. Although I am more than eighty years old, I still feel that I need to give myself in this way. May the Lord cover me with His blood. After two months we were finally able to lay a foundation. The serving ones now have some realization of what it means to translate the Bible, how they should use the reference books, and how to consult other material or versions. In the past they had the means, but they did not know how to use them. However, at the present time I have personally taken the lead to work through everything with them. While I worked, I also asked questions and directed them. In two months we finished the Gospel of Matthew, and then we moved on to the Gospel of Mark. Now the foundation is laid, but I am exhausted.

While I was working on the Recovery Version, I was also working on *Truth Lessons* and taking care of the English publications. For example, the messages for the International Elders' Conference have all been polished and are ready for me to read and review. After working hard this way, I was suddenly overcome two weeks ago by a general feeling of fatigue. Since then, I have been resting. Thank the Lord that He has given me a healthy body. If I did not have such a body, the result would have been unimaginable. I rested for four days, and by the fifth day I was able to resume meeting.

My point is that the enemy is attacking. When I was walking down to the basement of the meeting hall to join a truth class, I missed the last step of the stairs. Thankfully, the Lord protected me; my hand was still on the rail, but my body sustained a shock. At that time I did not feel anything, and I continued with the meeting. Since that time, however, I feel that my two feet have been weak and wobbly. I thought that it was caused by my fatigue and that with a little rest I would recover. The doctors suspected something was wrong with my heart and suggested an examination. The result of the examination was good, and the doctors declared that everything was normal. Still, I felt that my two feet could not bear my weight. The doctors suggested that I exercise more; they thought that I was tired from the desk work and that I needed exercise. But the more I exercised, the worse I felt. I could not explain this.

Last Friday I felt that I had to come and speak about the burden of prayer. Thank the Lord! Through this I realized that there is a spiritual battle here. On the one hand, the prayer last Friday sustained me, and on the other hand, it triggered something. The next day while I was in bed, I suddenly recalled a similar experience I had previously had with a backache. It was similar to this experience. I became clear that this was Satan's attack. He was doing a hidden work. I stopped all my work and lay quietly on my bed.

I give this little illustration to show that we need to pray. Do not think that Satan will work only a little. He sends these frustrations to us one after another. After my backache was somewhat healed, two days later I caught a cold and had a fever as well as diarrhea. The co-workers prayed for me on Monday morning for two hours, and then the full-timers prayed for me for one hour. The prayers were very effectual. In the past when I had a cold, I would struggle with it for at least a week, but this time I recovered in a day.

Do not think that all these things are accidental. We need to realize that we are in the midst of a spiritual battle. Yesterday I walked around my study for half an hour, and then I sat down to work on the manuscripts. The more I worked, the more alert and energetic I became. Now as I am speaking, the more I speak, the more strength I have. This shows that I am not sick. This is altogether Satan's attack in darkness. Of course, he does have some ground to attack; two months of work has drained all my energy. This gave Satan an opening to attack me. But thank the Lord for His protection! I was not hurt in any way.

A FIGHTING SERVICE

The brothers and sisters must realize that our work here is a fighting service. The elders in particular must receive the burden to build up the church in the homes. This is our undisputed goal. We need to make this successful. I hope that one day there will no longer be any big meetings among us, but we would have only home meetings. We can have more than three hundred thousand saints here in the church in Taipei without having a big meeting. Instead, everyone will meet in the homes. Yearly we can have a few special corporate gatherings, but we must never forget that the basis of the church is built upon individual families. This requires a long-term warfare. The co-workers in particular must see this and must endeavor in this way. We must build up the home meetings, teach the truth well, and give up the big meetings. If we do this, the clergy-laity system will be gone, and all the saints will know, speak, preach, and teach the truth. If we do this, we will no longer need a preacher among us; every saint will become a preacher.

A society is not propagated through teaching but through the begetting of offspring. Offspring are produced from the family, and they are also raised in the family. Through begetting, nourishing, and teaching, the offspring then produce their own families. In this way society continues generation after generation. Sixty years ago I was a single man. Later I married and had a family with eight children. Now these eight children have begotten more than twenty grandchildren in the third generation. This is the proper multiplication. It is the proper way for a society to propagate as a whole. The same is true with the church. It is through multiplication in the family that the church continues to prosper and spread generation after generation.

However, it is not easy to do such a work. Christianity is with us, and it affects us constantly. This "custom of the nations" is constantly frustrating us. This is what happened to Nehemiah when he rebuilt the city; Sanballat constantly opposed him (Neh. 2:19; 4:1-8; 6:1-9). This requires all of us to rise up to see this light and to struggle to fight. I do not mean to say that all of us must quit our jobs to serve as elders. I am saying that we must have an attitude of fighting. Even if we hold a job, we need to be for the Lord. If we do this, the Lord will bless us and our career. We are the Lord's recovery. If the Lord does not bless us, whom will He bless? If any man loves the Lord, this one is known by Him (1 Cor. 8:3). Those among us who have been loving the Lord and serving Him for decades have surely witnessed our families being blessed by the Lord. Today if we fight for His building, will He not bless us even more?

It is a great blessing for our families to be gained by the Lord and for our offspring to serve the Lord. We do not need to quit our jobs. God ordained that man labor to sustain his livelihood. Because this is God's ordained rule for man to exist after the fall, we need to keep our jobs. The young people especially should do their best to study well. After they graduate from school, they should take up a proper job. However, we should not fall into the trap of mammon once we take up a career. We should not try to become rich or to raise our standard of living. When we take a job, we must pray that the Lord will guard our heart for Him. Our time must be consecrated to the Lord. If we do this, the Lord will have a way in us. When Jacob was about to go down to Egypt, he first offered a sacrifice in Beer-sheba and consecrated himself to the Lord. God told him not to be afraid when he went down to Egypt, because He would make him a great nation (Gen. 46:1-4). We must have an aspiration and a burden from the Lord that even if we hold a job, we are still a full-timer. We are a money-making full-timer; we give all that we earn to the Lord for His use. The purpose of doing this is not only to save a few more souls and edify some saints but to build up the Lord's church in the homes. Today in Taiwan we have forty to fifty thousand brothers and sisters. If we can build up the church in every saint's home, we will replace the work of many preachers, and we will effectively teach the truth to the saints.

THE NEED FOR FULL-TIMERS

Of course, for the spreading of the gospel, the teaching of the truth, the ministering of life, and the building up of the church, we still need some full-time serving ones. For this reason, the support for the full-timers is very crucial. I would rather sacrifice the big meeting hall in Lin-ko than neglect the need of the full-timers. Whether or not we can build the big meeting hall is a secondary matter. The primary goal is to raise up two thousand five hundred full-timers. I have heard that some halls or churches feel that the burden for the support of the full-timers is too heavy, and they are considering "down-sizing," or "laying off," some of the full-timers. I beg you before the Lord, not to do this. This should never happen. We must have a strong resolution within ourselves that even if we must sell everything, we need to increase the number of full-timers. Even if we must sell our hall, we need to continue our effort to produce more full-timers. I feel that even if we must sell the land in Lin-ko, and even if we must borrow a few million dollars from other places, we need to do it to continue supporting the full-timers. We must reach the goal of having two thousand five hundred full-timers.

I also hope that we can increase the support of the full-timers. The budget for them is too small. They have given up their future, their positions, and consecrated everything to the Lord and the church. The church should take care of their needs. We should not be afraid of giving them too much. We are not afraid to do too much in other things. Why are we afraid to be too much when it comes to supporting the full-timers? This is an attack from Satan. It delays the work of the Lord's building. We must not be afraid of doing too much. We should only be afraid that we have not done enough. If the full-timers squander the support that the church gives them, and if they spend their money on unnecessary things, it proves that they are not qualified to be full-timers, and they should not serve full-time. When the full-timers hear this word, they should bow down to worship the Lord, and they should also serve with fear and trembling.

Let me give my own testimony. The Lord used me to spread

His work from Southeast Asia to the West. In twenty-three years, more than a hundred churches have been raised up in South America, North America, Europe, Africa, and Australasia. I admit that the Lord has used me to some extent, and the brothers and sisters have respected me and have supplied me abundantly. Still, other than expenses related to daily necessities, I have offered up all the money I have received year after year. During my twenty-three years in the United States, I have purchased only one small automobile, which was a second-hand car for which I paid eight hundred dollars. Eventually, I gave it away to a poorer brother, and I lived without a car of my own. What I am saying is that if the young people receive more supply from the Lord, they should learn to give. If we keep everything to ourselves, we are not qualified to be a full-timer. We must learn to take care of others.

As I have said before, years ago in Southeast Asia one brother received the burden to care for all the needs of the work in Taiwan. His offering not only made possible the purchase of the many pieces of property in Taiwan for building meeting halls, it also supported the livelihood of the full-timers. Beginning in 1950 there was a need to supply more than one hundred seventy people. Although not all their needs were covered, they were supplied enough to not experience total deprivation. Up until 1963 I was still supporting part of their needs from America. The churches gradually picked up the support, and by 1967 I was completely relieved of this burden. During this time, while I was in the United States, I experienced extreme hardship myself, yet the Lord did not fail to provide a bountiful supply.

Brothers, let me say a fair word. Those who receive the supply should realize that the money they are spending is the hard-earned money of the saints, who offer out of their love for the Lord. Such a love is priceless. The receiving ones should not take it lightly or spend the money loosely. At the same time, when they have an excess, they should take care of the needs of other saints. The church should be liberal in its support of the full-timers, but it should be careful in its own spending. On their part, the full-timers should be faithful in the way they handle money, and they should also take care of others.

By this summer at least a hundred full-timers will be produced in Taipei, but in order to gospelize Taiwan, we need to have two thousand five hundred by 1988. We need at least a thousand of them now. This is not an easy target to reach. I hope that we will be clear that the building of the big meeting hall in Lin-ko is not our primary goal. Our unique goal is the work of gospelizing Taiwan. For the need of the gospel in its various aspects, we need to work with what we have. If our finances permit us, we will buy gospel vans. If they do not permit us, we will use public transportation, but we cannot give up the work of gospelization. We do not want a big meeting hall without the power of the gospel or the practical spreading of the gospel.

Some may criticize me for always changing my way. In reality, as long as we want to improve, we need to change. The reason Taiwan is so prosperous today is that it does not limit itself to one method. It improves from one method to the next. This keeps us from failure. In the Lord's recovery I have worked from Chefoo to Shanghai to Taiwan, and from Southeast Asia to the West. I have had smooth sailing, and my morale is as strong as ever. The reason for this is that I vowed to succeed in all my endeavors. Of course, I have had failures, but I was not discouraged and did not lose heart. Instead, I considered the failures to be the predecessors to success. Failure or success lies not in the attainment of the goal but in the heart. The revolution of Mr. Sun Yat-sen experienced many failures, but in the end it was a success. It was a success because his goal was clear and his aim was single. I am clear that the new way of the Lord's recovery will become a success because our goal is right and our motive is pure.

We all admit that Mr. Sun Yat-sen rescued the Chinese nation. History has justified his achievements. In principle, this can be compared to the Lord's recovery today; its justification is undisputed. Six thousand years of human history have culminated in the consummate truth of the Bible, and this truth is what we are working out in the Lord's recovery. This is the reason we have the boldness and assurance to point out the mistakes of Christianity in the United States. Because of the slander of the evil ones, we were engaged in a legal battle. Thank the Lord that the truth eventually prevailed. One theologian even wrote a book to defend our position. This is because our goal is clear, our truth is accurate, and our motive is pure.

This litigation cost more than five million dollars. No one thought that we would have the courage to carry it out, but my mind was set. I would fight this battle even if it meant selling the hall in Anaheim. In the end, we did not sell our hall in Anaheim. Instead, we built the Irving meeting hall in the midst of the litigation. Do not think that I was fighting that battle alone. I did this in the Body and with all of you. Today we need to see that we are in the Body. We are co-workers together, and we have the same future. If today in Taipei we can reach the high ground of the new way, we will have secured a great victory for the Lord's recovery. We will build up the church in the believers' homes and accomplish God's eternal economy. Just as you encouraged me during the litigation process, I want to encourage you today, and I want to be encouraged through your encouragement.

CHAPTER FIFTEEN

HOW TO MEET

I have now been in Taiwan for almost three months, and I have tried my best to go to different meeting halls each Lord's Day to see how we are teaching *Truth Lessons.* On one occasion when I met with the elders, I spoke a few words to them, but I did not pour out all of my inward feelings because I never want to tell people what to do without first doing it myself. Empty knowledge is of no value; genuine knowledge is gained through experience. However, I am also clear that my commission in Taiwan is mainly for the translation of the Recovery Version into Chinese. I spend ninety percent of my time, and even one hundred and twenty percent of my energy, on this matter. For this reason, I do not have the time to talk in a detailed way about the change in the system.

TAKING CARE OF A MEETING— BEING BESIDE OURSELVES

When we began to change the system, I said that we are doing something new. We must, therefore, learn to do things one step at a time. I never expected that the new way would be successful within one or two years. This is not possible. We need to work this out gradually in one accord. Concerning the teaching of *Truth Lessons,* after much observation I can only shake my head in resignation. Our way of teaching is not correct. We do not even know how to take care of a meeting. Please excuse me for saying this, and please do not be discouraged. I am speaking honestly because I want us to grow. Let me demonstrate how we should take care of a meeting. I want us to learn something.

In taking care of a meeting, the co-workers and elders

must first be beside themselves. We must be "crazy" before God. The Lord Jesus was the first One to be beside Himself. Mark 3:20-21 says that He met so often that He did not even care for His food. His relatives came and pulled Him away, thinking that He had gone crazy. If the relatives of the Lord Jesus had not testified of this, we would never imagine that the Lord could be beside Himself for a meeting. We would have thought that the Lord met in an ordinary way and that the tone of His teaching was gentle and mild. However, if He had done this His relatives would not have said He was beside Himself.

The Lord Jesus was not the only one who was beside Himself; the apostle Paul was the same. In Acts 26:24, when Paul was defending himself before King Agrippa, Festus shouted, "You are insane, Paul. Much learning is driving you insane." This means that Paul was so intense in his defense that others thought that he was insane. The spirit within him burst forth, and his entire being was "exploding." In order to have an explosion, there must first be pressure. A deflated person can never be beside himself; he can never be "crazy."

The expression *beside Himself,* as in Mark 3:21, means that one is away from himself; he is delivered from himself. Humanly speaking, when a man is delivered from himself, he no longer acts according to himself. He has lost the form and expression that characterize him. For example, ordinarily we may sing in a very polite way, but suddenly we jump and shout as we sing. It seems as if we have lost our senses and are insane. This is what it means to be beside oneself. I believe the Lord Jesus was this way when He met on that day. This is the reason His relatives said that He was beside Himself. If the co-workers and elders are beside themselves in the same way, and they are so "crazy" that they sing, prophesy, and read the Word ecstatically in the meeting, irrespective of how many people are present, our meetings will surely be successful and full of the supply.

The same principle applies to the teaching of *Truth Lessons.* We need to be crazy, and our spirit needs to explode. We cannot be like a deflated tire. Who will receive the gospel if we preach lamely and tamely like a deflated tire? Similarly, if we are not beside ourselves when teaching *Truth Lessons,* if there is neither life nor vitality, the brothers and sisters will be killed. After I visited some *Truth Lesson* meetings in various places, I became quite concerned. We cannot build up the church by taking care of the meetings in that way.

BEING DELIVERED FROM
THE DEADENING INFLUENCE OF CHRISTIANITY

Whether it is the big meetings, the home meetings, or the meetings for teaching the truth, we first need to learn to lead the meeting in a proper way. Before we can speak to people, we must know how to begin the meeting properly and how to make people "come alive." If the brothers and sisters sit before us like blocks of wood, and we ourselves behave like pieces of wood, there is no way we can lead the meeting. In 2 Corinthians 5:13 Paul said, "Whether we were beside ourselves, it was to God; or whether we are sober-minded, it is for you." This means that in our daily life we should be sober, but in the meetings, in order to glorify God, we must be beside ourselves and ecstatic for God. If we are lukewarm in the meeting, we are not being sober but are in fact bound and dead.

History shows that Christianity has been under the influence of deadness, darkness, dryness, and desolation for a long time. Such degradation has continued until it has reached the lowest level. The Reformation did not reverse this situation of deadness. It was only one hundred sixty years ago when the British Brethren were raised up to release the light of the truth that men were delivered from darkness. However, although these truths were received in the spirit, they eventually led to an exercise of the mind. In the name of defending the truth, numerous divisions were produced. Within fifty years the entire situation dried up and the Lord was forced to raise up the Pentecostal movement as a reaction to the dead teachings of the Brethren. Those in the Pentecostal movement would shout, jump, and cry. They were no longer dead, but they had no regard for the truth. This went on until sixty years ago, when the Lord raised up His recovery through Brother Watchman Nee in China.

According to Brother Nee's realization, the Lord raised us up in China because deadness, oldness, tradition, and Pentecostalism had pervaded the West. The Lord did not have a way to go on and was thus forced to turn to the East. Since the day that the Lord raised us up in China, the light among us has been clear; we know that it is the Lord who has raised us up. He wants us to overturn the formalism of Christianity, the deadness of the Brethren, and the wildness of the Pentecostal movement. We take the truth of the Brethren, but we reject its deadness. We take the release of the spirit among Pentecostals, but we reject their wildness. Regrettably, the co-workers have not been sufficiently infused and impressed with these characteristics in the Lord's recovery. Today's Christianity is a killing religion. Subconsciously, we have fallen prey to its influence.

I am not selling my "seniority," but I have been conducting and holding meetings for more than fifty years. I have visited many places, and I am very familiar with the ways in which Christians meet. I have also read many books. I am clear about the deceiving, damaging, and ensnaring situation that exists today. We are still trapped in this snare. It is true that we are in the Lord's recovery, but we are not completely free from the snare of Christianity. We may have been saved in the Lord's recovery, but we still bear within our being the things that have ensnared Christianity.

This is the reason I put aside all considerations and openly rebuked the co-workers a year and a half ago. I did not "save their faces" or leave them with any place to turn. I did this because, more than anything, I hate being trapped in the snare of Christianity. I dearly love every co-worker, but I hate the things that issue from the influence of Christianity. Such things have been killing us from the day we were saved. Even today, we are still passing these things on to others. This is what grieves and cuts my heart the most.

The co-workers have been under my training for the past thirty years, but even today not too many are beside themselves. This is sad. It is a loss to the Lord. I hope that from today we can all learn to be beside ourselves in our homes before we come to the meeting. We should be "crazy," dancing before the Lord. This is not for men to see, but for the demons, the angels, and even that we would see. If we are "crazy" in our spirit, the brothers and sisters will be attracted and captured. In fulfilling my ministry in the United States, I did not speak beautiful English, and I certainly did not have any eloquence. Yet how did I attract so many brothers and sisters? I was able to be beside myself. We may have thousands of messages to deliver, and we may be full of God's economy, but if we are silent and reserved and do not exercise and release our spirit, we will kill everyone. Only those who are beside themselves and who are released in their spirit can lead the meetings properly.

In my natural constitution I am a reserved person. By nature I do not like to contact people. My mother told me that when I was five or six years old, I did not like playing with other children. I was always by myself. Later I received the Lord's grace and was forced by the Lord to learn to overturn my natural constitution for the sake of serving Him. Today I am an old person, yet it is still easy for me to be beside myself. I am ashamed to see co-workers who have been under my training for more than twenty years who are unable to be beside themselves. This is a shame to me, and it is a shame to them. Brother Nee once said that if a Christian has never been beside himself once before God, he is not qualified to be called a proper Christian. For this reason, all the co-workers must be beside themselves. We must learn to be "crazy."

When I pray to the Lord, many times I hit the desk or the bed. Sometimes I jump, skip, dance, and wave my arms. We must realize that the truth, the Spirit of truth, life, and the Spirit of life make us "crazy." In 1953 I conducted a formal training. I spoke to the trainees emphatically that they all needed to be "crazy" before God. When they set out to work for God, they needed to be beside themselves. Of course, this does not mean that we need to be crazy in front of others. We need to be sober before men but crazy in our spirit. Today when the full-timers visit people in the communities, they cannot act crazy when they come to people's doors. This will scare people away. We should be polite and sober but not bound. When we sit down, we must pay attention to our posture.

When we speak, our voice has to be gentle and kind. However, our spirit must be burning. If we can do this, the listeners will touch something in our inner being. They will think, "This man is attractive even while he is talking about Jesus. This is entirely different from what I have heard before." This shows that one recipe may make a dry and unpalatable dish in the hand of one cook but a delectable, juicy, and savory dish in the hand of another.

Hence, if we are crazy before God, our words will be full of power. At a crucial juncture, others will be convicted. Once they are convicted, we can have the freedom to be crazy before them. Then they will fully respect what we have to say. I believe this was what Paul did before King Agrippa. At a certain point in his defense, Festus shouted, "You are insane, Paul. Much learning is driving you insane." In visiting the communities, we should have similar experiences. I believe if we follow these instructions, many people will be convinced, and in the end they will be saved and baptized.

EXAMPLES OF PREACHING THE GOSPEL IN A CRAZY WAY

We must be persons who are burning in spirit and crazy before God. Whether we are visiting the communities or going to a meeting, we must prepare ourselves by first being crazy at home. I once said that John Sung was called a mad preacher. He was a person who was absolutely beside himself before God. Once, as a meeting was waiting for him, he suddenly appeared at the back door, singing as he entered, "Down with Satan, down with Satan; out with sin, out with sin!" As he sang, the entire congregation came alive. He was dressed in a traditional Chinese long gown. As he stepped onto the podium, he would pull out some gambling cards from his sleeves and sing, "Down with card games, down with card games; out with gambling, out with gambling!" or "Down with mah-jongg, down with mah-jongg; out with the devil, out with the devil!" At times he would hold out an opium pipe and sing, "Down with the pipe, down with the pipe; out with opium, out with opium!" At the end he would hold up a little coffin in his hand and say, "Do you want to go on with your gambling? Your gambling will lead you to the coffin. Do you want to hold on to your opium? Your opium will lead you down to the coffin." After this he would sing again, "Down with the coffin, down with the coffin; out with death, out with death!" Finally, he would make the call, saying, "All those who want to be finished with these things, please come to the front." A great crowd always would come to the front, weeping and crying as they walked forward, saying, "I want to be finished, finished, finished with these things!" This is the way John Sung preached the gospel.

THE CONDITION AND NEED FOR BEING CRAZY

In conducting any meeting and in working for the Lord, our first need is to be beside ourselves before God. Such "craziness" cannot be imitated. We must first pray thoroughly, confess our sins, and be cleansed before we can be filled with the Lord and His riches. Once His riches fill us, we will spontaneously be beside ourselves. Hence, in order to be crazy, we must first confess our sins, repent, pray, enjoy the Lord, contact Him, and be filled and clothed with His riches. Then when we come to the meeting, whether we sing or teach the truth, we will be full of impact. All those listening to us will be affected. After doing this once or twice, the saints will not need to wait for us to take the lead to be crazy; they themselves will become crazy.

Our meetings should not be old and stale, routinely starting with a hymn followed by some prayers. We should be beside ourselves in our homes before the meeting. We should stir up our spirit at home and then come to the meeting hall with singing or prayer. As we arrive, we should sing, praise, and pray with one another. This kind of meeting will surely bring in God's grace and His timely speaking.

During the past three months every time we met together, I sensed no living prayers. Most of the time it was the full-timers who prayed in a fervent way. The co-workers and elders were quiet and observing. If the co-workers and elders do not know how to be crazy and beside themselves, how can they lead the churches? In order for the churches to go on, there must be proper leadership, and in order to have proper leadership, the elders must be crazy. My wife often says to me, "The minute you speak, you forget about yourself. You forget about everything." This is what we all should do. As soon as we come to the meeting, we should be beside ourselves. As soon as we speak for the Lord, we should be crazy. Only a person with a crazy spirit can conduct a meeting and make it come alive.

LIVING AND WALKING BY THE SPIRIT

Being crazy has nothing to do with the outer man; it has to do with the inner man. We are crazy when our spirit is filled with the Lord's Spirit. If we are persons who live and walk in the spirit, as soon as we walk into the meeting the atmosphere will be changed. We have a spirit. If we use our spirit and live in our spirit as we choose a hymn, our choosing will be full of the spirit, and our singing will be full of the spirit. Our praying, reading, and speaking will all be full of the spirit. This is the basic qualification for conducting a meeting. If we do not use our spirit, our teaching of *Truth Lessons* will be nothing but dead reading, dead teaching, dead speaking, and dead listening. This is worse than the teaching in secular schools.

Not only do we need to live in the spirit; we must also stir up the spirit of all those in the meeting. The best way to stir up the spirit is to sing. I encourage us all to learn to sing our hymns. In particular, we should present this matter to the saints. We should tell them, "When we come to the meeting, we should not be bound and reserved. We are not here to attend a so-called 'worship service' of a denomination. We meet to release our spirit and to fellowship with one another in the spirit, receiving spiritual supply and spiritual infilling. In order to do this, we need to open up our spirit and stir up our spirit." As the saints come to the meeting, we must encourage them and instruct them in this way. They should pray and sing in threes and fives to stir up their spirit and to enliven the atmosphere of the meeting. If we do this, our meetings will be different.

HOW TO TEACH *TRUTH LESSONS*

Concerning the teaching of *Truth Lessons,* the first thing

we must remember is that we are not teaching a class in the public schools, we are teaching *Truth Lessons* in the church. This is altogether a matter of life and spirit. With a secular class, it is sufficient for the teacher to make the points clear. But with regard to teaching *Truth Lessons,* the focus is on the transmission of the Spirit and the dispensing of life. The Spirit is mysterious and intangible. How can we transmit the Spirit? Life is abstract and incomprehensible. How can we dispense life? Both the Spirit and life are in the truth. The reality of the truth is spirit and life (John 6:63). The real teaching of the truth is the transmitting and dispensing of the Spirit and life that is in the truth into people. For this reason, we must be those who live in the Spirit and in life.

Second, I have pointed out again and again that each lesson of *Truth Lessons* is a message in itself that does not need expounding or additional comments by the teachers. The materials in *Truth Lessons* are rich and clear. The teachers should take the lead to learn. The teachers should have this attitude: "I am not a teacher. I am a student who is learning with everyone else." If the teachers take the lead to learn and to lead the saints to read and absorb the lines, main points, outlines, big headings, and small items in *Truth Lessons*, what is read will become a supply to the saints. This is the reason I say, "Do not expound; simply read." However, the reading should not be done in a dead way but in spirit. Moreover, we should not ask only one person or even several persons to read the whole lesson. Rather, all the saints should read as one person with one voice. This will provide all the saints the opportunity to open their mouths to read, and this will also help them to practice speaking in the meetings. The reading must be done livingly. The saints can ask questions and answer them in a mutual way. This can be compared to playing basketball; when the players pass the ball smoothly to one another, they play a beautiful game.

Third, the teachers must release their spirit. They should not be shy or cowardly. Their spirit must come out to stir up the spirit of the saints so that everyone will not be loose but will enter into the lesson seriously and receive a transfusion.

Fourth, the teachers must be prepared before coming to the

class. Their preparation is mainly in studying the outline, not in searching for material. They must learn how to work the outline into the saints so that the saints may be deeply impressed.

Fifth, the teachers need to look for the important words in each paragraph and point them out to the saints.

Sixth, the summary at the end of each lesson is the key to entering into the lesson. Every point in the summary is the truth, every word is precious, and every sentence is excellent and full of life and light. The teachers should lead the saints to enter into the summary to enjoy it.

The *Truth Lessons* are rich in content, complete, and concise. Whether we can teach these lessons successfully altogether hinges on how we teach them. If we teach well, many will come to the meeting. There will be an atmosphere of desiring to attend these truth classes among the saints. The content of our ordinary meetings is a kind of communal cooking and is not too specific. The teaching of *Truth Lessons* is very practical and has a certain progression. This will help the saints to be solidly equipped with the truth and give them a taste of the riches of the Spirit and life.

THE SHARING AT THE END OF THE MEETING

For many years we have received a burden from the Lord to rid ourselves of the traditional way of meeting and have a proper practice. Therefore, at the end of a meeting, we should have a time for sharing. Without sharing, the meeting will be inadequate. The meeting for teaching *Truth Lessons* is no exception. There should be a period for sharing at the end of each lesson. Although we should ask one another questions and mutually answer and study in groups, we must still emphasize the sharing at the end. The purpose of learning the truth is to minister life and transmit the Spirit; it is not to find fault or simply study the wording. In particular, the prophecies and types require much time and effort to study; they cannot be thoroughly understood in three to five minutes by the saints in their groups. Consider the prophecy of the seventy weeks for example. The new believers do not need to understand everything about it. All they need to know is that there is the prophecy of seventy weeks in Daniel 9, and they should not try to be concerned with finding out its deep significance in the group study time. We all are "high school students." It is sufficient for us to understand the "high school curriculum"; we do not need to know the things that will be taught in "graduate school." The most crucial thing is not to give knowledge but to minister life and transmit the Spirit. Therefore, the saints must have a time for sharing at the end of the meeting.

A FEW POINTS REQUIRING PERSONAL ATTENTION

As teachers of *Truth Lessons*, we need to pay attention to this one thing: we should not dress sloppily; rather, we should dress neatly and properly. We need to dress as if we are delivering gifts to people's homes. Today even a salesperson dresses in a presentable way when he contacts his clients. If we do not tuck in our shirt and do not wear a tie when we bring a meeting to people's homes, they will think that the meeting we bring is not valuable.

Mormonism is a big heresy. For example, the Mormons believe that the Lord Jesus was born of Adam and Mary, and they also advocate polygamy. Yet their way of preaching is very clever. It seems that everything the Lord has led us to do in Taiwan has been "stolen" by them. They go out two by two, visiting people from house to house, bringing the meeting to people's homes, and teaching people how to begin a meeting at home. The most impressive thing is that all of their young people are in suits and are neat and tidy, giving people a very positive impression. They do not smoke or drink. Neither do they drink coffee or tea. They can gain people because they have this kind of outward appearance and a clever way of preaching.

Recently, in my visits to different places, I noticed that some of the brothers neither wore a tie nor a proper shirt when teaching *Truth Lessons*. This is to sell our "diamond" cheaply. I do not believe that anyone who sells diamonds would not wear a proper shirt and tie. Although we do not have any dress regulation or requirement, I hope that all the ones responsible for the truth classes will dress properly. In the full-time training, I once told the trainees that the colors of their shoes and their socks did not match, and the color of their ties also did not match. They needed to learn how to dress properly. In the same way, we also need to dress appropriately. If we are not properly attired, people will not be interested in us and will not believe what we say. Hence, we need to give people a feeling that we are proper and serious; moreover, we need to speak appropriately. Then people will think that we are weighty.

The same is true when we attend meetings. We should all dress in a serious manner. Today there is a heretical group in the Philippines that teaches people that Jesus Christ is not God, though they say He is a supreme human being. However, this group is very successful in the Philippines. The reason is that their meetings are orderly. Every attendant dresses properly, as if he were attending a banquet. The ushers wear nice uniforms, not extravagant ones but very proper ones. The area outside their compound is very messy, like all the streets in general. However, once one enters their compound, everything is orderly and regulated, and there are even attendants in the parking lot directing cars. In their meetings they exhort people to behave well, to be polite, moral, and loyal. They do not have much content in their preaching. They mainly teach people to be diligent and not slothful, to be honest and not tell lies, and to do everything by being punctual and by abiding by the rules. Many highly educated people agree with them, and many rich people like to hire members who belong to their group. Thirty years ago they had a membership of one million, and now they have four million. They surely are heretical, but because of their proper outward practice, they are very successful.

When I look at the situation of other groups and then consider the situation among us in the Lord's recovery, my heart truly aches. Please allow me to speak a frank word, for I do have the ground. In a training I held here thirty years ago, I spoke on thirty character points. I also built a simple, plain workers' home, but everything in it was orderly—even the plants were well trimmed and tidy. After I left for America and handed the home over to your care, it deteriorated year after year. Several times when I came back to Taiwan, I felt that the construction of hall one was good but that it had not been used properly. The entrance is not presentable. The books on the shelves are not tidy; some are worn out, and some have missing pages. Please consider this: If some educated ones who have a heart to seek the Lord, and who occupy high positions in society, came here, would they want to join us? We have erred in the Lord's work and misrepresented the Lord's recovery.

I am not asking that we build magnificent meeting halls. Our meeting halls should be simple, clean, tidy, and practical. I hope that the co-workers, elders, and full-timers would have a change in concept. Today the Taiwanese society has advanced. The shop fronts and restaurants have changed their appearances. Hence, we also cannot stay the same. We should neither be as crude and simple as in the past nor should we be fashionably extravagant. We must realize that we are representing the Lord to bring "diamonds" and "gems" to people. We are bringing truth, life, and the Spirit to God's children and God's chosen ones. Therefore, we should have a certain appearance, especially in our meetings.

Moreover, as teachers and leading ones in the meetings, we should pay attention to our speaking in public. Our natural man does not pay attention to speaking, so we need some adjustment and practice in this aspect. We should practice speaking to ourselves in front of a mirror at home and improve our speaking. Since we have received a commission to teach *Truth Lessons,* we should learn how to speak them. In particular, we should pay attention to our tone and speed. Sometimes we need to speak loudly; at other times we need to speak softly. Sometimes we need to speak fast, and at other times we need to speak slowly. Otherwise, even though we may have spoken much, people still may not understand what we have said. This is a waste. I hope that for the sake of the Lord's testimony, we all will learn this.

THE NEED FOR A CHANGE

If the Lord wills, I will gradually hold more trainings. In the past I have held trainings in the big meetings and for the co-workers. However, I feel sorry that these trainings were failures because the co-workers did not practice accordingly. We have a vast amount of spiritual assets in the Lord's recovery, yet our work has not been effective. This is because we have not paid attention to our appearance, and we do not have a practice that represents us well. Hence, we cannot break through in our work. The heretical group in the Philippines tripled its number in three years; however, our number has not increased; on the contrary, it has decreased. We have the truth and life, but because our method is inappropriate, we lack a proper practice to represent us. Since we have brought in the loose character of the Chinese, we are now in our current situation.

Please bear with me in my speaking. Today in Taiwan, people in the industrial, commercial, political, military, and academic fields are aggressively making changes. They discard old things and adopt new things. They are not the same as they were in the past. I hope that all the churches can have a big change, including the change of system that I introduced. Because of our weak foundation, our work will be quite complicated. I myself am not able to personally lead us in every detail. I hope that we all will seriously pay attention to what I have fellowshipped.

What I have shared is not merely related to changing our method of teaching *Truth Lessons*. I want us to see that meetings for the teaching of the truth are crucial. If the truth classes are carried out in a good way, all the other aspects of our work will be successful. The foundation of the entire church is the home meetings, and the key to successful home meetings is the teaching of the truth. If we are successful in establishing these two meetings, we will be able to spread to the communities, towns, and villages.

We cannot rely on big meetings in which one person speaks and everyone else listens. In the big gospel meetings that we have held in stadiums, we gained quite a number of people, but in the end only a few remained. Now we must concentrate on the home meetings. When the saints coordinate together to go door-knocking, the result is better than that of the big gospel meetings. Presently the full-time trainees go door-knocking twice a week in the communities; later they will propagate in the towns and villages. If we continue to labor in this way, we will give the Lord a way to advance.

We must clearly see that the change of system is intended to be a thorough change, a complete change. The change of system will enable the saints to have good habits and good character. For example, they will not dress casually for the meetings, but they will dress neatly and properly. When they go door-knocking, they will not be careless. Because we have neglected our outward appearance in the past and did not pay attention to a wise practice that could represent us, we encountered difficulty in every step of our propagation. The truths are here like a pile of diamonds, but we have treated them as if they were dung. This is the reason people do not recognize them as diamonds and do not want them. Now we need a big change to turn everything around so that people will see the diamonds and come for them.

I beseech that we pray much concerning the burden of this message and to ask the Lord for His mercy. We need to call on the Lord and tell Him that we truly need His mercy. In the past He gave us so many rich truths, but if we do not give Him the way today, He will not have a way to advance. May the Lord turn us absolutely and have mercy on us so that we will not receive His riches and grace in vain.

CHAPTER SIXTEEN

THE BURDEN AND PRACTICE
FOR THE BRINGING IN OF
A GLORIOUS FUTURE

First Corinthians 15:58 says, "Therefore, my beloved brothers, be steadfast, immovable, always abounding in the work of the Lord, knowing that your labor is not in vain in the Lord." This word by Paul was a conclusion to his teaching concerning the truth of resurrection.

Before speaking about the truth of resurrection, Paul first testified about the grace and his labor: "By the grace of God I am what I am; and His grace unto me did not turn out to be in vain, but, on the contrary, I labored more abundantly than all of them, yet not I but the grace of God which is with me" (v. 10). Paul said that through the work of grace he had become an extraordinary man. Yet he could not fully say what kind of a person he had become. He was able to labor more abundantly to bring God's economy to His children, not by himself but through the grace of God which was with him.

Following this word, Paul spoke about the truth of resurrection. At the end of this portion, in verse 58, he drew his conclusion, testifying that any labor and work in the resurrected Lord is not in vain. If our work today is in resurrection and not in the natural realm, it will not be in vain. Personally, I have always treasured this word of Paul. Since the day I began to serve the Lord, and for the past few decades, I have been constantly reminded, encouraged, and reassured by this word. I have said to myself many times, "I am laboring in the Lord. Yet this labor is not a work; it is grace, and it is not in vain. Therefore, I shall be steadfast and immovable, and I will always abound in the work of the Lord."

A REVIEW AND A PREVIEW

I have the burden to summarize or give an account of all that the Lord is doing among us in these days. We want to see what the Lord has shown us up to this point and what kind of future lies before us. This is a review of the past and a preview of the future.

When we began to change the system a year and a half ago, my main goal was to bring the church out of the old ways and to replace these ways with something new, to work from the inside out. Although we have not yet fully emerged out of the old "womb," at least by now a certain new shape has taken form. It now rests with the co-workers and the elders to ensure that we move onward steadily and steadfastly until the work is done and the delivery is complete.

I said that we should not only pick up the burden to ensure that the churches in the Lord's recovery increase in number but that the recovery as a whole would spread throughout the entire island of Taiwan. Whenever I speak of this matter, my heart aches within me. I feel deeply that we have come short of the Lord's calling. In 1948 the Lord brought us to Taiwan. By 1984 we had been here for thirty-six years. In our first five years in Taiwan, the Lord greatly blessed us. Not only did the number of churches increase rapidly, but the recovery was also spread throughout the entire island. The result of this increase and spread was a hundredfold increase from four hundred people to forty or fifty thousand people and from three or four churches to sixty or seventy churches. Later we suffered some frustrations, went downhill, and even stopped. Since that time there has been no increase or spread. The number of saints has remained the same, and the number of churches has increased only minimally.

In 1984 as I reviewed the situation of the previous thirty or more years, I was deeply bothered. Under the Lord's sovereign arrangement, everything on this island was ideal for the Lord's spread. From every perspective we were more than qualified to spread the Lord's kingdom. Yet we had not done this. I felt that I had truly failed the Lord. I felt that this was the time for us to receive the Lord's commission to pick up this burden once again and do everything we could to spread the gospel, the truth, and the churches throughout the entire island of Taiwan. At that time, I resolved to accomplish this task in five years. In order to do this, I spoke of the great need to add five hundred college graduates as full-timers every year. In five years we would have twenty-five hundred full-time serving ones.

When I brought up this need, I was very clear within that this was of the Lord. Now eighteen months have passed. We can only say that we are moving very slowly and doubtfully toward this goal. Yet if we measure ourselves against our past experience and consider all the present factors, we can say that the Lord has been very merciful to us. We must admit that the Lord's recovery does have a very strong foundation here. This has been proven by our faithfulness to the Lord during the past eighteen months. We have been willing to pick up the burden and answer the Lord's call About two hundred fifty young ones have given themselves to be full-timers. I hope that by the summer training two hundred more full-timers will be added. In this way, in another eighteen months, we will have at least seven hundred to one thousand full-timers. We hope that the preparation work for evangelizing Taiwan will be completed in three years. By 1988 we will be able to form an army and send it out.

There is still a year and a half to go. This is the time for us to train our army. In the full-time training these full-timers should spend at least two-fifths of their time to visit the communities, bringing the gospel and the meetings to people's homes and learning to speak properly in their visitations. The rest of the time they should be equipped in classes. By the time they set out in 1988, these trainees must be fully equipped. They will have learned the best techniques, and they will be trained to spread the Lord's gospel throughout all the towns.

After much consideration, the Lord gave us a good way. We will group the one thousand full-timers into one hundred teams. They will work in one hundred towns, visiting people and delivering the gospel and the meetings to the homes two by two. After a month, two will stay behind with the new ones in each town to do follow-up work and to establish the new church, and the other eight hundred will regroup and set out for eighty more towns, where they will work for another month. In this way, in five months we will establish churches in all three hundred eighteen towns throughout the island. The most important thing is to build up the gospel and the church meetings in the homes of all the new believers.

In the second five years, after the entire island is gospelized, and after the net of the gospel, the truth, and the church has spread over the entire land, we will move into the communities in all the major cities. We will also spread out from the towns to the nearby villages. In this way we will completely saturate Taiwan with the gospel, the truth, and the church. This is not a dream. It is not an idealistic goal. It is a workable plan. If we are faithful to the Lord and if we labor diligently, this future will become our reality.

Today we are in a different age. Taiwan has advanced and prospered in every area during its forty years of development. Communication is well developed. Education is widespread, and the standard of living is high. Industry and commerce are booming. Finance is strong, and the citizens are well off. The apostle Peter did not have the opportunities that we have. The condition in the land of Judea after the Lord's resurrection and ascension, at the time of Pentecost, was not similar to what we have today. At that time the Jews were under Roman domination. Its extortion and severe financial demands left the economy depressed and stifling. Education was limited, and communication was sporadic. One had to walk from Jerusalem to Capernaum; at the most, a donkey could be ridden. There were not the means of communication that we have today. Yet under those circumstances, Paul took the lead to preach the gospel from Jerusalem outward until it reached all of Judea, Samaria, Asia Minor, Eastern Europe, and even as far as Rome. All this happened within a span of thirty or so years. Today the Lord has furnished us with such a convenient and rich environment. If we do not labor, how foolish we are, and how much we come short of the Lord's grace!

Today we can use the telephone to call an elders' meeting. Saints from dozens of churches in Europe, Africa, and America can gather together and use the telephone to enjoy sweet fellowship. What a gracious provision we have from the Lord! We must all wake up to realize that this is an age for great actions. We need to seize the opportunities and achieve something. We look to the Lord desperately and pray that His blood would cover all of us to fight the battle for God's kingdom here in this land. We are not engaged in small-scale private enterprises. We are engaged in the universal enterprise of our heavenly King. We are here cooperating with the Lord, making ourselves available to Him for the spread of His kingdom. This is not a small thing. It requires our full effort and participation.

I say this as an encouragement. We are not forcing anyone to drop their jobs to serve the Lord full time. But we do hope that some elders would give themselves to serve in a full-time way. Even if we cannot serve full time for our whole life, we can at least try and serve full time during the ten years of our gospelizing Taiwan. We can go back to our jobs after all the cities, towns, and villages have churches. This is a glorious service. It is a service that is well pleasing to the Lord. This is a glorious operation in the Lord's recovery. I hope that we all will have a part in this operation.

THE BURDEN AND PRACTICE
TO REALIZE THIS GLORIOUS FUTURE

Building Up the Home Meetings

What should we do to bring in this glorious future and reach our goal? First, the elders in every local church should pick up the burden to build up the meetings in the saints' homes. Every saint should have a meeting in his or her own home. Last month there were forty-five hundred saints attending the home meetings in Taipei. Now the number has reached fifty-one hundred. We should be encouraged to continue advancing. Of course, we are not for numbers only. Our emphasis is to build up the home meetings.

The home is a steady and stabilizing unit. Those who are saved in the homes grow up in the homes. Since they are built up in the homes, it is not easy to lose them. In the past the church life was like a social club. When a person was saved, he was frequently ignored because of lack of care and concern. Now the church must be built up in the homes. When a person is saved and baptized, he will not be dropped. Rather, the fruit will remain and be strong. I hope that the elders will see this clearly. I have no intention to build up the big meetings centered on the meeting halls. We are for building up the home meetings. The home is the base for the building up of the church. It is the basic building unit of the church. This does not mean that we will give up the meeting halls. The halls are a means and a bridge for us to take advantage of and cross over. Our real goal is to build up the home meetings. If there are one thousand saints, there should be one thousand active homes. If there are ten thousand saints, there should be ten thousand active homes. If there are ten thousand homes in Taipei, and if every home brings in one person a month, in one year we will bring in one hundred twenty thousand people. This is a tremendous thing. If we take the old way, how many elders and co-workers will we need to appoint to take care of one hundred twenty thousand people? In the new way no such appointments are needed. All the homes can take care of these people.

The more we speak, the clearer we are concerning this matter. This is the life pulse of the new system, and it must succeed. With this in view, we should pay much attention to the full-time training. A plan has already been drafted with the trainers. In the future the full-time training will be carried out in the Full-time Training Center in hall three of the church in Taipei. All the trainees must reside in the center. Some churches may not be very happy about sending all these good young people to Taipei. They may ask, "What about our own locality?" Brothers, we need to have proper foresight. We should not let localism blind us from seeing the overall future of the Lord's recovery. These young people are being trained here temporarily. In the long run they will serve in all the localities according to the need. For the sake of the overall enterprise of the Lord's recovery, the elders and responsible brothers in all the churches should do their best to encourage the young people to attend the training and to send them on their way.

In order to meet the need of the full-time training and of the gospelization of Taiwan, there is a great need of financial support. The need for the full-time training alone presents a great burden to all of us. From the beginning, I fellowshipped that in the churches one out of every twenty saints should be a full-timer. The other nineteen should support his living and training. All the churches should strive toward this goal. At the same time we should do our best to be faithful in material giving. Some may say that the training and giving should be up to the Spirit's leading and stirring and that there should not be any human arrangements. But we need to understand that even though our personal walk should follow the leading of the Holy Spirit, the move of the entire church should issue from the leading of the Holy Spirit through the apostles' and elders' instruction. In Paul's Epistles, he directed Timothy and arranged for the movements of his co-workers.

The Lord willing, we should even specify the way we should dress and the way furniture should be arranged in the meeting. Every time we meet, we are before God; therefore, we need to be serious about our conduct. If we act loosely and carelessly, as we have in the past, we will be selling the Lord's recovery too cheaply. In the previous chapter I mentioned a heretical group in the Philippines. In their meetings everyone dresses properly and puts on proper attire. This is the reason high-class people are attracted to them and even pride themselves in being members. We should pay attention to this and reexamine ourselves.

Some may say that if we do this, we will be like those in James 2, who respect persons and prefer the rich to the poor. My response to this is from 1 Corinthians 11. At the time of the apostle Paul, when believers frequently gathered together for meals, the rich would bring better and finer food while the poor would bring little, yet everything was for mutual enjoyment. This was called a love feast (Jude 12). The Corinthians, however, did not properly take care of this matter. They did not wait for one another (1 Cor. 11:33). On the contrary, because each ate his own food, the rich became drunk while the poor starved (v. 21). This led to division and parties among them (vv. 18-19). For this reason, Paul rebuked them for despising the church of God. In the same way, if some saints are not able to dress properly, the rich ones should offer money to take care of them. I am not speaking this lightly. My point is that we cannot despise the church of God. We cannot sell the Lord's recovery cheaply. The Lord Jesus was not a wanton person. At the cross the soldiers cast lots for His garment. This proves that the Lord's garment was quite dignified. If He had dressed like a pauper, the soldiers would have thrown His garment away; they would not have fought over it.

Since we changed the system in October of 1984, there was a great turn within me. I did not want to initiate this change in the West. In 1949 the Lord sent me to Taiwan. Just as I began from Taiwan and brought in the present situation, in the same way I want to begin from Taiwan and spread outward from here, gradually bringing in a new situation everywhere.

Succeeding in the Truth-teaching Meetings

Second, the elders must build up the truth-teaching meetings. These meetings must become the center of all the meetings. In these meetings we must not only teach the truth but also help the saints to meet. In the future all large meetings and consolidated gatherings should be truth-teaching meetings. We do not have sermon meetings. Our sermon meetings are truth-teaching meetings.

Concerning the teaching of the truth, the Lord's recovery should be the most qualified and experienced among the Christian groups in Taiwan. Our teaching has spread even to other countries. No one's teaching can compare with ours. Our *Truth Lessons* have rich main points, clear outlines, simple and concise language, and are easy for new believers to understand. Of course, we should never be satisfied. We should study and improve our teaching and delivery skills.

The important thing is that we must not only teach, we must also make our meetings living. If we do this, we can bring our friends and relatives to the truth meetings. I hope that in the coming days, the truth meetings will be the most attractive meetings in the Lord's recovery. We need to turn with the age. Today everyone wants knowledge and information. Even an unbeliever wants to know the truth. If we preach in an ordinary way, others will not be attracted; however, if we speak logically, concisely, clearly, and with much content, others will be convinced. The whole world knows that Christianity teaches the Bible. Everyone more or less respects the Bible. If we can present the truth properly and clearly, based upon this well respected "classic," others will rise up to admire it.

Today most people have received a good education. Most people are college graduates. We cannot invite people to come listen for an hour and a half to a message given in a sloppy manner. This is what we did before. The truth meetings, however, present a simple and clear message that is packed with truth and logic. This will easily touch people. To the educated and thoughtful people, this is very effective and attractive. Hence, we must make the truth meetings our goal. We should even use these meetings to preach the gospel. If we would practice this, it will become a new move in Christianity; others will not be able to match us.

Actively Visiting
the Communities and the Campuses

Third, we need to actively engage ourselves in the visitation work in the communities and on the campuses. The co-workers and elders need to take the lead to do this work. Today Taiwan is growing rapidly. The expansion in the big cities mainly revolves around the new urban communities. There are high-class, young, and ambitious people living in these new communities. Some of these urban developments are more advanced than those in the United States. If we do not bring the gospel to them, we will miss the opportunity. We must take action and begin visiting. We are not the only ones who have noticed this phenomenon; the denominations are also paying attention to these new developments. If we take the initiative, we will gain people. If we wait until Christianity has started their work, it will be difficult to catch up. Hence, the co-workers and the elders need to wake up and take the lead to visit and work in these communities.

In the next term of the full-time training, there will be three hundred trainees. Every week they will spend two days visiting the communities. However, this work is not primarily theirs; this work belongs to the whole church. The elders must, therefore, stir up and encourage all the local saints to do their best to cooperate and coordinate together in the visitation work. In the future the spreading of the gospel will depend almost entirely on the communities. We must go to the communities. In addition, the campuses are important targets. In Taipei we should work to gain the students and to prepare the best material for the Lord's recovery. We should build up a strong testimony on all the campuses.

FOCUSING ON THE CAMPUS WORK

I have a proposal concerning the campus work. I hope we will fellowship thoroughly concerning this proposal. We must locate good meeting halls adjacent to good universities such as National Taiwan University. The location must be right, and the building must be large enough. Hall three was originally remodeled for this purpose. However, National Taiwan University is located near hall nineteen, and hall nineteen is not suitable for this use. I visited that hall once and was discouraged by what I saw. The location is hidden, and the hall is shabby. If I were a college student, especially from overseas, I would surely hesitate to go to such a hall. Even if I wanted to become a Christian, I would not want to enter such a shabby-looking place.

Let me say a word to the church in Taipei. For a brief time let us forget about Lin-ko. Let us focus on this goal and this burden. Secure a large and suitable building near the campus for a meeting hall. Find one that will hold at least three to four hundred people. National Taiwan University is the top university in this country. This university produces all the top people and has a large student population. We should have the foresight. If we want a campus work, we must work on National Taiwan University. I ask the co-workers to give me the liberty to bring up some old complaints. You have been under my training for many years and have been serving this entire time. Why have we not had this kind of view? We have always boldly declared that we are for the campus work, but what has been done on the top campus in the country? If I were taking the lead in the church in Taipei, I would surely go back to all of the meeting halls and fellowship aggressively about this burden. I would encourage all the brothers and sisters to make offerings for a new building near the campus. We should have this kind of spirit and this kind of view.

This is the reason I was merciless to the co-workers when I came back a year and a half ago. I was clear that if I was nice and polite, our work would not go on. I hope we will pray much before the Lord. Today we are engaged in the heavenly King's enterprise. We are building up His kingdom. This is a tremendous matter. We love the Lord. We want to be faithful to Him; for more than two or three decades we have given up everything and consecrated our all to Him. What have we accomplished? According to my observation, we have managed to hold on to a certain attainment; we have maintained a certain amount of truth and life. But what have we actually accomplished? In reality we are merely eking out a living. We should not be that passive and impotent. We should shake off this lethargy.

We should have a proper and practical plan concerning the campuses. Some meeting halls are five or six stories tall. What is the use of having such tall buildings in places that do not have a good campus? If the saints cannot afford to give for the campus, I do not believe we need to keep the big meeting halls. We can sell three or five of these halls and direct the money to a large facility by the campus. This is worthwhile. Even if we can gain only one hundred students from the campus, this is still worthwhile. When a nation launches a project, it cannot spend too much time calculating the cost involved; it can only count on the success of the project. If the project succeeds, it is worth the expense. I hope the elders will pray and fellowship thoroughly concerning this matter during the elders' meeting.

BUILDING UP THE ELDERS' MEETING

I hope we will overturn the Chinese disposition, which is to be nice and polite when sitting in a meeting. Even if everyone decided to visit hell, there would be no disagreement; at the most there might be an oblique suggestion to visit heaven instead. But after the meeting, everyone is freely criticized and condemned. When the elders come together, they can talk and debate about everything, but in the end everyone must be in one accord to carry out the decision. No one can act independently. Please remember that we are not serving merely as elders in our own little halls; we are serving as one of the elders of the entire church in conjunction with eighty other brothers.

In the past I told the senior elders that they should not carry the burden of the church in Taipei entirely on their own shoulders. They must build up the elders' meeting and let that meeting lead and direct the church. Only in this way can the church be strong and the Lord have a free way to go on. When I returned to Taiwan a year and a half ago, I appointed eighty elders. The purpose of my appointment was to build up the elders' meeting. I hope that we will learn to pick up the burden of the church and will learn to expand and head up the church in a good way. Only then will the church advance and have a good future.

In summary, our goal is very clear. We need to work on the communities because the general population is there. The church must follow the direction of the population. At the same time, we must work on the campuses. We need to gain the present generation of young people for the Lord's recovery. In particular, the church must do something at National Taiwan University. For this purpose, the elders need to rise up, pray much, and fellowship concerning what to do. For now, we will advance toward these two main goals. The spreading of the gospel in other areas will follow.

It is right to be careful and cautious, but "where there is a will, there is a way." The Lord wants our cooperation. The church is here, and it should have some action and endeavoring. Several times in the past I rebuked the co-workers. I pointed out that in Taiwan, industry, commerce, education, and politics are all advancing, but the church is not advancing. I have waited for many years, but nothing has changed; everything has remained the same. This is the reason I made the drastic decision to come back and do something myself. The elders can consider themselves a new generation. The senior elders should also consider themselves as young and vigorous. We should begin everything anew and build up the church anew. We cannot sit around and do nothing, merely conveying a little truth and life to the saints and expecting them to grow in life at their own pace. On the island of Taiwan the Lord has been delayed by our delaying for more than thirty years. There has been no gain, no progress. In the face of all the advances and prosperity around us, we must do something. We should strive with all we have. Only then will the Lord have a way. We must pick up these three burdens—building up the home meetings, having a success in the truth-teaching meetings, and aggressively developing the community and campus work.

MATCHING GOD'S WORK WITH OUR MATERIAL SUPPLY

In order to pick up the burden and to spread the work aggressively, we need to match God's work with our material supply. The present urgent need is to take care of the full-timers. Today the standard of living in Taiwan is high, yet our support for the full-timers is very low. These full-timers have given up their future for the spread of the Lord's recovery. In addition to taking care of their living, they also give away books and booklets to their contacts and the new believers. We need to take care of them. For this reason, I have seriously considered before the Lord to raise the support of the full-timers so that they will not need to worry about their living and can concentrate on the great work of evangelizing Taiwan.

I have presented all these needs to the churches. I hope we will see that the gospelization of Taiwan is not a slogan. We must give our all. The need of the full-timers is at least NT$120,000,000 (approximately US$4,000,000) per year. If we can raise this amount, we can be elders. If we cannot raise this amount, we are not qualified to be an elder. In order for all the saints to give everything to the Lord, the co-workers and elders must be in one accord. We must take the lead to charge forward. The result will surely come. However, if we expect the horses to run fast without supplying them with adequate grass, we are impractical. The Lord cannot bless this kind of attitude.

I say this because I am clear within that the Lord has blessed us greatly in material supply. Today the assets and income of most of the saints far exceed their need. The question is whether or not we are truly for the Lord. Have we truly consecrated our all to the Lord? When we all put our shoulders together, we can build a city. When everyone gives a hand, we can lift many things easily. If everyone puts in his share, we will more than meet our needs. This requires not only the churches' attention and the saints' awareness but also our practical consecration.

In addition to all this, should any church or meeting hall have some promising persons, I hope we would send them to the United States for special training. Their mind will be opened when they learn from other churches and fellowship with other churches. This is the way the world advances in science, education, and commerce. It encourages international exchange, and the result is phenomenal. We, however, are barely moving at all. We need to learn so that the church can catch up with the advance of the age.

SPREADING THE LORD'S TESTIMONY

Please forgive me for saying all these things. I may appear to be a foolish man. It may seem that I am beside myself. However, I have seen a vision and have received a burden to release the truth in the Lord's recovery item by item. These truths are published in books, but these books are only sitting on our bookshelves. Meanwhile, the entire Christian world, with all the children of God, is starving spiritually. We must realize that it is to our shame that these truths have not gone out. We have wasted the Lord's great grace upon us!

Thirty-five years ago I came to Taiwan with only my two hands. Among us we had only a few books by Brother Nee and a hymnal consisting of about one hundred eighty songs. I began to publish a magazine entitled *The Ministry of the Word* and a book entitled *Crucial Truths in the Bible*. At that time there were twelve members in my family, but we lived in a studio that was big enough for only eight beds. There was no desk; I had a rattan coffee table. I prepared all the publications from that table and began the work in Taiwan in this way. During the past thirty-six years, we have published many books, but they are all sitting on the shelf. This truly grieves me. I cannot bear to think of this.

By the Lord's mercy, I am sharing this with the co-workers and elders. I hope we will receive this fellowship from a "foolish" man (2 Cor. 11:16-17). The Lord did not have a way among us in the past. The tragedy is that we know what the way of the Lord is; our eyes are clear. We know that His truth is in our hands, but who will send this truth out? You may say you can sleep peacefully, but I cannot sleep peacefully. I am an old man, yet I still want to spend and be spent. I want to be able to answer to the Lord. For years there was no progress in the work of translating the Bible into Chinese. I have been here for two months, and there is now a good foundation laid in this work. On the one hand, this is not an easy task. On the other hand, this is not that difficult a task. It all depends on whether or not the brothers are willing to pay the price. I hope that from now on, we will all make a strong resolution to advance and make progress. Strive to produce some result, and labor to spread the Lord's testimony.

Brothers, I hope we will make a strong resolution to accomplish something while we are still young and capable. We must be like those in Judges 5 who made "great resolutions in heart" and "great searchings of heart" (vv. 15-16). We must achieve something for the Lord. We must never bury the grace that the Lord has given us or the gain that we have received from our training. When the Lord returns, we will be in trouble if the treasure within us is not dug out and the talents are not utilized. I hope that we will spend all we have and will not hold back anything. If we have a talent, we should spend a talent. If we have two talents, we should spend two talents. Only then will the Lord have a way to go on. Otherwise, we can wait for fifty years and nothing will happen. Today there are almost twenty million people in Taiwan. Only five hundred thousand are saved. Are we not ashamed of this? We have been here for more than thirty years. The gospel has not spread very far. Do our hearts not ache? Perhaps we have grown numb to this fact. I hope that this word will prick our hearts.

A WORD OF EXHORTATION

Dear elders, there are no easy tasks. Even to be a little elder is a difficult task. We need to struggle and strive. I believe we all love the Lord. All of us are willing to consecrate ourselves to the Lord and sacrifice for the Lord. Regrettably, in the past we did not receive this kind of help. That was a great shortage. I hope we will take this fellowship and the exhortation of the apostle in his revelation concerning resurrection: "Therefore, my beloved brothers, be steadfast, immovable, always abounding in the work of the Lord, knowing that your labor is not in vain in the Lord" (1 Cor. 15:58). The word used here is not *work* but *labor*. To labor implies not being discouraged, pressing on, and striving with all that one has. For any work, before success comes, there are struggles, frustrations, and failures. One has to strive and labor before he can reach his goal. In order to build up the home meetings, the truth meetings, the community work, and the campus work there must be this kind of labor and struggle.

I hope every elder will struggle and strive in this way. We should not avoid the difficult path and take the easy way. Nor should we settle for the light tasks. We must endure to the end. Nothing and no one should deter us, and we should never be discouraged or dejected. Success is not measured in a day. No account is settled until the Lord comes back. We were born here, raised here, saved here, and perfected here. This is our destiny. Today it is the Lord who has honored us by making us elders. We must respect this honoring and give our all to His commission. We must not only give our money and our career; we must give our blood and our life as well. If we have this kind of spirit, we will be successful elders.

Based on my experience of more than thirty years, and according to my studying and observation, I can say that the three ways that we have fellowshipped today are the best and most excellent ways. In addition to these ways, we have the richest inheritance, which is the truth among us. It serves as our shield and support. Everything depends now on how we conduct ourselves in the work. I hope we will take this word of encouragement and exhortation. I hope the elders will have an elders' meeting at least once a week to pray and fellowship much and to take up the burden of the church. May the Lord be gracious to each of us.

A PRAYER

Lord, we bring all the situations before You. You know everything. We believe everything is in Your hand. We believe that the recovery is Yours and that all the moves are Your moves. We believe fully that You will gain the glory in Taiwan and will spread Your kingdom here. For this reason, bless all of us. Bless the saints, bless their homes, and bless their service. Lord, especially bless the full-timers, and bless their training. May their work and walk in Your presence be burnt offerings on the altar, and may they be acceptable to You. Lord, we are full of peace and rest and are assured that this is what You want to do. You will accomplish this work for the coming of Your kingdom and the realization of Your will on the earth.

Lord, cover the co-workers and the elders, especially the elders in all the meeting halls, to take up this burden to build up the homes, the truth-teaching meetings, and the work in the communities and the campuses and to produce full-time trainees for the gospelization of every city. Lord, remember the brothers and sisters and bless them. May they consecrate everything on the altar for Your love's sake and for the sake of fulfilling Your work in this age. Lord, manifest Your riches in the midst of all the needs. May You gain a clear highway in Taiwan and gain a glorious testimony on this earth to be a model to all the churches. Lord, we look to You to accomplish this. We hide ourselves in You and exercise to put everything under Your care.

Lord, protect our coming in and our going out. Protect everyone and every home. Do not allow Satan any opportunity to attack, frustrate, or obstruct this move. Lord, take away our discouragement, our lack of confidence, and our fear. Make us steadfast and immovable, and give us faith in everything we are doing. We desire to see Your glory. May all the glory go to You! May the love of God, the grace of the Son, and the fellowship of the Spirit operate among us, and may we daily enjoy the dispensing of the Triune God. Lord, gain this earth and remember Your testimony on the earth. Amen!

CHAPTER SEVENTEEN

A SUMMARY OF THE FELLOWSHIP
CONCERNING OUR PRACTICE
RELATED TO CHANGING THE SYSTEM

Prayer: Lord Jesus, we worship You. Thank You that by Your sovereignty You have gathered us together once again. We do treasure this time. Lord, we offer up our worship, thanksgiving, and praise for Your recovery, for Your move among us, and for Your leading. Lord, bless this meeting, and fill this meeting with Yourself and Your presence. Lord, multiply Your blessing to us moment by moment. Let others see that You are in our midst, that You have a recovery on earth, and that this recovery is Your testimony, Your move, and Your spread on earth.

Lord, open our hearts in the same way that You have opened up Yourself to us. Grant us an open sky. May there be no veil, no shadow, and no hindrance within us, and may we be altogether shining within and without. Lord, remove all barriers and veils between You and us. Speak to us, Lord. We consecrate our hearts to You. We consecrate our entire being to You. We consecrate this entire move to You as a living sacrifice to satisfy Your heart. May You spread outward from us, and may You gain a free way through us. Lord, may none of us become a hindrance to You, and may there be no limitations or frustrations in us.

Manifest Your victory through us once again. May the victory at Calvary be realized, applied, and manifested once more through us today. May the enemy be shamed once more. Lord, this is Your move. You want to gain not only this land but also the whole earth. We thank You that there are hundreds of golden lampstands on the earth today. Bless Your work. We would like to see a brand new beginning. Lord, gain us, beginning from Taiwan. Gain every church and every saint. May every one of us be like David, who was according to Your heart. May Your light shine brighter and brighter, and may it be like the light of dawn, which shines brighter and brighter until the full day.

Lord, glorify Your name. Bind the power of darkness in Your name. Bind the evil one, Satan, Your enemy. Bind everything that opposes, destroys, and counters Your move. Lord, we exercise Your prevailing name to release Your children and loose the sinners. Lord, this is Your promise. You have promised us that whatever we bind will be already bound in heaven, and whatever we loose will be already loosed in heaven. Lord, release Your life, Your truth, and Your Spirit. In Your victorious name and according to Your word, we command You to act according to Your own glory. Lord, release Your riches, Your all-inclusive and unlimited Being, through Your victorious name.

Lord, we ask You to look at the situation on this earth! Destroy the power of darkness so that You can carry out the divine dispensing of the Divine Trinity in all the places. May all those who call on Your name be not only saved but also fully saturated and fully gained through the divine dispensing of the Triune God, and may this hasten Your coming back. Lord, we worship You and give all the glory and honor to You. We acknowledge You as the Head, both of the church and of all things. We call upon heaven and earth to testify to the fact that You have a recovery on this earth and that there are some who have placed themselves on the altar to satisfy Your heart. Lord, move freely without any hindrance. Amen!

FELLOWSHIP CONCERNING
THE CHANGE OF THE SYSTEM

We have been under the Lord's new leading since October 1984. During this past year and a half, we have seen the Lord's manifold blessings, both in an obvious and visible way and in a hidden and invisible way. In this meeting I would like to present a summary and some concluding observations.

I believe all of us are clear that the Lord gave us this fresh leading to bring in an increase in number in all the localities and to spread the work over the whole earth. Increase is a matter of number, and spreading is a matter of land. During the past year and a half, we have been following the Lord's leading step by step and have not paid much attention to the spreading; that must wait for a future date. Although we have not been as strong as we would like, we have done our best to take care of the increase in the localities. In Taipei we began the practice of turning from the small group meetings to the home meetings at the beginning of this year. Within three months the number in attendance increased from three thousand to more than five thousand. This is a sixty to seventy percent increase. Although the rate of increase has not come up to our expectation, it is nevertheless a great encouragement to us. Now under the Lord's new leading, we must pay attention to the building up of the church in all the localities by increasing our number. Then we should spread out upon this basis of building and increase.

I do not know how clear the brothers from different places have been concerning the new leading of the Lord in the vision of building and increase in the localities. Over the past eighteen months I believe we have seen something concerning this new leading from the Lord. What concerns me is that there may be a great difference in the degree to which we have seen the vision. This may be compared to taking an examination; some may obtain a score of sixty, and others a score of one hundred. I would, therefore, like to present once more in a concise way the vision of the Lord's new leading which He has shown us.

The aim of this new leading of the Lord is to totally deliver His recovery from the element, essence, background, environment, and tradition of Christianity. It is a deliverance from the inside out. Although this was the vision we saw sixty years ago, we have not yet fully and completely purged ourselves from Christianity; we are still dragging our feet, even after sixty years of struggling and striving. In 1984 I realized that we had actually moved backward rather than forward. Some things, which we had previously dropped, were picked up again. This disturbed me to the uttermost. So I considered the situation very soberly before the Lord.

At that time I was observing the situation not only in the Far East and Taiwan, but also in the United States and other areas in the West. I noticed that the main reason the Lord could not move much among us was that to a great extent we were still very much affected by the poison brought in by the element, essence, background, environment, and tradition of Christianity. Outwardly, we had rejected all the things of Christianity, but as far as the inward essence was concerned, to a large extent we were still entangled in these things. I received the commission from the Lord to "change the system," beginning from Taiwan. When I returned to Taiwan from the United States in October of 1984, I told the American brothers that this return to Taiwan would be different from all of my past visits. I wanted to have a brand new beginning with the view that the Lord would have a definite model for His entire recovery, a model that would satisfy His heart's desire. I initiated a thorough change as soon as I arrived in Taiwan.

<h3 style="text-align:center">THE FIRST CRUCIAL ELEMENT
IN THE CHANGE—
BUILDING UP THE HOME MEETINGS</h3>

Building up the home meetings in every believer's home is the first and foremost thing in our new beginning. This is not a matter of choice. As long as a person is a believer, he is our brother in the Lord, even if he is the weakest, coldest, and most indifferent, backslidden person. Therefore, we must make every effort to build up a meeting in his home. I said from the beginning that the small group is the foundation for the building up of the church, and that such a small group must be built upon the foundation of the home meetings.

The scriptural basis for the small groups and the home meetings is the expression *from house to house* in Acts 2:46 and 5:42. One and a half years ago I pointed out emphatically that on the day of Pentecost, as soon as the church was raised up on the earth, it began to meet from house to house. That was an unprecedented move; it was something that Judaism had never done before. It was not an idea that Peter inherited from the Jewish religion. Rather, it was a brand new thing, a creative act of God, and something that He ordained. Based on this, we were bold to say that we must have the small meetings, the group meetings, not only the big meetings. Eventually, the group meetings brought in the home meetings.

At the end of last year and the beginning of this year, we were clear that we could not be satisfied with the so-called small group meetings alone. According to my observation, however, the brothers in Taiwan and the United States have misunderstood the meaning of the small group meetings. They do not understand the small group to mean the home meetings, but merely a few brothers and sisters from the same area meeting together. Although these small group meetings were conducted in the homes, they were conducted in selected homes. That was not my original intention. I realized that our change was merely outward; there was no change in the inward substance. Our practice was still contrary to the revelation of the Bible. I felt that there was the need for more fundamental changes.

I was clear that the Lord wanted me to first build up a model in Taiwan. Because of this, I told the brothers from the United States that I did not want them to hear anything or to spread anything. It would be useless for them to copy Taiwan. They need to wait patiently until we arrive at some kind of result, and the success in Taiwan is realized. Our practice in Taiwan is a model, and all the practices will come out of this model.

When I returned to Taiwan, I emphatically told the brothers to divide up the small group meetings into home meetings. Actually, the term *small group meeting* is a temporary designation. In the Bible the only reference to the small groups is when the Lord divided the crowd into groups, in the story of the multiplication of loaves and fish. When we divided up the church in Taiwan into groups and homes thirty years ago, we based our practice on the grouping which the Lord practiced in the multiplication of the loaves and fish. The pattern we saw in Acts, however, was that as soon as the church was raised up, the believers met not by "groups" but by "houses"; the meetings were conducted in every believer's home. Based on this, we decided that we could no longer focus our attention on the big meetings. Instead, we must focus our attention on the home meetings. We need to do our best to build up the home meeting in every believer's home.

During this time we also learned some lessons on preaching the gospel. First, during the past year and a half the brothers from America saw the practice of preaching to people one-on-one. We should not use the big meetings, nor the small meetings, nor meetings with two or three to preach the gospel. Instead, we should preach to people one-on-one. This is a very effective way. We also began this practice in Taiwan. During the past two and a half years we have brought in many people. Such a practice was compatible with our emphasis of meeting "from house to house."

Based on such practices, the Lord showed us clearly that we need to bring the gospel to people's homes. We should no longer pay that much attention to bringing people to the gospel meetings for them to listen to someone preach the gospel. In spite of our strenuous efforts, we have experienced the futility of such work. New ones come to such meetings thinking that they are doing us a great favor. At the end of the meeting they usually fly away like birds in the air; with a "goodbye" they are gone, and there is no way to keep them. Now the situation is different. We no longer invite people to come and listen to a message. Instead, we deliver the gospel to their homes. When we deliver the gospel to their homes, we are spontaneously preaching one-on-one. If other family members are present in such a meeting, we have a home meeting.

Hence, not only do believers need such a meeting; a seeker of the gospel can also have such a meeting. There is no need to invite him to come to the meeting hall or to a small group meeting. There is no need to even invite him to a saint's home. We can visit him, deliver the gospel to him, and meet with him in his own home. Such a practice of delivering the Bible, the truth, the Lord Jesus, and salvation to a person's home is absolutely different from our practice of the past. Those who receive our message in such a way will truly have a different kind of feeling. Formerly, they had to come to us; they were granting us a favor. Now we are going to them; we are granting them a favor. They will surely be grateful to us for this.

We did not have such a practice when we were in mainland

China. At that time Shanghai was the largest city in China. It was an indifferent city. People could live in the same small street for more than ten years without speaking to one another. No one was interested in anyone else. If we visited them, they would peep through their door hole and ignore us as they would a stranger. The same was true in Hong Kong, where there was a lack of law and order; no one dared to open his door. But this was not the case in Taiwan thirty years ago; people were cordial and warm. Regrettably, at that time we did not see this way.

Today there are many new urban communities in Taipei consisting of blocks and blocks of high-rise apartment buildings. Every building houses at least eighty to a hundred units. When we visit these units, most of the occupants are very cordial and polite. Of course, some turn away from us, but it is difficult to find one family that strongly opposes the gospel, the Bible, or the Lord Jesus. As long as we can enter a person's home, we can meet in that home, and we can speak to people one-on-one. Sometimes we can find some dormant saints, and when we begin talking to them about the Lord, their cold hearts are rekindled. Visiting people from house to house is truly the best way and the God-ordained practice.

Recently the full-timers have been coordinating with the local saints to visit the communities twice a week. Every time they come back, they report to us cases of baptisms. This truly surprised the overseas brothers. They spend much time and effort to bring a person to the Lord. But when we knock on people's doors, the doors are opened, and when we enter to talk to them and read with them a portion of *The Mystery of Human Life,* they pray, believe, receive the Lord, and are baptized in their own bathtubs. Anyone who preaches the gospel to a person is qualified to baptize that person. This is something new. All the overseas brothers find this place too attractive and do not want to leave. They want to stay here to have a better taste of such a practice.

In the four Gospels we find an excellent example of preaching the gospel to sinners—the salvation of Zaccheus (Luke 19:1-10). Zaccheus was not saved through a "gospel campaign" conducted by the Lord Jesus. The Lord Jesus did not send Peter or John to invite him to come to a meeting. Rather, the Lord Jesus entered Jericho Himself and brought the gospel to Zaccheus's home. Eventually, He said, "Salvation has come to this house" (v. 9). Salvation did not come to Zaccheus alone; it came to his house. This is the proper and standard way to preach the gospel.

This year we have earnestly tried to practice this way. We no longer rely on the big gospel meetings. Last October we had a big gospel meeting in the stadium. Fourteen thousand people attended. It was a great scene, but there was not much result; only a few people were saved. The effect did not come close to what we have accomplished during the past six months by bringing people to the Lord one by one through visiting their homes. One point worth noting is that with our present practice we can immediately arrange for the next visit with the new ones. This means that we can arrange a time to have the next home meeting. In this way, the home meeting is established. The advantage is that we bring salvation not only to an individual but to a home, even to relatives and friends of that home.

THE SECOND CRUCIAL ELEMENT IN THE CHANGE—
TEACHING *TRUTH LESSONS*

In the new leading of the Lord, we first build up everything related to the church in the homes and not in the meeting halls. We should depend on knocking on people's doors and visiting them one by one and not on the big meetings. Second, we feel that God's desire is to raise up a group of people who are full of life and truth. They should be rich in life and clear in the truth. Paul said that God desires all men to be saved and to come to the full knowledge of the truth (1 Tim. 2:4). For this reason, we published *Truth Lessons*. We anticipate that these lessons will comprise four levels, with four volumes in each level. These are systematic lessons drawn from the light that the Lord has given us. They are put together in a proper way and according to the proper light. We are paying much attention to this work.

Besides the home meetings, we must pay close attention to the meeting for teaching the truth. Every class should not have too many people, preferably fewer than fifty. All the classes within the same hall should conduct the same lessons at the same time. We believe that as the new ones are saved in the home meetings, and as they receive edification from the new believer's lessons, they should subsequently be taught in small classes in the truth meetings. In this way they are equipped with the truth and are perfected by it. Hence, in our changing the system, the home meetings and the truth-teaching meetings are the two most basic and crucial meetings in the church life.

THE THIRD CRUCIAL ELEMENT IN THE CHANGE—
HAVING THE LORD'S WORD
AS THE CENTER OF THE MEETINGS

Besides these things, the most important thing is to read the Lord's word every day. Through this we enjoy Him and keep His word. We also need to break bread to remember Him on the day of His resurrection. This renders Him the true remembrance and affords us the solid feeding. In addition, every week we should gather together to pray. Through such prayer we cooperate with God's move. These two kinds of meetings can be carried out in the districts, in the small groups, or when the whole church comes together. The first Lord's Day of every month, all the saints in a particular hall should gather together for the Lord's table meeting. For the other Lord's Days they can meet in districts. The same principle applies to the prayer meetings.

In all our meetings we should emphasize the Lord's Word. During the bread-breaking meeting we can choose some practical, concise, and meaty portions for everyone to pray-read and enjoy. We can then share and testify concerning these portions. This will satisfy the Lord and minister to our needs. For the prayer meeting we can choose some messages on service that open up the basic spiritual principles of service. In the home meetings there should be some short messages for edification besides the fellowship, prayer, hymns, and greetings. This will help to raise up the new believers. We do not like to see people come to our meetings without learning something of God's Word or without God's Word being ministered to them. We hope that in every meeting some word from the Lord is released and ministered to the brothers and sisters. If we nourish the saints with these three kinds of messages in the bread-breaking meetings, the prayer meetings, and the home meetings, and if we teach *Truth Lessons* in a systematic, solid, and educational way, the saints will be helped and perfected.

Such arrangements will adequately meet the various needs of the saints and the church. Moreover, they will bring in an increase that is built on the basis of the homes. Such increase will be unlimited. If a believer opens up his home to have a meeting once a week, all his relatives and friends will identify his household as a believer's household. They will know that such a home preaches the gospel, reads the Bible, and teaches the truth. Most people today concur that Christianity is the highest and noblest religion in this world. The Bible is a well recognized and well honored book. We believe that even the weakest home can gain one person per month. If there are four thousand such open homes in Taipei, every month they will bring in four thousand people. The prospect of such a work is more than we can ask or think.

DELIVERING THE GOSPEL, THE TRUTH, AND THE MEETINGS TO THE HOMES

For this reason, we cannot remain the same. We cannot drag people to come to listen to the gospel. Instead, we need to go to them. We need to send the truth of the gospel to their homes. However, do not think that the gospel is merely a matter of saying, "God so loved the world that He gave His only begotten Son, that every one who believes into Him would not perish, but would have eternal life." This is the basic element of the gospel, but this is not the entire gospel. We must learn to adjust ourselves to accommodate others and speak according to man's needs. For example, if we see an upright person who loves famous quotes, we can read a few verses from Proverbs to give him a good impression of the Bible and to stir up his appetite. After this, we can give him the basic truth of the gospel. At times we can use some prophecies to show people the value and power of the Bible. This will stir up people's interest as well as command their respect. In particular, the Chinese people love Psalm 1; nothing in Confucius's teaching has the sweetness that this psalm has. We can also quote this psalm in a wise way in our preaching.

Since we are delivering the gospel to people's homes, our person must match the goods that we deliver. When we go to people, we must dress properly. First Timothy 2 teaches us that we should dress soberly, not adorning ourselves with braided hair, gold, pearls, or costly clothing (vv. 9-10). When others see us dressed in this way, they will open the door and welcome us, and it will be easy for them to receive what we have to say. All our books are nutritious food. Whether they are on life, truth, or the gospel, they all are what every man needs.

We must believe in the sovereign arrangement of the Lord. What He has done in Taiwan is to prepare the way for the gospel. Most of the people in the communities are very friendly. Even if they do not accept the gospel, seldom do they rail against us. Once some saints visited a community and met a woman who had just come back from the market. When she met the saints and observed how proper they were, she invited them in. After she heard the gospel, she received it with joy and was baptized in her home. Afterward she told the saints that her husband worked in Tainan and asked how the gospel could be preached to him as well. The saints told her that Tainan has a church with many believers and that they could take his name and deliver the gospel to him. This shows that when the gospel reaches one person, it can bring salvation to the entire family.

The Lord has indeed rendered unprecedented provisions for the new way. He has prepared man's heart. The minute we send the gospel to the homes, many doors are opened, and people invite us to come back. I hope that we will deliver the truth as well as the gospel to people's homes. In this way the new believers will be educated in the truth. We can use short twenty-minute videotapes to help the new ones, or we can take advantage of the telephone and teach them over the phone. In this way we deliver the gospel, the truth, and the meeting to people's homes. This is the best way to build the church locally in the Lord's recovery and to bring in the spread and increase universally.

We have clearly and adequately covered the above points in the past training meetings. I hope that we will change our concept from the big meetings in the halls to building up the home meetings in every believer's home. This is the foundation of the building up of the church, and this is the life pulse for the spread of the church.

EVANGELIZING TAIWAN

When we initially received this new leading from the Lord, we emphatically pointed out that we have enjoyed much blessing from the Lord in Taiwan. Our number is not small. However, for forty years we have not saturated the entire island with the gospel. This is our shame as well as our shortage. Where in Christianity can we find another group of people who have received as much truth from the Lord as we have? Yet we have locked up all these riches. We have not spread them. We have come short. Paul said that he was a debtor both to Greeks and to barbarians (Rom. 1:14). Today there are almost twenty million people in Taiwan, but the number of Christians is fewer than half a million, perhaps even fewer than three hundred thousand. We cannot blame the brothers and sisters in the denominations for not doing their job. They have not received as much light and truth as we have received. The truth that we release in our conferences and trainings is clear, transparent, and rich. Yet we have not brought many people to the Lord. This is the reason I say again and again that we have come short. We are indebted to the Lord as well as to our countrymen.

Hence, we have accepted a heavy burden before the Lord to pay back our debt and gospelize Taiwan within five years. We should even "truthize" and "churchize" Taiwan. The gospel, the truth, and the church need to spread all over this land. To achieve this goal, I have proposed that over the next five years we bring in five hundred full-time serving ones each year. They should be college graduates. We will form these two thousand five hundred people into an army and will evangelize all the towns and villages of Taiwan. Now we have two hundred sixty-six full-timers. In the coming term, perhaps two hundred fifty more will join them. We will then have more than five hundred. We hope that by 1988 we will have at least a thousand full-timers who are well equipped and trained to go out to spread the work.

After much consideration before the Lord, we propose to initially send these one thousand full-timers out in one hundred teams. Each team will have ten members. They will go to one hundred towns and will work for a month in the new way, visiting people, preaching the gospel, and building up the church. After this, two members will stay behind to take care of that locality. The rest will regroup into eighty teams and go to eighty more towns. In this way, in five months we will cover all three hundred twenty towns throughout Taiwan. Every town will have two workers remaining in the town to take care of the situation. This is six hundred forty people. The remaining three hundred sixty will return to the big cities to work with others in the community visitation. They will take every high-rise apartment as a "town." In addition they will also move aggressively onto the campuses to gain the students.

This is the way we are taking. In five years we will spread a big net over the entire island of Taiwan, a net of the gospel, a net of truth, and a net of the church. After this, we will have another five years to evangelize all the small villages and communities. By that time, every year we will have college graduates who will join our full-time training. After their training they will either go to the towns to strengthen the testimony, spreading the gospel to the surrounding villages, or they will cooperate with the work in the cities to gospelize all the communities and campuses. By 1994 all the cities, towns, and villages will be saturated with the gospel, the truth, and the church. This is not a dream. It is something that can be realized.

Forty years ago the Lord brought us to Taiwan. He has blessed this government, and after forty years of hard work, Taiwan has reached a state of prosperity. Communication is well developed, the standard of living is high, the educational level is excellent, and people's hearts are open to the gospel. Many brothers and sisters occupy top positions in various areas of society. This is the Lord's doing. He has done this for the gospel's sake. We must cooperate with the Lord's work and reach the three goals in our evangelizing work—to gain the communities in the big cities, to gain the towns and villages, and to gain the campuses.

According to statistics, there are more than forty thousand saints in the Lord's recovery in Taiwan. Of those, more than eighteen thousand meet regularly. If all these eighteen thousand saints rise up and consecrate themselves to function in an organic way, the dormant ones will follow. Everyone will be driven to pray, and everyone will offer himself to take advantage of the golden opportunity that the Lord has provided us. To gospelize Taiwan in five years will be light and easy. With such a situation before us, I hope that we will be wise and do everything to cooperate with the Lord.

THE FINANCIAL NEED

At present, although the amount we give to the full-timers is small, the total sum is sizeable. Every month the church in Taipei needs seven hundred fifty thousand dollars. For the whole island, the total is $1.82 million. In addition to this, there is the need of building the big meeting hall. Our present total offering per month for the entire island is about twelve million. In order to cooperate with the five-year plan of gospelizing Taiwan, and in order to produce more full-timers to meet His need and to have enough support to sustain them, there is the need for more brothers and sisters to give materially to the Lord in a more faithful way.

Prayer: Lord, what a glory that at this crucial time and place we have a part in such an economical move of this age— the move of evangelizing Taiwan in five years! Lord, thank You that You have chosen us to be the crucial persons. We all say Amen to this move. This is the King's business. This is a move from the throne. We will all rise up to join Calvary's host. Lord, we know for certain that this is not a dream or empty talk. It is our glorious future. You will help us to reach this goal. We say Hallelujah to this glorious and victorious move!

CHAPTER EIGHTEEN

PRACTICAL STEPS IN IMPLEMENTING THE NEW WAY

(1)

Prayer: Lord, we love Your dwelling place, which is Your Body, Your church. Thank You, for gathering us together once again. May Your presence be with us in the depths of our being so that we would not become an organization but would move together with You in one accord as Your organic Body. Lord, we desire to learn to fulfill our function as members of the Body and to promote Your new way under Your love and Your grace.

Lord, thank You that You have Your testimony here in Taiwan, and thank You for entrusting this testimony to us and showing us the clear vision and the great commission. Thank You for showing us the practical way and giving us the clear leading. We want to enter into a deeper fellowship with You, to touch Your heart's desire in a more practical way, and to be enlightened concerning the details of how we should go on. We ask that You grant us a definite leading whether in personnel arrangements or in the financial supply. Teach us how to trust in You, believe in You, look to You, and work by You with diligence. Lord, it is not of those who will or of those who strive but of Your grace and mercy. We look to You to grant mercy to Taiwan, to all the inhabitants of this island, that this land would not only be gospelized, but that everyone would be saved unto Your name and become a child of God. May You have a strong and powerful testimony at the end time before Your return, a testimony that will affect the entire earth.

Lord, fulfill Your word today. For the past two thousand

years the testimony of the church has not been fully manifested. Work this out today in Taiwan. Lord, give us this burden. We look to You not only concerning ourselves but also concerning the saints in all the churches. Just as You have visited us, cared for us, touched us, and moved within us, we ask You to do the same work within all the saints so that they will have the inner registration, the inner enlightening of their eyes, to clearly see the vision and to see the vanity of this world. May they see that everything is vanity, that there is nothing new under the sun, and that everything fails and can be compared to chasing shadows and the wind. Only You are worth anything, and only You are of eternal value.

Lord, we put ourselves, including what You have given us, all men and all things, on Your altar. Gain us. May we all be full-timers. May we live for You and unto You. Every day and every moment of our days are for You. Everything, every move we make, is for You. Lord, cleanse us, and may Your church be acceptable in Your sight. In Christ Jesus and by the Holy Spirit, we want to be priests, offering every saint in the churches under our care to You as a sacrifice. Lord, may they be acceptable to You. Sanctify them, and gain them in a deep way. Do a thorough work in them, a work beyond what we can ask or think. Lord, unless Your Spirit works deep within man, our work is in vain. May we all receive this burden to pray and to call on You day and night, until we see the New Jerusalem appearing as the praise of the earth.

Lord, accomplish an unprecedented work here in Taiwan. Do something earth-shaking in this age. Show the world a living testimony that is different from Christianity, a testimony that is the living expression of Yourself. Lord, fulfill this desire and answer our prayer. Hear our cry. We offer this as our sacrifice of a sweet-smelling savor for Your satisfaction. This is not a personal prayer; it is the cry of Your Body. Lord, may this touch Your heart, move Your heart, and move the throne, so that You in turn will move the universe, move the world, move Taiwan, move every heart, and even shake every heart. Lord, we have seen the signs of Your opening the door in Taiwan. Your promise to Philadelphia is also a promise to us. Give us an open door that no man can shut. Lord, open the door of every house, and open the doors of the hearts. Lord, grant all the saints this burden, the adequate prayer, a thorough appreciation, and a strong consecration. May everyone offer himself for Your glorious move. Amen.

A FIVE-YEAR SCHEDULE
FOR GOSPELIZING TAIWAN

In this chapter we want to speak of practical steps in carrying out the new way. We mainly want to show the brothers and sisters a schedule for gospelizing Taiwan in five years and some definite plans and actual implementations to achieve this schedule. For decades we have heard many spiritual terms and have become accustomed to them. We are used to terms, such as the "leading of the Holy Spirit" and "guidance of the Lord." As a result, we are not very concerned for the future. We do not make any plans. We only know to place everything in the Lord's hand and let the Lord do all the work. With this kind of understanding, all schedules and plans seem redundant and unnecessary. I have been saved for sixty-one years and have been working for the Lord for sixty years. As soon as I was saved, I loved to study the Bible, and through such study I entered into the realm of spirituality. I have accumulated sixty years of experience and have become very familiar with all kinds of spiritual principles. I have said many times that everything depends on the Holy Spirit and not on human arrangement. Therefore, I am very clear that the moment I mention the word *schedule,* we will think that this is a movement, and the moment I mention the word *plan,* we will think that this is organization. Actually, this is a wrong concept.

DEVIATIONS AND SHORTAGES
IN THE UNDERSTANDING OF BIBLICAL TRUTHS

It is easy for man to have a biased understanding of the Bible. When we consider creation around us and as we study the Bible, we find that under God's sovereignty everything physical and spiritual is not one-sided. It is not even two-sided. In most cases it is many-sided. This has been a big problem to students of the Bible throughout the ages. Those who are shallow in their understanding argue that the Bible is not consistent and that many passages do not agree with one another. Some have said that since the central thought of the Bible is consistent, we need only to lay hold of this central thought and not concern ourselves with the other things the Bible says. Some have even argued that all the contradicting portions are probably not God's own words. In reality, God's word is not only many-sided; it is all-embracing.

I have been studying this Bible for sixty years. Almost every day I open to it. How many sides are there to the truths in the Bible? Even today it is difficult for me to count them. We all know that there are four Gospels. They describe the Lord Jesus from four different angles. This may be compared to working on a sculpture; a man has to express the object from all four sides. However, if we study the four Gospels, we will see that there are actually more than four ways to describe the Lord Jesus. It is difficult to count how many sides the four Gospels depict.

I say this to give us a certain assurance. It is true that there are subjects, central thoughts, and lines of truths in the Bible. But in addition to these things, there are facets to the truths of the Bible. If we do not understand this principle, it will be easy for us to conclude that the Bible is not consistent. We will complain that God said one thing yesterday, another thing today, and still a third thing tomorrow. However, if we dive into God's word and dig into its depths, we will see that our God is very consistent, yet He is not simple. Take the human body as an example. No one can fully understand what the human body is all about. God created man with a body to support and sustain his spirit. With the body there is also a soul. With such faculties man is able to express God, receive God, mingle with God, and become one with God on earth. If the body that God created is so complicated yet consistent, the God who created it should be even more complicated yet consistent.

Today some people in Christianity are too simple in their mentality. In their simplicity they consider it a heresy to say that God and man can be mingled as one. Their argument is that God is great and man is small. How can the great Lord dwell in the small man? On the Mount of Olives the disciples saw with their own eyes that the Lord ascended with a physical body. Hence, to some today Christ is high up on the throne. These people argue that the Lord promised that He will come back again, and clearly He has not yet come back. How then can He be in us? They do not believe in Galatians 2:20, which tells us that Christ lives in us. They cannot understand this. They dismiss it, saying that although this is what the Bible says, it is not what it means. To them, the Lord's representative dwells in us—the Holy Spirit. They explain that this may be compared to a great king who cannot personally be present in a foreign country but who sends his ambassador to be his representative. Because they consider it impossible for the same Jesus to be dwelling in millions of Christians, they say that He puts the Holy Spirit inside the believers. This shows how shallow Christians are in their study of the truth.

The study of the truth is not a one-day affair. It has been going on for more than two thousand years. The completion of the New Testament was followed by the first generation of scholars known as the church fathers. They were the first group of people to study the truth. According to our research, these church fathers were higher and deeper than modern scholars in their understanding of the truth. After them, more studies were made concerning God. Some discovered that God is triune; He is not a simple monad. With Him there is not only the distinction of three and one but also the distinction of His economical aspect and His essential aspect. The essential aspect refers to His essence, His existence, and His being. The economical aspect refers to His move and His work. God is great, and His move constitutes His economy. According to His economy, He plans and works out everything. Such theological studies eventually produced three terms— *trinity, essence,* and *economy.*

Today almost all theologians have accepted the term *trinity.* Yet many are still ignorant, blind, and bewildered concerning the economical and essential aspects of God. When the Lord Jesus was baptized, it was the Son who was standing in the water, the Father who was speaking from heaven, and the Spirit who was hovering in the air like a dove. Therefore, some argue that this clearly depicts three persons in three places; how can we say that They are one? Such an argument sounds convincing, but I can defeat it with one stroke. I would ask them, "Before the Spirit descended on the Lord Jesus like a dove, did the Lord have the Spirit within Him?" They dare not answer me, for any answer would be a defeat to them. I would ask, "Since the Lord was conceived of the Holy Spirit, surely the Holy Spirit was in Him. The Bible clearly says that the One in the womb of Mary was begotten of the Holy Spirit. This means that the essence of His divinity was the Holy Spirit. At that time He was conceived, and He was begotten and born of the Spirit as His essence in His divinity. When He stood in the water, the Holy Spirit was already within Him. Why then was the Holy Spirit hovering like a dove above Him?" They would not be able to answer me.

We can say that God is three-one, and we can also say that there are two aspects of the Spirit. The Holy Spirit was in the Lord Jesus from the time He was conceived. Yet after thirty years, He also descended upon the Lord. Are there two Spirits or one Spirit? For those who have a shallow understanding of the truth, this is a thorny question. This shows that the truth is not that simple. There are at least two sides to every truth. Ancient theologians have delved deeply into the mystery of this issue. They have discovered that there are two aspects to God's being triune, the essential aspect and the economical aspect, that is, the aspect related to God's existence and the aspect related to His expression in His move.

Bible translation is not a simple task. For example, consider Matthew 1:20. The Chinese Union Version says, "That which has been conceived in her is of the Holy Spirit." This is clear, and no one would question it. But if we dig into the original language, we find that this verse actually says, "That which has been begotten in her is of the Holy Spirit." The Bible does not merely say, "That which has been conceived in her" but "that which has been begotten in her." This means that at the time the Lord Jesus was conceived in the womb of Mary, a certain One was born in her. Who is this One? To be sure, He is the Holy Spirit Himself. The Holy Spirit is not only the essence that brought about the Lord Jesus' conception; He is the very One who was begotten in Mary.

With such a consideration, we can readily understand the words of John 1:1 and 14: "In the beginning was the Word... the Word became flesh." How did the Word become flesh? It was by being begotten in the womb of Mary. This indicates that the God who was realized through the Holy Spirit was born into a man. This is a great truth. That which was begotten in Mary was the Holy Spirit Himself. Luke 1:35 proves this: "The Holy Spirit will come upon you, and the power of the Most High will overshadow you." The word *overshadow* connotes a hen brooding over her chicks. As God brooded, the Holy Spirit was begotten within Mary. Who is this Holy Spirit? He is the One who makes God realized and real.

This is a great truth, but it has been neglected through the limitation of man's knowledge. The Chinese Union Version is one of the seven best versions in the world. But even if we read this portion a thousand times, we will not be aware of the mystery and reality of God's birth within man. Actually, the revelation in the original language is plain and obvious, but because man's study of the Bible is inadequate and his understanding of theology incomplete, he becomes muddled and shortsighted.

SCHEDULING IN THE BIBLE

When we read the New Testament carefully, especially the Gospels and Acts, we find that both the Lord and the disciples worked with plans and arrangements. The Lord had a schedule and a plan; He did not pass His days on earth foolishly and carelessly. In Luke 13 the Pharisees threatened the Lord, saying, "Get out and go from here, for Herod wants to kill you." The Lord answered, saying, "Go and tell that fox, Behold, I cast out demons and accomplish healings today and tomorrow, and on the third day I am perfected. However, I must journey today and tomorrow and on the following day because it is not acceptable for a prophet to perish outside of Jerusalem" (vv. 31-33). This shows that the Lord had a schedule and an itinerary.

Actually, the Lord's itinerary was set from the foundation

of the world. His birth in Bethlehem, His flight to Egypt, His growth in Nazareth, and His being called a Nazarene were all prophesied long ago in the Old Testament. The same is true with His death. Daniel 9:26 prophesies concerning the year the Messiah was to be crucified. It was to be in the sixty-ninth week. Furthermore, He had to be killed on the fourteenth day of the first month during the Passover at Mount Moriah, which is Mount Zion. When the time came, the Lord delivered Himself to death. He acted according to God's plan, which was set before the foundation of the world.

First the Lord toiled and fulfilled His ministry in Galilee for three years. Then when the last year approached and the Passover was drawing near, He knew within Himself that He had to arrive in Jerusalem six days before the Passover to be examined by men as a lamb, so He set out from Galilee. When the disciples saw this, they marveled, and His followers were afraid (Mark 10:32). His itinerary was very definite; He needed to pass through Samaria on His way to Judea. He needed to arrive at His destination—Jerusalem—at the appointed time. He could not miss a day. If He arrived a day earlier or later, He would not have been crucified on the day of the Passover, and the prophecy of the Old Testament would not have been fulfilled.

This is not all. The Lord planned ahead of time. As He approached Jerusalem and came to Bethphage on the other side of the Mount of Olives, He sent two disciples and said, "Go into the village opposite you, and immediately you will find a donkey tied and a colt with her; untie them and lead them to Me" (Matt. 21:1-2). This was the Lord's planning ahead. No one brought a donkey to Him when He arrived. No angel appeared to the owner of the donkey in a dream the night before. The Lord planned this ahead of time. In addition to this, on the night of the Passover, when they were about to take the feast, and the disciples asked the Lord where they should prepare the meal, He answered, "Go into the city to a certain man and say to him, The Teacher says, My time is near. I am keeping the passover at your house with My disciples" (26:18). This again is an example of the Lord's planning.

Those who are too "spiritual" may say that since the Lord

Jesus is the Lord of everything, He could call a donkey into being and ride it into the city. If He wanted a place for the Passover meal, He could also call it into being. There was no need to make preparations ahead of time. It is true that He is God, but He entered into humanity and became the Son of Man. As far as His divinity is concerned, He did not need to ride on a donkey or a colt. He did not need to pass through Samaria on His way from Galilee to Jerusalem. But because He was a man, He needed to move step by step in the fashion of a man (Phil. 2:8). Since a man needs a certain number of days to travel from Galilee to Jerusalem, He made arrangements ahead of time. The Old Testament prophesied concerning His move, and He acted and made preparations accordingly to match the prophecy.

Since the Lord was a man, there was the need for Him to make many detailed arrangements involving persons and matters; hence, there was the need of schedules and budgets. The Bible shows that the Lord never acted hastily. He always worked according to His timetable. Even His visit to Lazarus and His raising him up was not done in a hurry; He followed His own timetable. Others sent men to plead with Him again and again, but He was not moved. At a certain point the disciples became indignant, but when the Lord's time came, He went. The disciples said, "The Jews were just now seeking to stone You, and You are going there again?" He did not listen to them, because He had His itinerary. The disciples might have been unhappy; however, they had no choice but to follow. They said in resignation, "Let us also go, that we may die with Him" (John 11:8, 16). This clearly shows that as long as we are human beings, we need schedules and budgets.

DETAILS OF OUR SCHEDULE AND BUDGET

Today it is not only the angels or only God Himself who is involved in the gospelization of Taiwan. It is we, such small people, who are involved in this work, and for this reason, there is truly the need for a schedule and a plan. For example, we need to learn the local dialects, such as Taiwanese or Hakka, before we can preach the gospel to others in an intimate way. At present, we have the following schedule. First, we visit the communities and the campuses. This is a warm-up exercise for our eventual expedition, comparable to the training and drills of an army before it sets out for the battlefield. We will have three years of drills. Then in the fourth year we will set out. Within five months we will establish churches in all the towns and cities. According to this schedule, we need at least one thousand full-timers in the first phase. Of course, we can get by with seven hundred, but the timing will be prolonged, the manpower stretched, and the impact reduced. There will not be as much force and success as we would like to see.

When I was young, I paid much attention to the world situation and to international developments. In 1924 the Whampoa Military Academy was established in China. After three years of preparation and training, the Northern Expedition for the unification of China began in 1926. I am not a student of politics or military science, but I was clear that as soon as the Northern Expedition set out, it would win, because the preparation work was more than adequate. In the same way, I believe three years of preparation is adequate for us. We will have one thousand full-timers who will be grouped into one hundred teams. Through visiting the communities and the campuses in a solid way, and through building up the home meetings and learning to have the proper meetings, we will accomplish the great task of gospelizing Taiwan in five years.

The next step in our plan is to produce another five hundred full-timers in the next two years. This will bring the number to fifteen hundred. We will then have a sufficient number not only to gospelize the towns but also to gospelize all the villages in another five years.

HOW TO PRACTICALLY IMPLEMENT
SUCH A PLAN

At present we have more than two hundred sixty young people in our full-time training. We anticipate that another two hundred or more will be added to the next term of training. Based on this number, we will need five hundred more next year. In order to reach our goal, all the elders and responsible brothers in all the churches need to pick up the burden in one accord. We need to encourage the young people in our respective localities to attend the full-time training. At the same time, the campus work should aim toward this goal. Based on the above considerations, we can probably get by with seven hundred, but one thousand is better.

I hope that we will consider this schedule and plan and bear this burden in oneness. I do not believe that I am asking too much. We all agree that it is more than right for us to gospelize Taiwan in five years. Without reservation we are declaring war on Satan. We are storming his house, breaking his forces, binding the strong man, and plundering his wealth. Although there are only eighteen thousand regular attendants in our meetings, any corporate effort will make our job easier; where there is the will of the entire Body, there is the way to win an "entire city." As long as we function and offer up our part, it will not be difficult to accomplish this momentous task. What we need now is to strive and struggle to realize our plan.

In order to realize our plan, we need practical ways to implement it. First, in order to produce one thousand full-timers, there is the need of our prayers. We need to ask the Lord to give us no fewer than a thousand persons. We even need to dream of these one thousand persons. Next, we need to operate according to some practical principles. Eighteen months ago I said that the basic principle in producing the full-timers is to have one out of twenty saints in every local church giving himself to be a full-timer. At present, we have eighteen thousand regular attendants in our meetings. This means we should produce nine hundred full-timers. The potential of our source is not poor. By next year the attendance may reach twenty thousand. This will be more than adequate to produce a thousand full-timers. Next, when we say that out of twenty saints we should have one full-timer, we are taking into consideration the source of our financial support. The nineteen saints should set aside five percent of their income to support the living of the one full-timer among them. This will not pose too heavy a burden on anyone. I believe that as the saints are faithful to the Lord, we will meet this budget.

Our statistics show that we are barely obtaining the number

of full-timers we need and our financial offering is still inadequate. I hope that as the elders return to their respective localities, they will fellowship the practical needs with the brothers and sisters. Although we are faithful in our regular offerings, we need to set aside five percent to support the full-timers. This will make up the lack. In the Old Testament, in addition to the regular sacrifices, God's people had to pay the temple tax, which was half a shekel of silver per person (Exo. 30:13-16; 38:26). Among the twelve tribes, the tribe of Levi served the Lord full time. The other eleven tribes took a tenth of their income to take care of the need of the Levites. I hope that all the saints will be faithful to the Lord to make up the portion that they ought to cover so that the Lord's work can go on in a smooth way.

For every saint to offer five percent of their income to support the full-timers does not mean that they should divert their regular offerings to this matter. Rather, they should offer this additional five percent over and above their regular offerings. This is only half of a tenth. It is strictly for the support of the full-timers. Only when we have such a budget can we move according to schedule. Even if we do not have a thousand full-timers by 1988, hopefully we will have seven hundred; however, if our financial support covers only five hundred, our move to gospelize Taiwan will be hampered.

We have received a new leading from the Lord to turn the church from the degraded situation of Christianity to the practice of the God-ordained way. We have also received a new commission to gospelize Taiwan in five years. For this, we need a schedule and a budget. We are clear about the schedule and the budget. What we need to do is to mobilize the entire congregation to obtain the people and the financial support so that we can carry out our plan as scheduled. May the Lord be gracious to all the saints in all the places, and may we set our eyes on this in steadfastness and one accord.

Although the churches in the Lord's recovery are a "little flock" (Luke 12:32), we thank the Lord that He has committed to us a great commission of gospelizing Taiwan in five years. This is an unprecedented task and a glorious enterprise. I hope that we will all see the bright future and share in this great enterprise. I believe the Lord will multiply His blessing on all those who spend themselves for the Lord and His gospel, and He will bless this country. The effect of this is far-reaching. May we all have the wisdom to receive this fellowship.

CHAPTER NINETEEN

PRACTICAL STEPS IN IMPLEMENTING THE NEW WAY

(2)

CONCERNING THE FULL-TIME TRAINING

Let us now fellowship further regarding the schedule and budget needed to practically implement the new way. First, concerning the full-timers, we need to realize that they must be trained. Whether or not one has passed through the training makes a great difference. However, we must avoid the ways of a public school. We are not operating a seminary; rather, we are being trained in various matters, such as being equipped in the truth, growing in life, carrying out the Lord's work, leading the meetings, establishing churches in different cities, and shepherding the saints.

In the past the move of propagation was mainly the result of the migration of brothers and sisters, who were led by the Lord to move to different cities for their jobs. In these new cities they brought some of their relatives and friends to be saved and started a meeting. Later other saints joined them to strengthen the testimony. This is how churches in different localities were established. This way is spontaneous but slow. Now the Lord is leading us to take a new way, which will enable us to achieve maximum results with less effort. There will be one thousand full-timers grouped into one hundred teams and sent to one hundred towns to establish one hundred churches in a month. This, however, will require much training and adequate preparation on the part of the full-timers. At present there are approximately two hundred sixty full-time trainees, which is seven hundred short of our target of one thousand. Perhaps more people will come to the training this coming year. This will be a great help to them.

For this reason I have paid much attention to the training. We cannot merely gather a group of people who do not have much knowledge, learning, or experience and send them to visit people in the towns. If we do this, they will not know what to say when people open their door to them. They will not know how to take someone on if he believes in the Lord. These matters require the teaching and practice given in the training. In the future all the trainees may need to wear "uniforms." This does not mean that they will wear official or distinctive outfits; they will wear something ordinary and uniform in style. In this way people will know that there is a group of Christians who are rich in life, clear in truth, thorough in expounding the Bible, weighty in speaking, noble in character, and neat and elegant in attire. Then they will spontaneously respect us, and they will welcome us when we go to visit them. This matter is of great importance.

Today many big companies in the world, especially in the United States, spend much money to hire fashion designers to design uniforms for their staff. The uniforms are neither extravagant nor military-looking but ordinary, yet elegant, solemn, and modest. No one would choose to go to a bank where the staff is dressed casually and behaves loosely. I hope that the co-workers and full-timers will pay attention to this aspect. Even though we are ordinarily dressed, we gain people's respect by being orderly, graceful, and dignified in our attire. Moreover, from now on, the books, pamphlets, and tracts we publish should be noble and attractive in appearance. In this way, the gospel and truth will have a way to go out, and our elegance and gravity will accompany our publications.

CHANGING THE APPEARANCE OF THE MEETING HALLS

To meet the demands of the change in our system, the elders should pick up the burden to fellowship with the brothers and sisters to be properly attired when they come to the meetings; they should not dress sloppily or fancifully but be modest and proper. Furthermore, the furnishings of the meeting halls should be changed. The meeting halls do not need to be extravagant or magnificent in appearance, but elegant, tidy, and clean, not giving the impression of being poor and cheap.

In the early 1950s Brother Nee brought in a revival in the church in Hong Kong. At that time I was starting the Lord's work in Taiwan. Brother Nee asked me to go to Hong Kong. As soon as I arrived, he brought me to the service meeting and asked me to make arrangements for all the services of the co-workers, the elders, and the deacons in the church according to the authority of the Lord. Brother Nee then returned to mainland China. After picking up the burden of taking the lead in the service in the church in Hong Kong, I first asked the elders to change the appearance of the meeting hall. At that time the meeting hall was on the second floor of an apartment building. In front of the door hung a lead wire with a drum hammer, which was used to knock on the door. Hong Kong is a world-renowned, first-class city, and people commonly install electric doorbells. Yet the meeting hall used this kind of "doorbell." Some saints furnished and decorated their living rooms with expensive items and had pianos in their homes. The meeting hall, however, looked like a meeting place for the poor. The mirror on the wall seemed as if it had not been dusted since the day it was hung, and everything in the room was topsy-turvy. No one was responsible. Furthermore, the meeting hall had only an old, dilapidated organ that had been donated to the church by a Western missionary, who had worked in the interior of China. I severely rebuked the serving brothers in Hong Kong regarding this matter. Thank the Lord, the saints were submissive, and the appearance of the meeting hall was changed that same day. After speaking to them in the morning, an electric doorbell was installed, the mirror was removed, and the dilapidated organ was replaced with a grand piano by the evening.

Later the church in Hong Kong formed a building group to purchase a piece of land for the building of a meeting hall. They found a field in Tsim Sha Tsui belonging to the Catholic Church, which cost HK$22 (approximately US$3) per square foot. They asked me how large a property they should purchase, and I told them to purchase at least two acres. This was twelve thousand square feet and would cost over HK$250,000 (approximately US$36,000). It was an enormous sum of money thirty-six years ago, so they asked me about reducing the purchase by one half. I replied, "This is your business. You can buy however much you want, but I must say that Tsim Sha Tsui is the main ferry station. Once you cross the harbor, you get to Hong Kong Island. Now since Hong Kong Island has undergone much development, any further development will be on the Kowloon side, where Tsim Sha Tsui is. Because Tsim Sha Tsui will be the center of both Hong Kong and Kowloon sides, you must purchase this piece of land as soon as possible."

While they were considering this, Brother Nee heard the news and charged them, saying, "Concerning the purchase of the land for the building of the meeting hall, just do what Brother Witness told you." They accepted it and planned to buy six thousand square feet, but when they were ready to purchase the land, the price had increased by one dollar per square foot. This meant they would need to pay six thousand dollars more than they intended. Then I said, "You must buy it no matter how expensive it is. If you do not buy it now, the land price will continue to rise. Later when you have the blueprint of the meeting hall and find that six thousand square feet is not enough, you will not be able to buy more land." After these words, they reluctantly bought three thousand more square feet and built the meeting hall. Now this piece of land is worth ten million U.S. dollars. The change of meeting halls resulted in an increase in the number of saints in the church. When I went there to hold conferences and trainings in 1954, the meeting hall was filled with more than one thousand people.

Concerning the church in Kaohsiung, a co-worker took me to see a piece of land that was originally a paddy field, for the building of a meeting hall. The land was about forty-six hundred square feet, at about NT$8 (approximately US$0.20) per square foot, and was located at the center of Kaoshiung. When I saw it, I was clear that later there would be much development in Kaohsiung. As a result, I told the brothers to purchase the land as soon as possible. A brother from Kaohsiung came, and I gave him the money from my ministry and charged him to be careful not to lose it on the way. Today that piece of land has a five-thousandfold increase in value.

We are not trying to attract people through outward, material things; however, in the twentieth century, everything has reached international standards, especially in Taiwan. Yet our meeting halls remain shabby and uncomely. This does not match our God and the gospel that we preach. Since God is holy and glorious, and our coming to the meetings is like coming to the "holy land," we must have the attitude to dress properly. Otherwise, when people look at us they will wonder what kind of God we have, and what kind of persons we are; they will question why do we not have an attitude of fear and respect toward our God. We are not imposing outward regulations, but we hope the brothers and sisters will have a clear realization and receive a proper leading.

In this way, we will have a shining testimony showing that we are a group of noble people. Today people with achievements, whether in the educational, industrial, or commercial fields, have proper and decent homes. We believers should be the same. This kind of testimony is very persuasive and can bring in the increase. Mormonism is one of the two groups commonly identified by Christianity as heretical; it has, however, been able to spread widely because of its outward appearance. Mormons are very attractive in their family and personal lives, as well as in their conduct, behavior, and appearance. They are honest, reliable, punctual, and proper. Hence, they are respected by others. In a previous message I mentioned a heretical group in the Philippines. They claim that Jesus Christ is not God but merely a noble and outstanding man and that they learn from His conduct. They are obviously heretical, but because they are honest, reliable, and well-behaved, they have spread in a prevailing way. Thirty years ago they had one million members, but now they have four million, many of whom are upper class people such as lawyers and doctors.

We have the truth, life, and the gospel as real diamonds, but we should not wrap them with tissue paper and sell them to people. Even though we may have the real diamonds, if we wrap them with tissue paper, no one will believe they are real

THE VISION AND DEFINITE STEPS

diamonds. Hence, the outward adornment is important. For this reason, there is a class in the full-time training that teaches the trainees to dress in a proper, neat, and tidy way. If we dress strangely, wear our tie sloppily, and leave our hair unkempt, even though we speak the truth, no one will listen to us.

There was a brother who in my eyes was simply "a little brother." One day he testified that he had finished reading all the Life-studies. I was very surprised because he looked unimpressive. Today, however, he is entirely changed. He dresses appropriately, without anything strange in his appearance. We cannot overlook our appearance. A diplomat must be particular in three matters: facial features, manner, and clothing. One's facial features are inborn and cannot be altered. One's manner of speaking, speech, and demeanor, however, can be trained. One's clothing can also be cultivated. Only when a person has proper facial features, good manners, and neat clothing can he appropriately represent his country. We, as representatives of the gospel and ambassadors of God, should have a dignified appearance.

ADDITIONAL POINTS REGARDING THE TRAINING

We have included some language classes in the full-time training. This is for the preparation of the gospelization of Taiwan and the whole earth. After we have gospelized the island of Taiwan, some full-timers will be sent abroad, in particular to South America, Africa, Australasia, Japan, and Korea. Hence, they will need to learn the respective languages. Moreover, for the purpose of understanding the Bible and reading the reference materials, they will need to learn Greek. We have invited teachers from different places to come, so that on the one hand, they can teach the trainees different languages, and on the other hand, they can live the church life here. This is "killing two birds with one stone."

Concerning the furnishing of the training center, everything should be simple, dignified, and harmonious. There must be some who would specifically manage affairs and finance. Since we will have the full-time training every year, we must set up a standard. If the Lord wills, after the meeting hall in

Lin-ko is completed, we will move the training center there, and it will be on a larger scale. We must now establish a good foundation so that there will be no difficulties in the future.

I hope that all the churches will try their best to encourage the young people to join the full-time training and help in handling the applications. I do not insist on my own view. If you want to have a full-time training in your own locality, you may do so, but I would rather that you do it together with some other localities. In this way, the teaching staff and the content of the classes will be enriched and strengthened. This also saves much energy. There are two terms of training in a year, with each term lasting four months. For the remaining months in the year, the trainees can return to their respective localities to help and strengthen the churches, or they may stay in Taipei to propagate in the communities. This will further strengthen the steps we take for the propagation.

CONCERNING EXPENSES FOR THE TRAINING

All the churches must bear the burden to share the expenses for the training. In principle, one full-timer should be produced out of twenty people. Owing to different circumstances, some churches may not have suitable young people to send to the full-time training, but they should still be faithful in the matter of financial support. In contrast, some churches or halls may have many students that can be produced as full-timers but have some difficulties in the matter of support; other churches and halls should make up this lack. If all the churches in Taiwan are one and all the saints endeavor together in one accord, producing as many full-timers as possible and giving as much as possible, the Lord's grace will enable us to reach our goal of having one thousand full-timers to evangelize Taiwan in five years.

FELLOWSHIP REGARDING
THE MEETING HALL IN LIN-KO

We are producing a model in Taipei for spreading the gospel to the entire island of Taiwan. Our basic principle is to build up the church in the believers' homes so that the preaching of the gospel, the teaching of the truth, and the edifying of the saints are in the homes. However, Christians still need big meetings, because the atmosphere of the big meetings can never be replaced by small meetings. For this reason, we need a big meeting hall that can afford us a place for corporate meetings once a month and can be used on a regular basis for the long-term training. Once the meeting hall in Lin-ko is completed, it will have an occupancy of fifteen thousand so that saints from various localities can take turns to come and have corporate meetings.

According to the principle in the Old Testament, God ordained that His people gather in Jerusalem three times a year. This was very helpful to the establishment and unity of the nation of Israel. If the church is built up only in the homes, the building will be scattered, and the saints as a whole will not be able to join and blend with one another. Hence, there is the need for a big meeting to join and blend the saints together. Moreover, some high-peak truths cannot be released from house to house through the ministry; rather, they need to be released in the big meetings. The release of the high-peak truths in the big meetings will become the truth lessons for the saints to mutually teach and ask questions in the homes. Furthermore, international conferences and trainings can also be held in Lin-ko. This will blend the churches on the earth into one Body. Hence, the meeting hall in Lin-ko is not merely for the need in Taiwan but for the entire earth.

All that we are doing is beneficial to our country. Our effort to bring the gospel and truth to the homes to gospelize, truthize, and churchize Taiwan is the real reformation of the people's heart. This will have a far-reaching influence on people's morality and conduct. After the meeting hall in Lin-ko is finished, it will be used as the training center. Like a factory, the training will be very profitable for the building up of our nation. Therefore, all the saints should pray much that the government will have the foresight to approve our request to build.

The budget for the construction of the meeting hall in Lin-ko is around NT$400 million (approximately US$13 million). The need for the full-time training and propagation is about the same amount. It will be too heavy for the churches in Taiwan to bear the entire burden. I hope that the saints from overseas, especially the churches in the United States, will share this burden. This requires much prayer. In terms of priority, the full-time training and propagation should be given priority. The move of gospelizing Taiwan will begin in January of 1988, but the construction of the meeting hall in Lin-ko depends on the approval of the government and the giving of the saints; thus, it may take some time.

THREE CRUCIAL MATTERS

I hope that when the co-workers and elders go back to their localities, they will fellowship with the saints regarding these three great schedules, plans, and needs: first, there is the support and quota for the full-timers and the financial need; second, there is the expenses of the full-time training and propagation; and third, there is the need for the construction of the meeting hall in Lin-ko. Although the full-time training is in Taipei, the full-time trainees come from all over Taiwan. After they are trained, they will be for the whole earth. Hence, this financial burden should be shared by all the churches in Taiwan and not borne exclusively by the church in Taipei. I hope the brothers will encourage the saints to rise up to respond to these three matters. If we succeed in these three matters, the Lord's recovery will have a broad way on the earth, and the prospect of the Lord's recovery will surpass our expectation.